D1526212

Information Sciences Series

Editors

ROBERT M. HAYES
University of California
Los Angeles, California

JOSEPH BECKER
President
Becker and Hayes, Inc.

Consultant

CHARLES P. BOURNE
University of California
Berkeley, California

Joseph Becker and Robert M. Hayes:
INFORMATION STORAGE AND RETRIEVAL

Charles P. Bourne:
METHODS OF INFORMATION HANDLING

Harold Borko:
AUTOMATED LANGUAGE PROCESSING

Russell D. Archibald and Richard L. Villoria:
NETWORK-BASED MANAGEMENT SYSTEMS (PERT/CPM)

Launor F. Carter:
NATIONAL DOCUMENT-HANDLING SYSTEMS FOR SCIENCE AND TECHNOLOGY

Perry E. Rosove:
DEVELOPING COMPUTER-BASED INFORMATION SYSTEMS

F. W. Lancaster:
INFORMATION RETRIEVAL SYSTEMS

Ralph L. Bisco:
DATA BASES, COMPUTERS, AND THE SOCIAL SCIENCES

Charles T. Meadow:
MAN-MACHINE COMMUNICATION

Gerald Jahoda:
INFORMATION STORAGE AND RETRIEVAL SYSTEMS FOR INDIVIDUAL RESEARCHERS

Allen Kent:
INFORMATION ANALYSIS AND RETRIEVAL

Robert S. Taylor:
THE MAKING OF A LIBRARY

Principles of
Information Retrieval

MANFRED KOCHEN

Professor of Information Sciences
Urban/Regional Planning
Research Mathematician

University of Michigan
Ann Arbor, Michigan

A WILEY-BECKER & HAYES SERIES BOOK

 MELVILLE PUBLISHING COMPANY
Los Angeles, California

Copyright © 1974, by John Wiley & Sons, Inc.
Published by *Melville Publishing Company,* a Division of John Wiley & Sons, Inc.

All rights reserved. Published simultaneously in Canada.

Library of Congress Cataloging in Publication Data:

Kochen, Manfred.
    Principles of information retrieval.

    (Information sciences series)
    "A Wiley–Becker & Hayes series book."
    Bibliography: p.
    1. Information storage and retrieval systems.
I. Title.
Z699.K583   029.7   74–1204
ISBN 0–471–49697–9

To my mother,
who taught me the value of order

Information Sciences Series

Information is the essential ingredient in decision making. The need for improved information systems in recent years has been made critical by the steady growth in size and complexity of organizations and data.

This series is designed to include books that are concerned with various aspects of communicating, utilizing, and storing digital and graphic information. It will embrace a broad spectrum of topics, such as information system theory and design, man—machine relationships, language data processing, artificial intelligence, mechanization of library processes, nonnumerical applications of digital computers, storage and retrieval, automatic publishing, command and control, information display, and so on.

Information science may someday be a profession in its own right. The aim of this series is to bring together the interdisciplinary core of knowledge that is apt to form its foundation. Through this consolidation, it is expected that the series will grow to become the focal point for professional education in this field.

Foreword

Information retrieval as a discipline stands in need of a conceptual and theoretical framework, of an articulation of its fundamental principles, and identification of key issues and problems. It is particularly curious, in the light of its importance in bringing order and structure to other disciplines, that it itself has been so deficient in these same qualities. Kochen in this thoughtful and cohesive book has taken what I believe to be an important step toward overcoming these deficiencies.

How might one begin to think about information retrieval and its principles? My own preference is to consider, as a reasonable point of beginning, the problem of selecting, from a collection of documents, one or more which is expected to be useful. Now why is there a problem, and what is its nature? Notice that, if we think small enough, none need arise. For if the collection is sufficiently small, then all of the documents therein can be delivered to any interested user who can examine each one in turn until satisfied. Clearly any retrieval problem, as such, emerges and takes shape only if the size of the collection is so large that it must be organized for partial search, or equivalently that a selection must first be made by someone, or some system, other than the user himself. The selection would have to consist of a subset of documents few enough in number to be examined directly by the requester. The nature of the problem is then this: the requester must somehow describe to the system the attributes of the documents which he wishes to inspect, and the system in turn must be able to identify and search these attributes. Furthermore it would have to operate with attributes appropriate to many requests from many users, and so in effect operate as though there were agreement among users as to the set of potentially useful attributes for describing documents. It is in this hypothetical area of common agreement that one encounters problems of indexing, classification, subjects, topics, and other forms of description. The most useful description of a document clearly depends on the point of view one takes toward it and on its expected future use. Such description depends as well on the specific size and type of collection in which the document is embedded. It may be enough to describe a document as being about "birds" if the collection to be searched consists of a few thousand documents on diverse topics, but the description is far from adequate for searching the Library of Congress.

The formidable problems arising from the diversity of users, uses, and collections are compounded by the fact that the world's total quantity of recorded information of course continues to accumulate, and so there is a tendency for most collections to grow. Such growth is often described as exponential, or explosive, which invites extrapolation of ominous and absurd conditions. A sense of perspective can be attained by examining the causes of such growth and by developing suitable models to describe the situation. Documents do not beget documents, and so the biological connotation of the word *growth* itself can be misleading. The rate at which new documents are produced is proportional to the number of people who write them, since it is plausible to assume that the average rate of writing per author remains more or less constant. It seems likely also that the ratio of readers to writers would not be subject to any very large changes over the years. Is there then any solid basis for the sense of crisis or inundation which for the past 300 years has surrounded the growth of recorded information? I believe there is, simply because the backlog accumulates. Thus the ratio of the total number of documents to the total number of readers increases perpetually. The idea of discarding the obsolete seems not too popular, perhaps because of the difficult questions it raises. Who is to decide what is obsolete, and on what basis? Certain corrective forces are present, however, for the use of library collections tends to be concentrated on more recent materials, but we must ask whether this merely reflects the fact that the more recent materials are proportionately more numerous, the growth rate indeed being exponential, or whether older materials really are, in effect, being discarded through disuse. And if so, are they in fact obsolete?

Finally the question seems inescapable — will we one day reach the point where it is virtually impossible to win new knowledge because it takes more than a lifetime to prepare ourselves adequately by learning what has gone before? The question is posed not because an answer is to be expected, but because it invites attention to other basic questions of how knowledge is organized, classified, and communicated, and how subject specialties for research are defined and chosen. The nature of the problem thus outlined provides context within which we can join Kochen in a quest for the principles of information retrieval.

Authors, readers, documents, and topics are the building blocks of Kochen's conceptual structure. The systems-oriented approach which he takes facilitates the identification of important questions, issues, and problem areas that heretofore have not been well integrated into the field of information retrieval, and whose significance, I think, has not been sufficiently appreciated. For example, the role of reference citation nets, and issues related to the familiar but usually misunderstood information explosion are illuminated and find their place readily in the overall scheme. The aim of developing basic principles and theory is kept in focus throughout.

This book does not attempt to substitute for more detailed and comprehensive works on vocabulary control, subject indexing, classification, and retrieval systems evaluation. The author does provide a perspective and a systematic development that is unique; he offers much that cannot be found elsewhere.

The mathematical apparatus necessary to develop and clarify the models used seems to me neither excessive nor too advanced. It may in places give difficulty to those with little mathematical preparation, but the principles are in the main understandable even to one who skips the formulas.

Chicago, Illinois   DON R. SWANSON

Preface

It has been said that there is nothing as practical as a good theory. The need for a theoretical foundation underlying the analysis and design of information retrieval systems has been expressed by many students, users, designers, and researchers. Information retrieval is of potential interest to nearly everyone, for who does not occasionally need aid with where to turn, how to cope, how to keep up, and how to file?

During the past two decades there has been great growth in the number and variety of information retrieval systems on the market. Practitioners and researchers in medicine, engineering, law, and social work face bewildering choices. At the same time, the luxuriant growth of innovative developments in many directions seems to be reaching a plateau. The time is ripe for a synthesis with a unifying point of view.

The nonprofessional user is becoming more aware of his right of access to information and the growing gap between the information-rich and the information-poor. The threat of possible misuse of unified computerized data banks of dossiers concerns everyone. The study of information retrieval can benefit every school child or educated person.

Information retrieval, aside from its how-to-find-out interpretation, is a fascinating challenge to science. How do people or animals store and retrieve information? What are the biochemical, physiological, and psychological mechanisms of this mysterious phenomenon? At the larger level of entire intellectual communities, what principles govern the growth of knowledge? Molecular biochemists are increasingly dealing with concepts of information and information use. Computer scientists are beginning to use the term *organization of knowledge* to refer to one of their key concerns.

A really useful aid to orient all these potential students of information retrieval requires some theoretical underpinnings. In this book we aim to help develop such a theory. We do this by clarifying the notions of *information* and *information use*. We point out the emergence of a new paradigm. *The main thrust of this book is an approach to analyzing the growing knowledge system for how well it helps people recognize, select, and cope with problems.* Information retrieval systems are effective to the extent they mesh with the knowledge system in which they are embedded.

The book is addressed to (*a*) all those who want to join this theory-building, paradigm-shaping enterprise, (*b*) those who want to use it in its present state, and (*c*) those who would like to enrich their appreciation of intellectual developments.

The first group includes the increasing number of scientists and engineers who want to switch toward more socially relevant and better-supported areas, which are also exciting and challenging. Ever since Bush suggested this area as a likely successor to the large wartime scientific enterprises, this field has held that promise. It also includes a large group of doctors and researchers in biomedicine and social science who have a taste for theory blended with interests in practical and experimental information retrieval questions. It is essential for the further growth of this paradigm that a sufficiently large community of information scientists, researchers concerned with the research process, molecular biochemists concerned with communication in cells, and philosophers and social scientists concerned with the growth of knowledge—who all share a liking for theory—begin to build upon some of the ideas in this book. Hopefully they will be stimulated to design new experiments or to improve some of the theoretical developments presented here. They may also find this work a source of orientation that enables them to look at their problems in a different light. The rewards are new and rich avenues of exploration and publication and more vigorous cross-fertilization of ideas.

The second group includes experienced users and designers of information retrieval systems who are concerned about what direction to pursue, and who also have a liking and appreciation of applied mathematics. With modern educational programs in management science becoming increasingly sophisticated in their use of mathematics, most of the new generation of designers and managers should be familiar with the mathematics used here. They may welcome seeing it applied in this area. The book may help provide them with some rationale for their decisions. Managers in private or public enterprises with large computer facilities which they are considering for use in information retrieval should find it useful. The decisions they make help determine how the market will change, which, in turn, will affect them. It is of great value to them to be fully aware of the consequences their decisions are likely to have.

Because the state of theory in this field is still immature, managers and designers should not expect to find field-tested design equations, recipes for choosing a system, or algorithms for decision-making. In this book we offer first steps toward such a mature theory. The prescriptions offered are necessarily tentative and incomplete. We point to some basic design principles whose specific applications may take many diverse forms. As the theory develops, these should be of considerable future benefit to users, designers, and managers of IR systems.

The third group includes students. College or graduate-level courses in information or library science have often lacked sufficient substance at a real college level. This book can be used as a main text or as a supplementary text for a one-semester course on information retrieval. An early version was, in fact, so used for a graduate-level course in the Computer and Communication Science Department of the University of Michigan. Such courses are offered in various departments, including computer science, library science, electrical engineering, and industrial engineering. The book can also help introduce courses on information retrieval into departments of sociology, political science, urban planning, economics, education, English, journalism, philosophy, psychology, history of science, and applied mathematics. For students in any of these fields, or in continuing education, the book may open a door to a new field, new ideas. It will acquaint them with and orient them to an area no educated man today can afford to be ignorant of.

For all its readers, I hope that this book will provide useful new ways of looking at information problems, orientation toward trends and enlightened policies, stimulation of ideas for new services and investigations, unification, and synthesis.

We tried to make the level as high as possible. The algebra learned by most U.S. high school students today is quickly forgotten when they do not get opportunities to keep in practice or to see where it useful. Most conscientious high school graduates with an above-average degree of mathematical sophistication should be able to follow and appreciate most of the mathematics in this book. This assumes some introduction to computers, a working knowledge of elementary mathematical analysis, and some appreciation of logic and probability theory. Calculus, probability theory, and matrices are used in one or two places, and sections for which a reader's mathematical background is inadequate can be skipped without losing the logical thread. College graduates with some exposure to these topics and some mathematical maturity should have no difficulty.

To reach the various audiences to whom this book should be useful, we tried to make sure that every reader will at least come away with a few general ideas of an importance comparable to, say, Simon's "satisficing." The key feature of this book is that it develops *one* key idea of considerable novelty and importance: how information retrieval systems help people cope with problems. We have brought together evidence and arguments, using methods from various disciplines, for a unified new approach that captures some other important points of view as well. We hope that it will stimulate and orient readers to use and enrich the principles of information retrieval.

This book was started in 1964 while I was in Euratom, in Ispra, Italy on leave from the IBM Research Center. It was subsequently revised several times at the Mental Health Research Institute of the University of Michigan. The generous support of all these institutions made completing it a possibility. The intellectual debts to pioneers in information science are so numerous that they are better represented by the large, yet highly selected bibliography at the end than can be done here. Nonetheless, the influence of Derek de Solla Price, Thomas Kuhn, Karl W. Deutsch, my various mentors in physics and mathematics, as well as several colleagues in the library world is readily apparent and gratefully acknowledged. The manuscript was considerably improved by comments from R.M. Hayes, D. Swanson, and H.P. Edmundson, whom I thank greatly. The finishing touches were added at Harvard, where I was on sabbatical leave when the manuscript was completed.

Several students and assistants at the University of Michigan contributed greatly with their comments and aid. A. Bert Segur was most helpful in his careful reading of an earlier draft. The assistance of Gail Raimi—Dreyfuss, Wendy Lehmann, and Linda Silverman in improving both content and style was most valuable. Mrs. Barbara Badre's expertise—almost wizardry—as typist and artist made what are normally painful chores of book-writing a distinct pleasure. To all these people, and not least Paula, David, and Mark, who tolerated many long evenings with a preoccupied husband and father, goes my sincere appreciation and gratitude.

Ann Arbor, Michigan   MANFRED KOCHEN

Contents

Chapter Eight

Problems and Issues   156

SYMBOLS*

Symbol	Meaning	Where introduced
t	Time (years)	15
P	No. of people	15
D	No. of documents	15
S	No. of topics	15
$\mathcal{D}$	Set of documents	16
d	A document	16
$C(d)$	Set of documents that d cites	17
$C^{-1}(d)$	Set of documents that d is cited by	17
$A\mathcal{D}(t)$	Set of documents added in year t	20
$\|S\|$	No. of elements in a set S	20
$C(t_2/t_1)$	No. of documents published in year t_2 which cite a randomly chosen document published in year t_1	20
$C^{-1}(t_1/t_2)$	No. of documents published in year t_1 which are cited by a randomly chosen document published in year t_2	21
T	Set of topics	22
$R(d)$	Set of topic–descriptors assigned to d	22
R	Average number of topic descriptors (index terms) per document	22
U	Set of document users	27
A	Set of authors	27
$I(P)$	Set of disciples on whom mentor P exerted intellectual influence	34
p	Probability that a randomly chosen document is relevant to a given query topic	75
C	Probability that a randomly chosen document cites a given document known to be relevant	75
C'	Probability that a randomly chosen document cites a document known to be irrelevant	75
a	Acceptance rate or precision ratio, extent to which an IR fails to retrieve irrelevant items	75
h	Hit-rate or recall ratio, measures the extent to which an IR system retrieves relevant items	75
L	Request load, no. of requests per hour	140

*For other symbols, see p. 156.

Chapter One

Background to Development of Theory

1.1. NEED FOR A THEORY OF INFORMATION RETRIEVAL

When an information technologist speaks of an information retrieval (IR) system, he usually means a way of providing people with documents they need. H.P. Luhn (Schultz, 1967) was among the first to design general purpose IR systems; he used a computer to generate indexes and abstracts. Since then, many clever inventions have enriched the literature on IR systems. Their supply on the market has grown greatly. This resulted in a large variety of commercial and academic IR systems which many potential users find bewildering.† As resources available to potential customers of IR systems become more scarce, IR system designers, managers, and technologists must become more discriminating in their evaluations. Guidance is welcome by users and designers alike.

When a psychologist or biochemist speaks of information retrieval (Byrne, 1970; Tulving and Donaldson, 1972), he usually refers to the process of selecting

---

†Even the number and size of surveys, computerized bibliographies, and directories to IR systems being marketed, developed, proposed, and written about has become staggering. In the U.S. Federal Government alone, the number of major mechanized information systems selected for exposition by Herner grew from 13 in 1968 to 35 in 1973 (Herner, 1970; Herner and Vellucci, 1973; Slamecka, Zunde, and Kraus, 1969). Information technologists who specialize in advanced computer sciences tend increasingly to use "information retrieval" to mean programming techniques for the use of various data structures, retrieving subroutines from a large computer-stored library of these in programming, deductive question-answering, and automatic report-generation and tabulations. In this technically sophisticated specialty, the advances have been as numerous and rapid as they have been of impressively high quality.

1

and extracting from an organized collection of stiumlus–response associates a more-or-less specified one. For example, if a psychologist asks a person to memorize a list of paired associates, such as 1–bun, 2–shoe, and 3–tree, and if he subsequently asks the subject to name the associate paired with 3, he regards the subject to have *retrieved*[†] "tree" in response to stimulus "3." If a neuroscientist trains an animal to respond in a specified way to a stimulus and then disturbs the animal so that it fails to respond, he attributes the failure to lack of registration of what is to be remembered, to erasure from memory, or to lack of appropriate retrieval.

Decisive experiments to distinguish between registration, retention, and retrieval are about as difficult to design as are controlled experiments with IR systems. A major reason is that the basic concepts are not yet clearly explicated. This is one of the first tasks for theorists. When advances in conceptualization lead to more revealing facts, a second task for theorists is to organize these facts and to connect them with what is already known. Finally, theory is needed to explain, to raise deeper questions, and to synthesize a coherent whole.

The notion of information, which is the central concept, is still as unclear as it is pervasive. It is used in the discussion of genetic codes and in the transmission of culture. It appears in economics and influences psychology. It seems impossible to discuss either computers, brains, or libraries without using this notion. Yet only in communications engineering does it have a well-explicated meaning.

The primary task of an IR systems theory is to clarify the meaning of *information* in information retrieval. We need a paradigm to direct research developments and decisions regarding IR systems. We need new ways of thinking about how information can be represented and recorded for later use. In the larger area of information systems, of which IR systems are part, "we are cursed with the problem of the large, complex system. . . for which there is neither an adequate science nor an adequate engineering discipline" (Auerbach, 1971).

As a vehicle toward theory development we focus on the technologist's concern: design of information retrieval systems to help specified users cope with specific classes of problems, for which documented knowledge is required. The main phenomenon calling for explanation is the remarkable way in which the literature has served the healthy growth of knowledge, especially science, despite its exponential growth and the concern this has caused among many users and IR system builders. Some important tasks for theorists are: explication of the notion of "representation" as it relates to data structure, to organization of knowledge in the literature, and to organization of knowledge made possible

---

[†]Actually, the preferred term is *recalled*. This differs from *recognized*, where the subject locates the word in a list that includes it.

by information technologies; analysis of questions, from both the point of view of logic, computer science, and behavioral science; analysis of processes like question-answering, question-asking, knowledge synthesis, knowledge utilization.

We chose the design of IR systems as our vehicle for two reasons. Considerable empirical knowledge about the growth of literature has accumulated. The problems related to stability and normalcy in the growth of knowledge appear to be central and common to the alternative vehicles that might have been chosen to investigate principles of information retrieval.

1.2. STEPS AND BARRIERS TOWARD THEORY-CONSTRUCTION

Information retrieval as a term denoting a topic was originated by a theorist, C. Mooers, in 1951. He viewed an information retrieval system as a machine that indexes and selects information in a library. He was struck by the similarity of such a machine and multiplex communication systems used in telegraphy. This led him (Mooers, 1954) to use the methods of information theory to calculate the efficiency and error probabilities of various ways of encoding.†

The coordinate index notion was introduced by another theorist (Taube, 1953). Here a conjunction of descriptors (another concept explicated by Mooers) is assigned by an index to a document. The user can assume that the document pertains to each of these descriptors. He can request a search for all documents pertaining to a conjunction or coordination of the descriptors he specifies.

An obstacle to sound theory-construction was lack of mathematical sophistication on the part of early theorists. Designing an IR system is a rather sophisticated engineering problem, and the use of mathematics is no less essential here than it is in the design of communication systems. While in principle Mooers seemed justified in using heuristic rather than rigorous arguments in these first days of the IR art, this lack of rigor left many obscurities and possibly errors. By contrast, the level of rigor used by von Neumann (Burks, et al., 1946) at a comparably early stage of the computer art was high, and this proved its utility in terms of the designs that followed.

It should be noted, however, that the design of computers lends itself more naturally to mathematically rigorous analysis than does the design of IR systems. This is because a computer is essentially a mathematical machine. It is therefore

---

†This early work seems to have been overlooked by subsequent theory-builders. With suitable refinements it can contribute toward a more adequate analytic methodology for evaluating IR systems.

questionable whether mathematical sophistication and precision could have done for IR what von Neumann did for computers. When the study of IR started, a high degree of rigor might well have been premature. We may question whether even today the analysis of IR systems is amenable to existing mathematical concepts and methods. New mathematical ideas and techniques may well be called for and inspired by the problems of IR. Eventually, an appropriate level of mathematical sophistication and rigor will very probably be used, and this will indicate that information science is maturing as a scientific discipline.

The first book on theory[†] appeared in 1961 (Vickery, 1961). A deeper study of principles for index-construction or subject-description of documents was the theme of that book. This was motivated by the presumed greater complexity of indexing methods caused by the growth of literature. IR was viewed in the tradition of problems in librarianship. By 1965, when a second edition of this book appeared, it was generally recognized that the key problems were not primarily those of coping with large volumes and complexity of indexing. By then, quantitative analysis of retrieval efficiency, costs, and performance had begun to predominate. By 1972, emphasis had shifted toward revolutionary changes in the ways problems are or should be solved, not only in science but in the sociopolitical arena as well.

The 1965 edition of *On Retrieval System Theory* (Vickery, 1965) portrayed the state of theory at that time rather accurately. It was not a body of theorems, nor empirical generalizations, nor general principles that might guide designers or analysts of IR systems. There were predictions that "mathematical logic will aid us in the organization of descriptors and the operation of selectors"; the most sophisticated application of a concept from logic was the application of Boolean lattices to logical combinations of descriptors (Fairthorne, 1955, 1956, 1958). There were hopes that information theory would help us encode descriptors in the data base,[‡] that linguistics would aid the selection of descriptors, and that linear programming might help us design search strategies. This had not yet happened to a significant extent, and the contemporary fashion in theory construction is to replace concern about selection and encoding of descriptors and design of search strategies with interest in methods for efficiently structuring very large files (Knuth, 1968). This was already of increasing concern by 1965, and appeared in several semitheoretical works (Becker and Hayes, 1963; Belzer

---

[†]This is theory in the more restricted sense of IR systems. In the broader sense of "theory" which we hope to discuss, IR systems are a vehicle, and the first seminal work that stimulated many of the ideas developed here was *Science Since Babylon*, (deSolla Price, 1961).

[‡]Very recently a major contribution in this area appeared (Elias, 1973); it is described in Section 3.5. A Ph.D. thesis extending these results to the updating problem is underway in the M.I.T. Electrical Engineering Department by R. Flower, under the supervision of Peter Elias.

and Goffman, 1964; Bourne, 1963; Buchholz, 1963). With the current shift in emphasis toward the role of IR systems in the newer methods of problem-solving, it is possible that priorities of concern with file organization and data structures will be reversed toward more stress on what it takes to help the problem-solver rather than how to optimally utilize computers and their programs.

One of the most erudite theoreticians (Bar-Hillel, 1960), reacting to attempts by Fairthorne, Mooers, and Vickery toward defining useful measures of distance between topics and documents, felt that the concept of a descriptor network did not appear promising. Nonetheless, subsequent work in which functions for comparing any pair of document-descriptions which makes a set of "documents" a metric space (Goffman, 1970; Salton, 1968) began to yield modest theorems. The applications to logic, algebra, and topology began to be studied more seriously (Hillman, 1964; Opler, 1964).

At the same time, there were several contributions to the methodologies for evaluation of IR systems (Borko, 1962; Cleverdon, 1965, 1967; Cuadra and Katter, 1967; Giuliano and Jones, 1966; King and Bryant, 1972; Lancaster, 1969; O'Connor, 1965; Pollock, 1968; Rothenberg, 1969; Saracevic, 1970; Swanson, 1965; Swets, 1963), to the clarification of such few fundamental laws as characterized information science in 1972, (Booth, 1967; Fairthorne, 1969; Goffman, 1966; Leimkuhler, 1967; Price, 1965; Sharpe, 1965), and toward providing a better rationale underlying their design (Holt, 1963; Kent, 1963; Meadow, 1967; Williams, 1965).

1.3. RESOURCES FOR THEORY-CONSTRUCTION

One of the most important resources toward the development of theory in the information sciences was born in 1966 when Cuadra initiated the ARIST[†] Review Series (Cuadra, 1966–present). In response to the rapid growth of information science and technology, this series aimed at consolidating results and providing good critical reviews, in depth, of selected areas. This need was recognized by two of the leading theoreticians, D.R. Swanson[‡] and R.M. Hayes, as well as by Mrs. H. Brownson (Brownson, 1960) of the National Science Foundation, and this helped launch the series.

[†] Annual Review of Information Science and Technology.

[‡] This is about when *Information Science* emerged from *Documentation* as a new profession, aspiring to become a scientific discipline alongside the other sciences. It was physicists like Swanson and mathematicians like Mooers who led the way (Mikhailov, et al., 1966; Mooers, 1959; Otten and Debons, 1970; Swanson, 1961; Yovits, 1969). For an analysis of how the terminology switched, see Wellisch (1972).

The first volume contains very little of direct use for theory-construction. Indeed, it indicates failure to apply existing theory where it should have been. For example, sampling theory and related statistical methodologies, which had been highly developed and widely used in the behavioral sciences, were not employed in many studies of the behavior of scientists and technologists and their needs for and uses of information systems. Consequently, there was little reliable evidence about the needs of users.

The chapter on evaluation of indexing systems showed that very few of the key variables and criterion measures that had been proposed prior to 1965 had been systematically explored. The most theoretical chapter in Volume 1 was "Content Analysis, Specification, and Control" by P. Baxendale. Of the 300 1965-publications which fit into the scope of her chapter, she selected about 200 as pertaining more to the theory and methodology of the indexing process than to experiences with particular indexes. The nearly total absence of a generally accepted theoretical framework is indicated by the following quote (Baxendale, 1966): "This lack of recognition of the similarities between current problems and previous solutions leads to the third observation: the unfortunate introduction of needless ambiguities in the language of documentation."

In 1967, ARIST's reviewers (Herner and Herner, 1967) still found the techniques used to study information needs and uses "extremely crude and precarious." Again they suggested that a possible cause was in the "diffuseness of the language of the field" due to the variety of backgrounds and orientations of the people coming into it. In the chapter on evaluation (Rees, 1967), it is stated that "Confusion still exists regarding appropriate objectives of testing and evaluation" and "One wonders why systems analysis techniques, so helpful in developing information systems themselves, are not applied to the development of tools for evaluating these systems."

In 1971, Cuadra suggested that a comparison of the activities reported in Volume 6 with those in Volume 1 would be instructive. The most noticeable shifts, however, were in technology—toward remote access by terminal and toward public and commercial data bases—and in applications—toward more socially relevant topics such as law enforcement and toward a more business-like approach—but not very much in the development of theory. There was an attempt to connect the most important empirical research with a model of how scientists exchange information (Crane, 1972; Price, 1965), and this is an important indication that a major resource for theory-construction has been recognized.

The research findings emerging from this "invisible college" of investigators on "communication networks" (Allen and Marquis, 1963–; Crane, 1972; Crawford, 1971; Gaston, 1970; Griffith and Miller, 1970; Hagstrom, 1965; Hutchins, Buchanan, Michael, Sherwin, Real, and White, 1963; Menzel, 1966; Mullins, 1968; Newcomb, 1966; Price, 1970) are very important, and provide not only a challenge but a basis and resource for theory-construction. The contributions to theory cited in ARIST Volume 6 (Coleman, Katz, and Menzel, 1966; King and Bryant, 1970; Kuhn, 1962; Sparck-Jones, 1970; Toulmin, 1971), however, contrast somewhat with the picture presented in the anthology *Introduction to Information Science* (Saracevic, 1970), which presents evidence of puzzle-solving activity. The Saracevic volume is a rather important recent landmark in the development of theory. Although it is an anthology, it does suggest the work and ideas of W. Goffman on epidemiological and similar mathematical models for the diffusion of knowledge and the role of documents as a central theme. Another important work on theory, which is not as widely known as it should be, presents the less mathematical and equally profound thoughts of leading social scientists such as Karl W. Deutsch, Norman Storer, Talcott Parsons, Herbert Menzel, William Garvey, and Belver Griffith, and leading library/information scientists like Jesse Shera, Eugene Garfield, and Harold Borko (Montgomery, 1968).

In sum, the raw resources to use for theory-construction in information science appear to be available. The intellectual climate and the time appear to be right. These resources need now be *developed* into a structure of theory. Despite the organizational excellence of Saracevic's anthology and the comprehensive thoroughness of Cuadra's ARIST series, there is little evidence in these works that enough resources have been developed in response to the shift of the intellectual climate toward concern with new methods of problem-solving.

1.4. INFORMATION PROBLEMS: A POINT OF VIEW

There is not just one information problem. There are many. If some information system could save λ% of the average time an American physicist needs to spend on communication, it would be worth 3λ–6λ million dollars per year to the U.S. (Bromley, 1972). How to do it economically is one information problem. Getting libraries and information centers who would voluntarily cooperate to do what is necessary so that they can pool bibliographic and material resources is another information problem. There is already a trend toward this and an organized effort (UNISIST) to foster it (Brown, Miller, and Keenan, 1967; Carter, 1967; Henderson, Moats, and Stevens, 1966; Knight and Nourse, 1969; OECD, 1971; Oettinger, 1972; Rubinoff, 1965).

Which set of problems are picked and how they are formulated and ranked to exhibit the *key* problems depends on a point of view. The point of view which has shaped this book is that of an inquiring system (Churchman, 1971). It stresses concern primarily with the question: how can a decision-maker utilize existing wisdom for more effective real-world problem-solving? At the same time, in recognition that our wisdom is less than our knowledge, that our wisdom is less than adequate for our problems, it stresses the continued growth[†] of wisdom. It is in this context that we ask *why we need IR systems, what kinds we need, and under what conditions they are worth the total effort required to create and maintain them* as viable entities.

"The thing that has saved man from his limited visions in the past has been the difficulty of devising suitable means for reaching them," said the Director of the Division of Biological Sciences at Cornell (Morison, 1962). This was meant in the context of genetic control. But it applies equally well to innovations or modifications aimed at social or intellectual control. When we introduce a new IR system, we plant it inside some living institution. The IR system is not merely a collection of machines, programs, and operating protocols. Like its host institution, it is a living system, including its human users, servers, and monitors. Installing an IR system is like grafting. To understand conditions under which an installed IR system will grow viably is to understand its host institution and the system it replaced or modified which performed its function prior to its installation. Nor can we expect to be sufficiently wise to say, on behalf of all people and all time, whether the modifications a major new IR system effects on the existing system are evolutionary or maladaptive (Kochen and Cason, 1973; Medawar, 1960).

All we can hope to do is to increase our awareness that we are asking deeper questions so that we can recognize and appreciate more keenly the favorable, evolutionary changes when they occur. We can realistically hope to understand how IR systems can fit into the newer conceptions of problem-solving. This requires a better understanding of the functions of IR systems, which have evolved in societies over the centuries. The key problems for which IR systems ought to be created have for some time plagued the "natural" systems. They were recognized at least 40 years ago as somehow screening the billions of words of recorded knowledge, deciding which of these articles and books to study more intensively, and utilizing such knowledge, understanding, and wisdom as may be arrived at this way (Bernal, 1939; Wells, 1938).

An IR system is a product of information technology. IR systems will evolve with that technology (Shaw, 1963). The evolution of technologies has been analyzed into three stages (Fubini, McKay, Hillier, and Hollomon, 1969). The first stage in the evolution of technologies is one in which what is being done now can be done cheaper, faster, and better with the help of that technology than without. IR systems with good coordinate indexes, full-text searches, or

---

[†]In an age where "limits to growth" of all kinds is the most popular slogan, this kind of growth may be the only one likely to survive.

permuted title† indexes illustrate this stage of technological evolution, for they enable us to do subject searching faster, though at a higher cost, than with conventional subject indexes.

The second stage in the evolution of a technology occurs when we can do things we could not have done without that technology. A citation index, which enables us to find all papers subsequent to 1965 which have cited a specified 1965 paper, illustrates IR in this stage.

The third stage occurs when we change our behavior and our ways of doing things because of the new technology. The car, the telephone, and Xerox machines are examples, with the latter two relating to IR systems. Micrographics has not yet reached this stage, and CATV (cable television with the potential for revolutionizing IR) is about to make its bid for entering this stage (Parker and Dunn, 1972).

The third stage is one of great risk. The advancing technology can cause irreversible effects. Careful engineering alone does not guarantee that the net result of the advances will be beneficial. Certain radical innovations in publishing or library practice which are recommendations from sound engineering of limited scope may well turn out to be detrimental, and irreparably so.

That is why we must probe more deeply into the functions of IR systems than is done in most cost–benefit analyses. Rather deep questions about the dynamics of the growth of knowledge, in which an effective IR system would intervene, must be discussed from a variety of viewpoints, dominated by one that is humanistic (Kochen, 1969).

1.5. METHODOLOGY

Ideally, a theory is a set of sentences in a formal language with a few powerful axioms, some special rules of inference, and a rich body of true theorems that capture the essential phenomena and concepts. We want to capture the concepts of *information* and *use of information* in IR systems. The first and hardest part in constructing a theory is developing the formal language and its system of interpretation: picking a suitable set of variables, predicates, and functions. What makes it hard is the difficulty of specifying what the theory is to do with sufficient specificity and logical precision.

---

† Various types of indexes and indexing methods are discussed extensively throughout the literature. Most of them are quite familiar to every user of books and libraries. The permuted title index was developed by H.P. Luhn into a practical innovation of considerable impact (Edmundson and Wyllys, 1961; Fischer, 1966).

Then a set of bold, yet plausible, assumptions must be made. Here we compromise between realism and deductive power.

This is followed by the classification and compilation and synthesis of problems, solutions, and models into patterns and more general classes. There the detection of analogies plays an important role. This requires a degree of luck, insight, and intuition. Sometimes this is unavailable, and there is only a scattered compilation of unrelated models, isolated problems, fragmented answers. Sometimes, also, such intuition precedes and influences the creation of specific models. It is this latter approach that we try here.

Consider the following three analogies: (*a*) a human being stands in a relation to *his* nervous system which is similar to the relation between an institution and *its* information system; (*b*) that part of the human nervous system responsible for remembering is analogous to our IR system; (*c*) the world system of knowledge and communication, including the literature, is to mankind as a person's nervous system is to him. The value of such general analogies is in the suggestive insights, a stimulation for more exact thinking, they lead to. They can mislead if stretched too far or taken too seriously.

The human nervous system can be studied in isolation provided it is viewed in the context of the entire person, partitioned into a circulatory system, a digestive system, etc. So can memory. We can attempt to dissect it and analyze the pieces one at a time. That is the method of science.

It applies well to systems such as a gas in a closed container of volume V under pressure p at temperature T. We can heat the gas and observe the pressure p' when the temperature becomes T'; we know that the volume has remained constant during heating. We can try to express pressure as a function of temperature for that volume; if it is a linear function, the coefficient is a function of V: $p = c(V) \cdot T$. Repeating the experiment with a different volume may lead us to Boyle's law, $c(V) = k/V$, or $pV = kT$.

To take another example, in counting tasks a person can keep in mind about 7 ± 2 items at one time (Miller, 1956). This seems to be a property of "short-term" memory, where information is organized into "chunks." A large number of components can be identified in stimuli with a large number of variables as long as the number of components per variable is 7 ± 2 (Pollack, 1968).

To understand human memory more deeply, however, we have to study it in the context of the entire nervous system and the entire person. Separating memory, attention, learning, etc., is more useful to a textbook author than to the scientist seeking to understand. The methods of information theory, the behavioral sciences, computer sciences, biology, and information sciences in the technical sense (Kochen, 1973c) can all contribute toward a theory of memory in the sense of IR. Our contribution to developing such a theory is restricted by the use of methods in information science primarily.

Attempts to dissect such an entire nervous system so as to study the relation between just pairs of variables at a time is not always possible; the attempt to keep the other variables constant can impair the very functional relation to be observed in an essential way. To observe necessitates, sometimes, such a violent interference with what is to be observed that only the effect of the observer's intervention is observed, and not the function of interest.

The chief criterion in scientific theory-building is, of course, experimental corroboration. The first steps toward a theory advanced in this book are not yet at that stage except in special areas. Nonetheless, it is important to bear in mind at the outset the kinds of experiments that will have to be done, particularly since there may be basic limits to what we can observe experimentally[†] (Elsasser, 1958). There is, of course, considerable historical data that can be used to test certain hypotheses, as in historical research and in research on the history of science in particular.

1.6. PLAN

Our two primary[‡] objects of analysis are (*a*) an IR system and (*b*) system of knowledge and communication in which it functions. We will, for the most part, think of the knowledge system concretely as that by which people with problems use, and add to, the literature. On dissecting this knowledge system, we find three major ingredients: people, documents, and topics. People generate, digest, and utilize information. Documents record and transfer it. Topics organize it. The first class of ingredients corresponds to Sebeok and Fairthorne's (Fairthorne, 1961) "source and destination," and Bühler's "Kundgabe and Appell." The third corresponds to Sebeok and Fairthorne's "Designation," and Bühler's "Darstellung."

An IR system exists to serve the needs of the information-processors, the people. It responds to their requests for specified knowledge. They pose questions or queries to the IR system which indicate that they know they need some

---

[†]Does that mean the analysis of some human behavior, of cognition, and of more complex IR systems involving human behavior, is beyond the limits of scientific investigation? Much of it has been fruitfully attacked by the traditional scientific method. But the behavioral sciences and the information sciences should and can bring about a radical change in our views of, and in our ways of doing, science. Psychology must eventually become a state-specific science (Tart, 1972) concerned with states of consciousness. This will bring about a reorientation in the very notion of what we mean by an experiment. A person's awareness that he knows something must again become admissible evidence just as we admit observable behavior. Rather than continue with reductionism in the behavioral sciences, to fit it into the mold of classical science, the pioneers in the study of the mind and of knowledge must rise to the challenge of leading and revising science itself.

[‡]Though only Chapters Seven and Eight are devoted to (*a*), the relation to IR systems appears throughout Chapters Two through Six, which discuss (*b*).

knowledge that they do not have. Only documented, authenticated knowledge is demanded and supplied. It is of value only insofar as it fits into some representation in the user's mind. This representation must somehow be coupled with the organization of knowledge provided by the IR system.

We have used the term knowledge rather than information, though information has, so far, been used quite loosely and broadly. The distinction is important. All the terms used here to suggest vague concepts will be subsequently defined as technical terms and explicated. Information is a cost, says Boulding (1966), while knowledge can be an economic good.

The three types of ingredients in Figure 1.1 will be explicated in some depth. Three approaches will be used. The first two are approaches borrowed from engineering. In the first, each component—the rectangle, circle, and triangle of Figure 1.1—is viewed as a black box and described behaviorally by its input–output or stimulus–response relations. In the second, each unit is described by possible algorithms that could generate such behavior. The third approach is that of analyzing relations and interactions among documents, people and topics. This resembles some of the newer ways of looking at sociological phenomena. These stress the rational and nonrational elements in the behavior of people interacting with one another and their culture. Each information-processor (author, reader), document, and topic has an intellectual signature. It is known, to some extent, by the company of authors, readers, documents, and topics with which it is most closely associated.

In addition to developing mathematical models of the information-processing agents, documents, and topics by themselves, we can analyze the six possible couplings among and between them. In Chapter Two we study four of these interactions: among documents, between documents and topics, between documents and agents, and among agents. Some of the basic relations among the number and growth of these three constituents of the knowledge system are derived. This chapter lays the groundwork for our definition of "information" and of "use of information" in an IR system, which is developed in the subsequent chapters.

In Chapter Three we introduce our explication of information as needed for a study of IR. We are now, and at various other points in the book, using *information* in its nonscientific, generic sense to include data, documents, knowledge, understanding, and wisdom as well as information in its technical sense. The central theme of Chapter Three is the concept of a *topic* as a device for organizing knowledge. We indicate in Figure 1.1, by numbers in parentheses, which chapter discusses the various components in Figure 1.1 and their interactions. Thus, (3) is associated with the triangles. In Chapter Three we use the algorithmic or second approach.

In Chapter Four we investigate the *document* concept, or circles in Figure 1.1. Here, as in Chapter Five, we use the black-box stimulus–response (S–R)

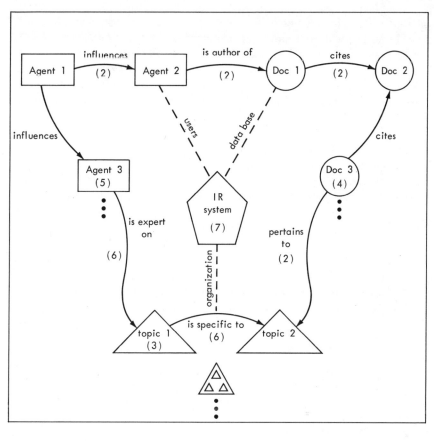

Figure 1.1. Conceptualization of knowledge system.

approach. In both Chapters Five and Six we use the algorithmic approach also. Wherever it is useful, we use differential equations, matrices, probability, logic, and all the other mathematics of modern systems theory with which nearly every contemporary college graduate with a serious interest in information science should be familiar.

In Chapter Five we examine the concept of an *information-processing agent*, interpreted as a user at an IR system who adds to or utilizes the knowledge system to recognize and cope with problems. This corresponds to the rectangles in Figure 1.1. The remaining two interactions that we postponed in Chapter Two, between agents and topics, and among agents, are taken up in Chapter Six.

The central object of study, an IR system, which appears throughout all the chapters, is the theme of Chapter Seven, which summarizes design principles. Chapters Five and Six develop a basis for classifying IR system users and uses (problem-classes, in topics), and in Chapter Seven the theme of matching classes of IR systems with user and use classes is taken up.

Chapter Eight presents a mathematical analysis of an illustrative problem of special interest and summarizes the key issues raised throughout.

Several themes weave through the text. One is the ubiquitous tradeoff between errors of omission and commission. Another is that of nature's self-regulatory mechanisms by which the knowledge system remains viable, functional, and stable. Yet another is that of skew distributions which appear nearly everywhere. They are all part of the central theme of information (in the popular sense) and its use to help people recognize and cope with problems.

In sum, we ask, in general, for conditions in a knowledge system under which various kinds of IR systems contribute more than they cost toward the healthy growth of knowledge. This type of question ought to be of some concern to mathematical sociologists. Whether it is or not, it is of central concern for information science, and will be approached with the help of all the relevant mathematical tools and concepts at our disposal.

Chapter Two

The Environment of an Information Retrieval System

2.1. OVERALL PERSPECTIVE

We conceptualize the knowledge system into which an IR system is implanted to consist of three kinds of component parts: (*a*) people in their role as information-processors, (*b*) documents in their role as carriers of information, and (*c*) topics as representations. We are concerned with the life cycle of each of these three objects and with the dynamic interactions among them. Therefore we consider a basic variable common to all three: time. We take this to be a continuously varying (real) number t with an arbitrary zero-point.

The number of people, documents, and topics are, respectively, the functions of t: $P(t), D(t)$, and $S(t)$. Though these are most naturally to be considered as discontinuous in t, it will, for purposes of mathematical analysis, be useful to treat them as continuous functions; this will permit us to replace difference equations by differential equations, which are easier to solve, and the resulting general conclusions we seek are qualitatively the same for both the differential and the difference equations.

There are six possible couplings among these three functions. For a document, which is the basic ingredient of an information retrieval system, there are three: document–document coupling, such as the number of papers citing or being cited by a given one; document–topic coupling, such as the number of topic-descriptors used to index the document or the number of documents indexed under a given topic-descriptor; and document–people coupling, such as the number of authors or users of a document or the number of documents authored by or used by a person.

The estimates we derive are of the kind usually sought by engineers or scientists to get an overall and preliminary assessment of the feasibility of an idea or technique. The finer details sometimes require better approximations and more specialized assumptions. In most of our estimates, this is not the case, and the finer details can obscure the most salient features of the large pictures more than they help.

Of course, all these coupling constants must be described more precisely, their choice justified, and their utility shown by deriving interesting results. To reduce our conceptualization to one that is mathematically tractable, it is necessary to simplify—to make rather bold decisions that only three variables and six coupling constants are more fundamental than the hundreds of other variables necessary for a complete description of a complex institution. In trade for such incompleteness we gain logical precision. Idealized models enable us to chart the logical boundaries of our domain of inquiry and to formulate plausible assumptions and separate these from less plausible conclusions derived from them. All this will lead to insights, ideas, and hypotheses to be empirically tested—tentative formulations of principles that would not have occurred otherwise.

2.2. DOCUMENT–DOCUMENT COUPLING: CITATION NETS

We can analyze some of the quantitative aspects of citation nets even before we have a fuller and deeper analysis of what a document is. We need merely assume for now that documents exist as identifiable units, each of which has explicit links with other documents. To fix ideas, think of a document as a computer-stored record that can be called by a tally or address with pointers to other such addresses or tallies.

Logically, the verb *cites* is a two-place predicate;[†] it designates a two-place relation defined on all possible pairs of document-tallies. To be precise, let $\mathcal{D}(t)$ denote the set of all the $D(t)$ documents in the library of an institution at time t. A two-place relation is any subset of the set of all ordered pairs (d, d') with d, d' both elements of $\mathcal{D}(t)$. For example, if $D(t) = 3$ and $\mathcal{D}(t) = \{d, d', d''\}$, and if d cited d' and d'' while d' cited d'', then the *cites* relation is the subset $\{(d, d'), (d, d''), (d', d'')\}$. Such subsets are determined empirically. They can also be represented by an *incidence matrix* or a *graph* (Figure 2.1).

In the incidence matrix, we place a 1 in a cell whose row corresponds to a citing document d and whose column designates a document which d cites. We place a 0 in a cell if the row-document d does not cite the column-document.

[†]We use this term here in the sense that it is used in mathematical logic (Carnap, 1934), as the *name* of a relation. The same relation—for example, $\{(1,2), (1,3), (2,3), \ldots\}$—may have two different names such as "is less than" and "is softer than." This interpertation of *predicate* resembles its use in grammar and is less likely to cause confusion between *use* and *mention* than do other interpretations in logic (Fairthorne, 1965).

The 1s in the incidence matrix correspond to lines with arrows in the graph. The graph is the citation net.

Corresponding to the predicate *cites* is the inverse predicate, *is cited by*. This is represented by transpose of the incidence matrix for *cites*; If $C = (c_{ij})$ is the matrix for *cites*, then $C^T = (c_{ji})$ is the matrix for *is cited by*. The incidence matrix and graph for the previous example are shown in Figure 2.2.

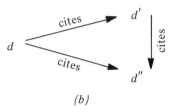

	d	d'	d''
d	0	1	1
d'	0	0	1
d''	0	0	0

(a)   *(b)*

Figure 2.1. Illustrating the relation *cites*. (*a*) Incidence matrix for *cites*. (*b*) Graph for *cites*.

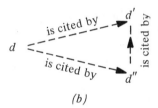

	d	d'	d''
d	0	0	0
d'	1	0	0
d''	1	1	0

(a)   *(b)*

Figure 2.2. Illustrating the relation *is cited by*. (*a*) Incidence matrix for *is cited by*. (*b*) Graph for *is cited by*.

We now introduce some mathematical notation for the purpose of deriving some statements about properties of citation nets. To start, we examine the collection of all documents citing any document that is cited by a given one.

Let d denote any document and $C(d)$ the set of all documents that d cites. Let d' be such a document in $C(d)$. Let $C^{-1}(d')$ be the set of all documents which d' is cited by. This will surely include d. In plain words, if we form the collection of all documents cited by a given document d, and we adjoin to that collection all the documents citing any of these cited ones, the resulting collection will surely contain d. This proves Theorem 1.

THEOREM 1. $$d \; \epsilon \bigcup_{d' \epsilon C(d)} C^{-1}(d')$$

This states an obvious relation in a formidable notation, but it is useful to get acquainted with this notation because it is necessary for stating less obvious relations about citation nets.

THEOREM 2. If there is just one document which cites no other in the set of all documents, then

$$\mathcal{D} = \overset{\infty}{\underset{j=1}{\cup}} C_j$$

where

$$C_j = \underset{d_i \in C_{i-1}}{\cup} [C(d_i) \cup C^{-1}(d_i)]$$

and

$$C_0 = C(d_0) \cup C^{-1}(d_0) \quad \text{for some} \quad d_0 \in \mathcal{D}$$

By starting with any document and collecting all the documents that it cites or that cite it, and adjoining to that all those that cite or are cited by any document picked up so far, and continuing, we will eventually pick up all documents. The condition for this is that there be just one document without references to antecedents. The set C_j is the collection of all documents which cite, or are cited by, some document in C_{j-1}, for $j = 1,2,3, \ldots$, and C_0 is the set of documents which cite or are cited by a given one.

Proof: Pick any $d_0 \in \mathcal{D}$; $C(d_0)$ is the set of all documents that d_0 cites and $C^{-1}(d_0)$ is the set of all documents citing d_0. Then C_0 is the set of all documents which either cite d_0 or are cited by d_0. At most one document in C_0, indeed in $C(d_0)$, will have no citations. For each document d_1 in C_0 except possibly that one, we can form $C(d_1)$ and also $C^{-1}(d_1)$ if this is not yet the empty set. We call C_1 the set of elements in either $C(d_1)$ or $C^{-1}(d_1)$ for all the possible d_1 in C_0. We can continue until both the set $C(d_i)$ contains only the document that cites nothing and $C^{-1}(d_i)$ is empty. We will then have exhausted every element of $\mathcal{D}$.

To prove this, suppose, to the contrary, that some d were in $\mathcal{D}$ which had not yet been found by this process, *because it was not at all cited.* Either it is the nonciting document or else it cites the simple nonciting document directly or indirectly, in one or more removes. In either case, there can be no documents other than d or the ones it cites in one or more removes, or else there would have to be more than one simple nonciting document, as hypothesized. Hence d must have been cited, and it would therefore have been located by this algorithm. Indeed, every document in $\mathcal{D}$ must be cited at least once, or there would have to be more than one nonciting document.

If d was cited by some other document d', then this argument can be repeated by applying it to all the d' that cite d. By induction, Theorem 2 follows.

The proof of this theorem makes an important and somewhat controversial assumption. We assume that if d cites d', then d' cannot also cite d. This is justified by our precise explication of the concept of a *document* in Chapter Four as something citable. A well-defined birthdate is associated with each document. It is the time that a publisher acknowledges receipt of the manuscript for the intended document. Prior to this birthtime a manuscript is not, according to our conceptualization, a document, and it cannot be cited in the sense we wish to define *cites* as a technical term (Section 4.5). Thus for d to cite d', d must have a birthtime after that of d'. If d and d' have simultaneous birthtimes, then neither should cite the other at that time.

What is more commonly understood by the word *cites* does not correspond completely with this assumption. Some publications cite (in the popular sense) unpublished manuscripts, preprints, work in progress, private communications and numerous items that we would not wish to call documents. The bibliography of this book, for example, contains several references to publications in process, especially the author's. Many manuscripts are revised after they have become documents in our technical sense. The revised version of such a manuscript d could cite a later document d', which cites d as well.

We could define a *citable document* in such a way that the above could not be said to occur. For now, we would like simply to point out that the popular use of the terms *document* and *cites* is too imprecise for deriving useful theoretical results. It does not violate the essence of the relation of citation, which is analogous to that of parenthood in one respect, to require it to be antisymmetric and irreflexive. These assumptions prove their utility by implying interesting results.

The main hypothesis of Theorem 2 is that there be just one nonciting document. There must be at least one. If every document cited some other document, then some earlier documents would have to cite later ones, violating the above assumption.

If there were more than one nonciting document, then the document collection could be divided into separate parts. The algorithm implicit in the proof would then locate all the documents in a part which contains the document used to start the search. This algorithm can be used for computer-aided search of a citation index to compile a rather complete and up-to-date bibliography for a retrospective search. This can be used to explore the interiors and boundaries of topics.

A real citation index (Garfield, 1955) does not, of course, cover all the literature. It begins with a sample (profile) of the documents published in a certain year, say 1964, chosen by a searcher as representative of what he needs. It lists all the earlier documents cited by any of these. In each subsequent year, say 1966, etc., it lists not only all documents in a specified set of journals which cite any articles prior to 1964, but it indicates for each 1964 article which 1965 and which 1966 articles cited it. A searcher can then pick a particular 1965 article and do a *forward trace*: he can look for all 1966 articles that cited it. He can also do several backward traces; for each 1966 article he found, for example, he can determine the earlier papers it cited.

We will discuss the potential and limitations of this powerful basis for information retrieval later. It works because the authors of the papers a searcher knows to be relevant usually make a relevance judgment in the papers they cite that is more useful to the searcher than comparable relevance judgments made by the average indexer. Another reason citation indexes are so useful is their independence of topic-descriptors, avoiding the imprecision and inconsistency inherent in the use of topic-descriptors.

We can partition the set of documents $\mathcal{D}(t)$ which exist in a library up to and including time t into the set of documents published in 1960, or in 1959, or in 1961, etc. If t is measured in years, then we denote the set published during the year t_1 by $\mathcal{D}(t_1 + 1) - \mathcal{D}(t_1)$, which we abbreviate by A $\mathcal{D}(t_1)$ (A for *Added* documents). By convention we will sometimes denote the number of elements in a set S by $|S|$, so that $D(t) = |\mathcal{D}(t)|$, and $|A\mathcal{D}(t_1)|$ [or more simply $N(t_1)$] is the number of documents published during year t, and

$$\frac{dD(t)}{dt} \quad \text{or} \quad D'(t) = \lim_{\Delta t \to 0} \frac{1}{\Delta t} |\mathcal{D}(t + \Delta t) - \mathcal{D}(t)|$$

is the instantaneous publication rate at time t.

Consider any randomly chosen document published in year t_1. Call it d_1. Among the $|A\mathcal{D}(t_2)|$ documents published in year t_2, for $t_2 > t_1$, there will be $C(t_2|d_1)$ which cite d_1. Because d_1 is selected at random, $C(t_2|d_1)$ varies with d_1 as a random variable, which we shall denote by $C(t_2|t_1)$. Its mean $\bar{C}(t_2|t_1)$ is one of the document–document coupling constants. Indeed, t_2 and t_1 need not be years but could be any pair of real time-values, making $\bar{C}(t_2|t_1)$ a function in t_1 and t_2 and $C(t_2|t_1)$ a two-parameter stochastic process. It seems plausible, however, to assume independence: that the probability of $C(t_2|t_1) \leq c$ and $C(t_3|t_4) \leq c'$ equals $P(C(t_2|t_1) < c) \times P(C(t_3|t_4) < c')$ for any t_1, t_2, t_3, t_4, c, c'. Also plausible, but more in need of empirical verification, is the assumption of stationarity: that the probability distribution of $C(t_2,t_1)$ does not depend on t_1 or t_2 but only on $t_2 - t_1$. This implies that $\bar{C}(t_2,t_1)$ is a function of $t_2 - t_1$ only, which means that the average number of citations per article is the same today as it was 100 years ago or will be 100 years hence.[†]

[†]This is an instance of a hypothesis to be empirically tested.

Note that $\overline{C}(t_2,t_1) \cdot N(t_1)$ is the number of document pairs, with one document published in year t_1 and the other published in year t_2 and citing the one published in year t_1. If the incidence matrix had as its rows only the documents of $A\mathcal{D}(t_2)$ and as its columns only those of $A\mathcal{D}(t_1)$, then the above product is the total (exact) number of 1s in the matrix. This can by anything from 0 to $N(t_1)N(t_2)$; in the former case, no document published in t_2 cites any document published in t_1; in the latter, each document published in t_2 cites every document published in t_1. The average number of 1s in a column is $\overline{C}(t_2|t_1)$.

Consider any randomly chosen document published in year t_2, and call it d_2. Among the $N(t_1)$ documents published in year t_1, for $t_1 < t_2$, there were $C^{-1}(t_1|d_2)$ which are cited by d_2. As before, $C^{-1}(t_1|t_2)$ is a random variable. $\overline{C}^{-1}(t_1|t_2)$ denotes the average number of documents published in t_1 cited by a document published in t_2, averaged over the citing documents. It is the average number of 1s in a row of the $N(t_2)$ by $N(t_1)$ incidence matrix.

Note that $\overline{C}^{-1}(t_1|t_2)N(t_2)$ is again the same total number of 1s in the incidence matrix that was computed above. This proves Theorem 3.

THEOREM 3. $\quad \overline{C}(t_2|t_1)N(t_1) = \overline{C}^{-1}(t_1|t_2)N(t_2) \quad$ for each t_1, t_2

The numbers $C^{-1}(t_1|t_2)$ form another set of document–document coupling constants. If any three of the four numbers used in Theorem 3 are given, the fourth is determined.

This theorem states that the mean number of references to articles published in year t_1 (called t_1-papers) which are found in the bibliographies of t_2-papers, multiplied by the number of t_1-papers, is the same as the average number of t_2-papers cited by t_1-papers, times the number of t_1-papers. This result can be used to estimate the number of documents likely to be retrieved during the various steps of citation tracing using an algorithm such as described in Theorem 1.

Example: Suppose the library contains $N(t_1) = 20$ documents published in year t_1 and $N(t_2) = N(t_1 + 5) = 25$ documents published five years later. Suppose that a paper published in year t_1 is cited, on the average, by $C(t_1 + 5|t_1) = 10$ papers that are published five years later. Then the number of references by a paper published in $t_1 + 5$ to some paper published five years earlier must be, on the average

$$\overline{C}^{-1}(t_1|t_1 + 5) = \frac{(10)(20)}{25} = \frac{200}{25} = 8$$

Theorem 3 is easily generalized in that $N(t)$ can be replaced by the publication rate $D'(t)$. In all the interpretations we must then replace the phrase "published in year t" by "published during the time interval $(t, t + dt)$."

It follows, as a corollary, that if the growth rate is constant, then $\overline{C}(t_2|t_1) = \overline{C}^{-1}(t_1|t_2)$: the average number of papers citing a randomly chosen cited article is the same as the average number of articles cited by a randomly chosen citing paper. If the growth rate increases, then the latter average is correspondingly less than the former. During the period of history when the total number of documents grew exponentially, the growth rate must have been increasing. During such a period a paper could be expected to receive more citations on the average than it gave. We may still be in such a period now.

The greater is $t_2 - t_1$, the greater is this effect. For large $t_2 - t_1$, the average paper gets more citations $t_2 - t_1$ years later than it gives. Its half-life should grow with the growth rate of the literature.

2.3.   DOCUMENT–TOPIC COUPLING: SUBJECT CATALOGS AND INDEXES

The notion of a topic is even more elusive than that of a document. We defer an attempt to analyze it as a representation of information. We need only assume that people behave as if there were at times a set $T(t)$ of distinct topics denoted by the subject-headings used by subject-catalogers of a library. Let $S(t)$ or $|T(t)|$ be the number of topics of concern to a particular institution at time t. This, like $D(t)$, has a growth rate (see Section 6.3 for data).

Logically, the verb *pertains to* is a two-place predicate and denotes a two-place relation which either holds or does not hold for any document–topic pair. Corresponding to it is the inverse predicate *is treated in*. For example, let d stand for a particular patent by Edison and s for the topic of *incandescence*. If some cataloger asserts that d pertains to s, then he should also admit that s is treated in d, and conversely. Any searcher expecting this logical equivalence should be justified in his expectation.

We can again represent these two relations by two incidence matrices or two graphs. It is now quite easy to prove an analog to Theorem 3. Consider document d chosen randomly from $\mathcal{D}(t)$. Let $R(d)^\dagger$ denote the set of topic-descriptors from $T(t)$ assigned to d prior to time t. Let $R(t)$ denote the average number of such descriptors per document. Figure 2.3 illustrates a document–topic coupling table. Imagine it to represent a directory to about 10,000 documents which have appeared in periodicals or been issued as patents. These are designated by tallies, say the numbers from 1 to 10,000. An article, say Number 59,

---

†We use the letters R and R as mnemonics for *relevance*. We need not discuss this here, because we make only formal if–then statements: for example, if relev(d,s), then relev$^{-1}(s,d)$.

might have been described by a human indexer with a set of 10 descriptors chosen from a list of 500 possible index terms. For example, Document 59, entitled "Lattice Parameters of Zn_3As_2," might be assigned descriptors 3, 7, 23, and 472 which could be looked up in a codebook to stand for semiconductors, crystals, cubic lattice dimensions, and Zinc–Arsenic, respectively. Document 21, which was cited by Document 59, reported a much smaller size for the same cubic lattice than did Document 59; it should have been assigned the same four descriptors, but since another indexer might have done it, only the terms 23 and 472 might have been assigned.

Recording such a directory is equivalent to storing the information content of a table with 500 rows and 10,000 columns. Each row represents a descriptor, each column a document; 1s are placed in cells corresponding to the descriptor for that row which has been assigned to the document for that column.

If a searcher wants to consult this directory for all documents reporting measurements of the size of the cubic lattice of the zinc–arsenic crystal, he would scan both rows 23 and 472 across the entire table, and mark those columns in which there is a 1 in *both* of these rows. He would then search for the documents designated by those columns, 21 and 59 in the above illustration. In the above matrix, $\bar{R}(t)$ denotes the average number of 1s in a column, if no account is taken of t.

Similarly, consider a topic s randomly chosen from $T(t)$. Let $R^{-1}(s)$ denote the number of documents which have been said by catalogers to treat s, and let $\bar{R}^{-1}(t)$ be the average number of documents per topic. This is the average number of 1s in a row of the directory-table of Figure 2.3.

Clearly, the total number of 1s in the directory table is expressible, equivalently, as $\bar{R}(t) \cdot D(t)$ or as $\bar{R}^{-1}(t) \cdot S(t)$. We therefore have Theorem 4.

THEOREM 4. The average number of descriptors per document times the number of documents is equal to the average number of documents per descriptor times the number of descriptors.

This result appears to have been first mentioned in print by Taube and Wooster (1958). Though quite evident and easy to understand, it is still not as widely known among practitioners and students of the information sciences as might be expected. It is important for the design of IR systems.

Example: Suppose a library has 100,000 books and a subject-heading list of 50,000 terms. If the average number of subject-headings assigned by catalogers to books is 1.6, then the average number of books on one subject heading must be

$$\frac{\text{Number of descriptors/document} \times \text{Number of documents}}{\text{Number of descriptors}} = \frac{100,000 \times 1.6}{50,000} = 3.2$$

It is perhaps plausible to assume that neither $R(t)$ nor $R^{-1}(t)$ varies greatly with t. There is some data to suggest that during the history of indexing practice, the average number of descriptors per document has increased. But it is a rather slow increase, with fairly definite bounds. A document cannot pertain to too many descriptors and still preserve the unity which makes it useful.

If we assume $\overline{R}(t)$ to be constant, and regard $D(t)$, $S(t)$, and $R^{-1}(t)$ as continuously differentiable functions of t, then from Theorem 4 it follows that

$$\overline{R}D'(t) = \overline{R}^{-1}(t)S'(t) + S(t)\frac{d}{dt}\overline{R}^{-1}(t)$$

Except for the last term, this is similar to Theorem 4 with D' and S' in place of D and S. From this we can derive some interesting implications about $S'(t)$.

Documents	1	2	3	$\cdots$	21	$\cdots$	59	$\cdots$	10,000
1	0	0	0		0		0		0
2	0	0	0		0		0		0
3	0	0	0		0		1		0
$\vdots$	$\vdots$	$\vdots$	$\vdots$		$\vdots$		$\vdots$		$\vdots$
7	0	0	0		0		1		0
$\vdots$	$\vdots$	$\vdots$	$\vdots$		$\vdots$		$\vdots$		$\vdots$
23	0	0	0		1		1		0
$\vdots$	$\vdots$	$\vdots$	$\vdots$		$\vdots$		$\vdots$		$\vdots$
472	0	0	0		1		1		0
$\vdots$	$\vdots$	$\vdots$	$\vdots$		$\vdots$		$\vdots$		$\vdots$
500	0	0	0		0		0		0

Descriptors

Figure 2.3. Illustrating the relation *is discussed in.*

THEOREM 5. If the literature growth rate, the average number of descriptors per document, and the growth rate of the average number of documents per topic are all constants, then the number of topics varies inversely with time.

Proof: If the average number of papers per topic grows at a constant rate, then $\overline{R}^{-1}(t)$ grows linearly with t. The other two conditions of the theorem imply that $\overline{R}(t)D'(t)$ is a constant, say $\overline{R}D'$. Substitute these two results into the differential equation derived above. Solve the differential equation for $S(t)$ to obtain $S(t) = S_0/t + \overline{R}D'/k$, where S_0 is the (initial) number of topics at $t = 1$ and k is the constant rate at which the average number of papers per topic grows.

The conditions of this theorem assert a constant growth rate for documents. If population, particularly the intellectually productive subpopulation, reaches a state of zero-population growth, then this condition is plausible. The condition that the average number of papers per topic grow at a constant rate also implies a steady growth for each specialty. In practice, of course, such growth can continue only up to a limit. When a topic becomes too overcrowded, it begins to split into subtopics. But continued linear growth of a topic can occur for a limited period of time. The implication is that the number of topics declines during that period. Since this is not a likely situation, the assumption that a topic grows at a constant rate is not very likely either. The condition of zero growth rate for a topic is more plausible, and is explored in Theorem 6.

Can $S(t)$ ever decrease? Even though *phlogiston* is no longer a topic-descriptor, it once was; searchers might still, in a historical inquiry, want documents on this topic. Suppose the library is weeded of all documents on obsolete topics or that such documents as are kept are recataloged. Then $S(t)$ could decrease.

THEOREM 6. If $(d/dt) R^{-1}(t) = 0$, then $S(t)$ grows the way $D(t)$ grows.

Proof: The differential equation is simply $S'(t) = (\overline{R}/K) D'(t)$, where K is the average (constant) number of documents per topic. Hence $S(t) = (\overline{R}/K) D(t) +$ const. In particular, when D grows exponentially, so does S.

If the number of articles per topic stays fixed, then the number of topics must grow just as fast as the number of documents to be "pigeon-holed" into the set of topics. An interesting corollary is that if $D(t)$ ever begins to decline, then so does $S(t)$, under these conditions.

It is suggestive to call the set $R(d)$ of topic-descriptors assigned to document d the *topic-profile* of d. This is part of what we have called the *intellectual signature of d*. The set $C(d) \cup C^{-1}(d)$ of documents cited by or citing d should be called the document-profile or citation-profile of d, and it is another part of ds intellectual signature. Let us abbreviate this union by $C^*(d)$.

If $|C^*(d)|$ is large, say 20 or more, and $C^*(d) = C^*(d')$ for two documents d and d', the probability should be close to 1 that d and d' are *closely related*, perhaps copies, revisions, translations, or simply different physical forms of the same work. Even if one indexer formed $R(d)$ and another one generated $R(d')$ for such closely related documents d and d', there should be considerable overlap of the topic-profiles:

$$\frac{|R(d) \cap R(d')|}{|R(d) \cup R(d')|}$$

should be close to 1. The above measure is a variant of one used by Rogers and Tanimoto (1960) and Augustson and Minker (1970), and the literature contains a number of other measures that have been proposed (Stevens, Guiliano, and Heilprin, 1965). Let us denote such a measure by a function $\sigma_t(d,d')$ and call it a *topic-profile similarity function*. A similar function, $\sigma_c(d,d')$, for example,

$$\frac{|C^*(d) \cap C^*(d')|}{|C^*(d) \cup C^*(d')|}$$

would be called the *citation-profile similarity function*. A plausible hypothesis to be tested empirically could now be formulated as $\sigma_t(d,d') = k\sigma_t(d,d')$ for some constant of proportionality k. Indeed, there have been experiments (Kessler, 1965) to show the connection between the *backward citation profile* and the *topic-profile* of documents. This is partial support for the statement made in the previous section about why citation indexing is useful.

There are many reasons[†] why an author of d cites a prior document d'. If $R(d') = R(d)$, with $|R(d)| > 3$ or so, then he very probably cites d', *if he knows of d'*, because he owes an intellectual debt, has found a discrepancy, has checked a prior claim, or in some way advanced knowledge in an intersection of topics which is rather specialized and in which he should indicate the relation to prior work. Let us suppose that the only reason d' would not be cited is that the author of d failed to retrieve d' during a search with topic-profile $R(d)$. If indexers would indeed assign $R(d')$ to d, then the author's failure to retrieve d' must be due to his not having assigned the same topic-profile to his own document for use as a search specification, $R(d)$, as would the indexer, according to this simple model. The IR system might use a less stringent criterion than an exact match between the search specification and the topic-profiles. The greater chance of retrieving d' is paid for by retrieving also numerous other documents, which the author of d would now find an undesirable distraction when he is looking for relevant prior works. The greater the variance among the topic-profiles assigned to the same document by various readers, the more the payment in having to screen "false drops" to attain a desired probability of a "hit."

[†]In compiling the bibliography for this book, for example, we tried to include any key contributor to theories concerning IR or knowledge systems whose work had ever come to our attention. But, to keep the bibliography from being much larger than it is, which would have rendered it less useful, we had to carefully omit references to numerous authors whose work we knew but did not judge as relevant or significant for our purpose as the works that were cited.

This is what Ziman (1969, p. 80) calls the fundamental law[†] of information retrieval. In his words, "If you try to get hold of nearly every paper that there is in your chosen subject, you will be faced with a collection in which a high proportion of the material is obviously irrelevant; in your attempt to find out all about the percolation of electrons in semiconductors, you will be inundated with papers about the percolation of water through the foundation of dams."

2.4. DOCUMENT–AGENT COUPLING: AUTHORSHIP AND READERSHIP

The three objects of study in this simplified description of the environment of IR systems were people, documents, and topics. The notions of document and topic still need to be explicated in much greater depth. The preceding section, for example, concluded at just the point where the ambiguity and flexibility of the topic-descriptor *percolation* could be recognized as the fundamental cause of the tradeoff between recall and relevance ratio in this instance. We hope to approach a more comprehensive understanding of *topic* gradually. We have so far introduced a few relations between documents and topics in the hope of shedding light on both these notions in small steps.

This approach is also used with our third object of study, people. In this context we study people only in their role of processing information connected with the production and utilization of documents. The reader and the author, as people, are, of course, the most important links in the entire system. But for them, there would be no need for an IR system or its institutional environment. Yet, for the purpose of analysis, it is useful for a time to disregard the human side of these information-processors which generate and utilize documents; they could, in principle and up to a limit, be automata. Let us call them information-processing agents, or just agents. The essentially human role played by people in the production and utilization of knowledge is what transcends the theoretical limits of a valid model for their function in terms of information-processing automata, and these limits and the nature of these human roles are of the greatest interest.

In the library of a given institution at time t, an author is anyone who has ever generated a document in $\mathcal{D}(t)$. Let $A(t)$ denote the set of authors. If the institution records each recipient of each document, then there is another set $U(t)$ of document users. Their union constitutes the population of information-

---

[†] Some information sceintists (e.g., H. Wellisch, private communication, August 1972) question whether this should be assigned the status of law. Underlying this phenomenon may be a theorem somewhat analogous to Shannon's coding theorem for noisy channels (Kochen, 1973c).

processing agents $\mathcal{A}(t)$. Let $P(t) = |\mathcal{A}(t)|$, which is almost all the agents in the institution involved in communication. Insofar as each author will have used (read) at least one document in $\mathcal{D}(t)$—surely his own—$A(t) \subseteq \mathcal{A}(t)$. Equality would hold only if there were no user who is not also an author.

Document—agent coupling is described by the two-place predicates, *is an author of* and *is a user of,* and by their inverses, *was authored by* and *was used by.* The first designates a relation which holds or does not hold for any document—author pair; the second designates a relation on $\mathcal{D}(t) \times \mathcal{D}(t)$.

Let d be a document chosen randomly from $\mathcal{D}(t)$. Let $\overline{A}(t)$ be the number of authors per document averaged over all d. Alternately, we could confine attention to $\overline{A}_1(t)$, the number of authors per document averaged over all the documents generated in just the year ending at time t, or in $\mathcal{D}(t) - \mathcal{D}(t-1)$. An increase in $\overline{A}(t)$ or $\overline{A}_1(t)$ (it would be more evident in $\overline{A}_1(t)$) indicates a tendency towards more multiplicity of authorship, presumably due to the trend toward "Big Science" with more emphasis on teamwork.

Similarly, let $\overline{U}(t)$ and $\overline{U}_1(t)$ be numbers of users per document who have ever used it prior to t, averaged over all $d \in \mathcal{D}(t)$ and $\mathcal{D}(t) - \mathcal{D}(t-1)$, respectively. A plausible hypothesis for empirical verification is that $\overline{U}(t)$ is proportional to $|C^{-1}(d)|$ averaged over all $d \in \mathcal{D}(t)$. The greater the average number of times papers are cited, the more they are used. Citation frequency may be a good indicator of general usage.

Let $\overline{A}^{-1}(t)$ be the number of papers per author averaged over $A(t)$ and $\overline{U}^{-1}(t)$ be the number of papers used per user prior to t averaged over $U(t)$.

THEOREM 7.

$$\overline{A}(t)D(t) = \overline{A}^{-1}(t)|A(t)| \qquad \overline{A}_1(t)D_1(t) = \overline{A}_1^{-1}(t)A_1(t)$$

$$\overline{U}(t)D(t) = \overline{U}^{-1}(t)|U(t)| \qquad \overline{U}_1(t)D_1(t) = \overline{U}_1^{-1}(t)U_1(t)$$

Proof: As in the previous two sections, we can represent the authorship and usership relations by incidence or relation matrices or, equivalently, graphs. Each row corresponds to a document. The columns represent authors or users. $\overline{A}(t)$ and $\overline{U}(t)$ are the average numbers of 1s per row, and $\overline{A}^{-1}(t)$, $\overline{U}^{-1}(t)$ are the average number of 1s per column. The product in each side of the two equations represents the (same) total number of 1s in the two incidence matrices, respectively.

THEOREM 8. Let a be the fraction of users who are authors. If there is at least one document or user, then

$$a = \frac{\overline{A}(t)\overline{U}^{-1}(t)}{\overline{A}^{-1}(t)U(t)} = \frac{\overline{A}_1(t)\overline{U}_1^{-1}(t)}{\overline{A}_1^{-1}(t)\overline{U}_1(t)}$$

Proof: Let $U(t) = |U(t)|$ and $|A(t)| \doteq aU(t)$. Rewrite the pair of equations in Theorem 7 in matrix form as

$$
\begin{pmatrix} \bar{A}(t) & -a\bar{A}^{-1}(t) \\ \bar{U}(t) & -\bar{U}^{-1}(t) \end{pmatrix} \begin{pmatrix} D(t) \\ U(t) \end{pmatrix} = \begin{pmatrix} 0 \\ 0 \end{pmatrix} = \begin{pmatrix} \bar{A}_1(t) & -a\bar{A}_1^{-1}(t) \\ \bar{U}_1(t) & -\bar{U}_1^{-1}(t) \end{pmatrix} \begin{pmatrix} D_1(t) \\ U_1(t) \end{pmatrix}
$$

This pair of simultaneous linear equations in $D(t)$ and $U(t)$ can have a nontrivial solution $(D \neq U \neq 0)$ only if the determinant is zero. That is the equation of the theorem.

Observe that $\bar{A}(t)$, the average number of authors per paper, is small, between 1 and 2. The average number of papers per author per year is also small, perhaps near 2. Hence, approximately, $a \doteq \bar{U}_1^{-1}(t)/\bar{U}_1(t)$. For this to be less than 1 the average number of papers read by a user in a year should be less than the average number of users per paper during one year. At first sight this seems implausible, but if the user population is large and varied, then it will include many users who read at most one document per year. This makes the average $\bar{U}^{-1}(t)$ very small.

The users include both scanners and serious readers. The number of serious readers of a scientific article is, however, known to be small, not more than 7 or 8. Then the average number of papers read by a serious reader during a year must be less than 7 or 8, which is quite counterintuitive. It must imply a skew distribution of reading rate among the serious readers, too. A very few read very many articles per year, while most read perhaps less than half a dozen.

If the number of documents generated by an author is constant, then the number of documents grows in proportion to the number of authors; if the number of documents per user is also constant, then the number of users grows in direct proportion with the number of authors. That is, the a of Theorem 8 which is the ratio of $|A(t)|$ to $U(t)$, is then a constant; $1/a$ is the average number of users (consumers) per author (producer). Though $D(t)$ might grow exponentially, this does not constitute an "information explosion."

The notion of *explosive* is connected with *out of control, dysfunctional*, or *malignant*. If the number of papers grows exponentially and at a much faster rate than the number of uses, that might be an explosive condition. This can occur only if the number of authors grows exponentially. The number of uses might grow exponentially, too, but at a slower rate. The actual growth law of both author and user communities is most probably one characterized by the logistic curve, which is approximately exponential for some of the time (Price, 1961).

To explore the logical boundaries of this result a bit further, consider an extreme condition in which each author uses only his own documents, and there are no users other than the authors. Here $a = 1$. Two appropriate words for this condition would be *fragmentation* and *disintegration*. They are near-synonyms of *explosion*, somewhat more precise (though still not sufficiently so), and a lot more appropriately suggestive. This condition can occur even if $D(t)$ does not increase, but we would not call it explosive then.

At the other extreme is a condition in which there are only users and no authors. There is nothing for them to use. Here $a = 0$. Appropriately descriptive terms for this condition are *sterility, inertness*, and *death*.

Neither of these extreme conditions is desirable. This suggests that there might be a most desirable condition in between. Perhaps the actual value of a fluctuates within safe limits around this optimal value of a in viable systems.

A possible natural mechanism for regulating this value of a is based on the following plausible assumption. Authors will tend to reduce their production of documents for which there is no user demand, and to increase their production of documents for which there is user demand. Some authors help shape the demand for documents, however, by helping users recognize problems of which they were previously unaware. For example, Carson's *Silent Spring* helped shape the demand for subsequent documents like *The Hidden Persuaders* by making the reading public aware of problems in the quality control of food, drugs, air, and water.

Another regulatory mechanism was pointed out by Swanson. Every author is also a user. If the authors produce excessively, then they probably also read more. This leaves them less time to produce. As a result, the supply of literature is kept in check.

An important class of documents provides valid answers to well-defined significant questions. The literature of most of normal science (Kuhn, 1962) should contain solutions to puzzles. How does all this puzzle-solving activity originate? The published solution of a puzzle by one author often stimulates another (or the same) author to formulate another puzzle in such a way that it now becomes solvable when it was not before, or when he would not have thought of it before. Thus documents may beget documents. This increases the demand for documents, but only by users who are also authors. It is the condition of a tight little puzzle-solving community of authors who produce documents for one another. We could still have $a = 1$.

This condition is not as undesirable as the one in which each author was his only user and used only his own documents. Here the authors at least use the documents of other authors as well. It is, however, still undesirable† if the only users are authors in their sole role as authors. Some of the extremely specialized communities of scientists approximate this condition in their document usage and citation patterns. ‡

There is little danger that authors will run out of puzzles to solve. A sample study of the use of literature in physics (Bromley, 1972) revealed that 33% of the papers were judged to make "additions of conceptual and lasting value." If and when normal science enters a crisis stage (Kuhn, 1962) because of too many anomalies, unsolvable puzzles, contradictions, and paradoxes (or perhaps also too few puzzles), these conceptual advances will have contributed toward the shaping of a new paradigm. When it replaces the existing paradigm in a scientific revolution, normal science or puzzle-solving activities start over once more.

But there is more. By solving puzzles, authors add to knowledge. Their documents also add conceptual value and stimulate users to *add* to knowledge in these ways. But some authors stimulate some users to *use* knowledge by helping them recognize real problems other than the well-defined puzzles of their specialty. Many of the users who are not also authors or who are authors on different topics will be such problem-solvers. *What is critical is that there be enough successful problem-solvers to keep pace with the rate at which serious problems are recognized. It is equally critical that major problems be recognized at the rate at which they arise and in time for solutions to be effective.*

The nonauthor users as well as the authors recognize problems. Recognition of a major problem is usually documented, hence attributable to an author. An important source of the real problems we refer to is the users themselves. Having solved the medical problems which kept life short centuries ago, medical scientists now have to solve different medical problems which occur in older people. Analogous remarks apply to organizational problems.

Users are often practitioners of a profession such as engineering or medicine. They face real problems in their professional practice. Some of their problems eventually become known to those likely to become interested in and capable of solving them even when they themselves do not have the time or ability to solve

---

†To be defended in later chapters. We take the position that the need to advance knowledge and understanding is not a primary, basic human need. It is one derived from a need to eventually use such knowledge and understanding for improving the quality of life more generally.

‡Another instance of an interesting hypothesis worth testing. In advanced mathematical research, for instance, the specialized publications at the frontier of the field are generally understood, and read, only by a dozen fellow specialists. Nonspecialists often have trouble even understanding the title, much less appreciating its significance. This is in part due to the jargon, stylized notation, and excessively technical vocabulary that is used.

them. This happens through consultation, through meetings of professional societies, and through their literature. Unfortunately, it does not happen enough. Practitioners do not always have the time, energy, interest, and concern to submit papers for publication or to attend professional meetings. Even when they do somehow acquaint others with their problems, their thinking and ways of expressing themselves are often so different from those of the audience they ought to reach, that this audience often fails to become enlightened by what the practitioners have to teach them.

Being an author is much more essential for a *pure* researcher than for an *applied* scientist. The latter is much closer to the practitioner, in that he is more concerned with solving a problem which may or may not add to knowledge or understanding. The key difference between a worker in pure and applied science, according to Brooks, is not their motivation but their strategy. The pure researcher's strategy is governed primarily by the internal logic of his field. The decision about which experiment he does next is determined mainly by whether it would deepen understanding. In his publications he tries to meet such a criterion, and his work is evaluated by his peers according to such standards.

The applied researcher, more like the practitioner, selects his problems and chooses his experiments according to whether the results are likely to be useful. It is the applied researcher who needs the teachings from the practitioner about his real problems. Quite often he, or his colleague in pure research, works on a problem which he can later connect with some real problem of a practitioner. But the task of transferring the fruits of research, pure and applied, to practitioners, and that of acquainting the researchers with the practitioners' needs, remains one of the most challenging and important obstacles.

Failure to recognize or solve real problems which arise has noticeably undesirable consequences for an institution. If the institution is viable, the demand for some documents recognizing problems and for others contributing to solutions increases as the undesirable consequences become more severe. When they are not severe, the normal activities of authors motivated by the need to understand and appreciate will tend to increase the production of documents recognizing real problems, existing or potential. In this way the fraction *a* varies with time, but remains regulated within safe limits around an optimal value.

If we may call the recall–precision tradeoff the first law of information science, we suggest that this is the second law or principle.

2.5. AGENT–AGENT COUPLING

A study of the information system among U.S. physicists (Bromley, 1972) concluded that while the primary journals are the most important source, informal oral communication is a close second. Communication among people describes generally (and as yet vaguely) what we mean by agent–agent coupling. Communication has many aspects: intentions, contents, and forms. One of the most important communication links among people is the one that bonds them together in the same intellectual community or institution. We shall denote this by the general term *exerts intellectual influence on*.

This is viewed as a two-place predicate which denotes a two-place relation on $U(t) \times U(t)$. Its inverse, *is intellectually influenced by*, also denotes a two-place relation which holds or does not hold for any pair of users or members of the community. One way to specify the boundaries of this community is to include all people who are connected to everyone else in the community by *either* of the above two relations, either directly or indirectly. As in the case of citations, this specifies a graph (Ore, 1962) with all people as its nodes. Intellectual communities will then appear as special subgraphs.

One person exerts intellectual influence on another if the second behaves in roles requiring cognition according to norms specified by the first. For example, suppose that a professor of history asserted that the most significant problems for historical research are those which can be answered with the direct help of primary sources, and not circumstantial evidence, or indirect inferences. If another historical researcher who was the professor's student, in selecting his research problem, conforms to those norms, we would say that the professor has exerted intellectual influence upon him. Intellectual influence is also a mentor–disciple relation. The agent who is influenced is a disciple. The influencing agent is a mentor.

The growth of a field of knowledge is intimately related to the process by which intellectual influence is propagated over the generations. Every mentor begins as a disciple. As a disciple, his goal is to develop and utilize his information-processing resources to their fullest to play the roles in which he is cast. Moreover, he aims to be cast in those roles which maximally use his resources; he aims to concentrate upon those fields of knowledge, and to become part of those professional societies, which are best matched to the unique set of capabilities with which he is endowed. The developing agent cannot always rationally choose from the many alternatives which exist and which may not be known to him. He needs guidance and direction.

The more mature agent, through the intellectual influence of his mentors, has already selected from these alternatives. He professes a direction implicitly by his behavior, if not explicitly. He normatively specifies the roles he plays, at least by example. He professes the significant, true, and relevant sentences of his chosen topics, both those known to be known and those known to be unknown. He does this in his own characteristic style. To the extent that he is intellectually influential, he sets examples which may become behavioral norms, goals for disciples to follow.

Opinion leaders play the same role in intellectual networks that politicians play in a contact net of political influence (Milgram, 1967; Pool and Kochen, 1958; White, 1970). They are articulation points in the net, forming bonds with a great variety and number of other people. It is because of and through them that a contact chain with one or more links can connect any member in the large community with any other. The key role played by opinion leaders in the utilization of knowledge for problem-solving and decision-making in government (Havelock, 1971) supports a conceptualization along the above lines.

A result parallel to Theorem 3 for citation nets can be immediately derived. Consider an agent P chosen at random from the population or community $P(t)$. Let $I(P)$ be the set of all people in $P(t)$ on whom P has exerted intellectual influence, and let $I(t)$ denote the number of such people averaged over all $P(t)$. Let $I^{-1}(P)$ denote the set of all people who have exerted intellectual influence over P and $I^{-1}(t)$ be the number of such people averaged over $P(t)$. For example, if P is an influential scholar who has seven disciples and had, during his turn, three mentors, then $|I(P)| = 7$ and $|I^{-1}(P)| = 3$.

The incidence matrix for this relation corresponding to *exerts intellectual influence on* has the elements of $P(t)$ as rows and as columns. There is a 1 in row i and column j if P_i exerts intellectual influence over P_j or if P_j is intellectually influenced by P_i; 0 if not. The average number of 1s per row is $I(t)$. Therefore $I(t)P(t)$ is the total number of 1s in the incidence matrix. This is also $I^{-1}(t)P(t)$, since $I^{-1}(t)$ is the average number of 1s per column.

Let us call people on whom P exerts intellectual influence P's disciples and call people who exert intellectual influence on P his mentors. Then $I(t) = I^{-1}(t)$ can be stated as Theorem 9.

THEOREM 9. The average number of disciples per person is equal to the average number of mentors per person.

This result seems counterintuitive. The source of this is the use of averages. Suppose that in a community of ten there were just one master with nine disciples, none of whom had any disciples; nor had any of them mentors except this one, and he had no mentor. The *average* number of disciples per person is (9 + 9 × 0)/10 = 0.9. The average number of mentors per person is also (1 × 0 + 9)/10 = 0.9.

The coupling variables we have considered so far were all random variables or continuous parameter stochastic processes with t as parameter. Only if they were Poisson processes (or had Poisson distributions) would their means (averages, expected values) describe them completely.[†] For $I(t)$ to be a Poisson process, $I(t_4) - I(t_3)$ and $I(t_2) - I(t_1)$ must be statistically independent for any t_1, t_2, t_3, t_4 satisfying $t_1 < t_2 < t_3 < t_4$. But this assumption surely does not hold;

[†]In the Poisson distribution, a one-parameter distribution, the mean and variance are both equal to that parameter (Feller, 1950, 1966).

$I(t_4) - I(t_3)$ is the number of disciples a randomly chosen person has acquired in the time interval (t_3, t_4), which might be the later half of his most influential and productive period. Suppose (t_1, t_2) is the earlier half. For people who acquired very many disciples during the period (t_1, t_2) the probability that they will also acquire many during the period (t_3, t_4) is surely higher than it is for people who acquired few disciples during (t_1, t_2). If $I(t_4) - I(t_3)$ and $I(t_2) - I(t_1)$ were independent, then the probability distribution of $I(t_4) - I(t_3)$ would be the same no matter what the value of $I(t_2) - I(t_1)$.

An argument formally resembling the above can be made for each of the coupling variables.

What is a plausible and yet workable basis for deriving the distribution of $I(t)$? To facilitate the derivation of results, let us make some simplifying assumptions. First, we will not count disciples of disciples. Second, we will not take cognizance of psychological and sociological factors such as dominance and Zeitgeist. We will consider only the excellence with which the master plays his role in determining the number of his disciples.

It seems reasonable to suppose that with a small increment in t, Δt, say 1 day, at most 1 disciple is added to or leaves the retinue of the master; also that $I(t)$ is a Markov chain with parameter t. The latter assumption is that the distribution of the number of disciples at time t (in days, after t) depends only on the number of disciples at $t - \Delta t$, and not on how the latter got to be what it is. Consider the three conditional probabilities p, r, q of $k + 1, k, k - 1$ disciples at t, given k disciples at $t - \Delta t$, respectively. In general, all three depend on t, Δt, k, and a parameter α $0 \leq \alpha \leq 1$, which measures the excellence with which the mentor played his role at t. Since t does not refer to the age of an individual, but to the age of an information system—for example, an epoch in history—there is little reason to suppose that p, r, q vary significantly with t. The number of disciples per mentor should be no different in 1960 than it was in 1760, other factors being constant. But it is reasonable to assume a bandwagon effect by letting p increase with k and α, perhaps as $p = (\alpha/2)[1 - B(k + 1)^{-b}], 0 < B < 1, 0 < b < 2$. There may also be a sliding effect in that r is greater if k has decreased; but to take this into account would no longer allow analysis as a Markov process. Hence we shall assume that $q = 1 - \alpha/2$; hence, also, $r = 1 - p - q = (\alpha/2) [B(k + 1)^{-b}]$. Letting $p(k,t)$ be the probability of k disciples at t, we have:

$$p(k,t) = \frac{\alpha}{2}[1 - B(k + 1)^{-b}] \, p(k - 1, t - 1) + \frac{\alpha}{2} B(k + 1)^{-b} \, p(k, t - 1)$$
$$+ \left(1 - \frac{\alpha}{2}\right) p(k + 1, t - 1)$$

$$k = 1, 2, 3, \ldots; \; t = 1, 2, 3, \ldots$$

$$p(1,t) = \frac{\alpha}{2}(1 - B) p(1, t - 1) + \left[1 - \frac{\alpha}{2}(1 - B)\right] p(0, t - 1)$$

The probability $p(1,0)$ of having one disciple at the outset is p_0; and $p(0,0) = 1 - p_0$; also, $p(k,0) = 0$, $k > 2$. The solution of this partial difference equation in k and t gives $p(k,t)$ in terms of the parameters of α, B, and b.

To illustrate the stationary distribution for this process, take $B = 1/2$, $b = 1$, $\alpha = 1/2$. The stationary distribution is, approximately, $p_0 = 0.42$, $p_1 = 0.42$, $p_2 = 0.105$, $p_3 = 0.029$, $p_4 = 0.008$, and $p_5 = 0.0042$. The mean number of disciples would be about 0.8. This mean is, of course, computed over all mentors whose excellence measure is 0.5. The parameters B and b may vary from one field of knowledge to another.

There is likely to be considerable stratification in the aggregation[†] of disciples and mentors. Given two disciples A and B of some common mentor M, and given that N is a second mentor of A, the conditional probability that N is also a mentor of B is greater than the corresponding unconditional probability. Also, the conditional probability that N is the mentor of B, given that A and B do not have a common mentor, is less than the unconditional probability.

More precisely, consider two agents A and B each of whom has n mentors. By chance alone, the probability of exactly k mentors-in-common is

$$ B\left(k\right) = \binom{n}{k} \prod_{r=0}^{k-1} \left(\frac{n-r}{N-r}\right) \prod_{s=k}^{n} \left(1 - \frac{n-s}{N-s}\right) $$

Here N is the size of a random sample of N agents. If N is large compared to n, this may be approximated by the binomial distribution

$$ B\left(k\right) = \binom{n}{k}\left(\frac{n}{N}\right)^k \left(1 - \frac{n}{N}\right)^{n-k} $$

with mean (n^2/N). We now save those samples which had at least k mentors-in-common, and select a random one from among the samples retained. Let C_k denote the event that among the N agents, there are at least k who are mentors of both A and B. We now consider the conditional probability $P(C_{k+1}|C_k)$. If $k = 0$, we expect this to be what would be obtained by chance alone for $P(C_1)$. If $k = 1$, $P(C_2|C_1)$ should be higher than the $P(C_1)$ obtained by chance alone. Suppose that

$$ P\left(C_{k+1} \mid C_k\right) = (k+1)\, e^{-k/(m+1)} \sum_{i=k+1}^{n} B\left(i\right) $$

The sum on the right-hand side represents the value of $P(C_{k+1})$, if chance alone were in effect. The term $(k+1)e^{-k/(m+1)}$ rises until $k = m$, then drops

---

†This phenomenon applies to documents and topics as well. Documents are aggregated into classes, classes of classes, etc., as in the case of books shelved according to the Dewey decimal classification.

exponentially with k. The parameter m is related to the average *cluster* size. The disciples within such a cluster—or stratified aggregate—belong together, because they all share more mentors with each other than they would share with other agents by chance alone.

The distribution of $I(t)$, the number of mentors/disciple, could be further specified. If a stratified aggregate of disciples consists of, say, m' closely coupled disciples, then there is also associated with this aggregation a cluster of masters, namely, those mentors whom most of the disciples have in common. The number $C[a(t)|a(t + T)]$ is thus a sum of several terms, the first being the number of masters associated with the cluster to which the disciple belongs.

In general, a disciple belongs to more than one such cluster. These clusters will differ in the strength of the bond among the disciples and in the number of disciples in the cluster. The strength of the bond is the number of mentors, each weighted by the number of disciples in the cluster who share him. Let C_1 be the number of mentors/disciples contributed by the cluster to which he belongs with the greatest bond strength. Let C_2 be the number contributed by the cluster, to which the disciple also belongs, with the second greatest bond strength, and so on.

There is no reason to suppose that $C_1, C_2, \ldots$ are correlated. Indeed, it may be reasonable to assume that the conditions of the Central Limit Theorem can be applied to enable us to state that $C[a(t)|a(t + T)]$ is approximately Gaussian. Its mean and variance would, in general, vary with t.

There is empirical evidence that $I(t)$ has a very skew distribution: a few people have very many disciples; a few more have a moderate number; a large number have few disciples; very many have just one; and the vast majority of people have none. This is also often called an 80%–20% law: 80% of the disciples are distributed among 20% of the mentor population. Income, word frequencies, city sizes, species per genus, and many other phenomena are distributed similarly. Eighty percent of the country's wealth may be concentrated among 20% of the population. Eighty percent of all the words in a book or used by a person in one day are really just 20% of all the words in a dictionary, many (such as *the*) being used over and over.

Distributions to describe this are the log-normal, the negative binomial, and one associated with Zipf, Mandelbrot, and Bradford (Bradford, 1948; Zipf, 1949; Mandelbrot, 1960). This general phenomenon of skewness is so pervasive in information science that it might be the germ of a third law or principle. We will discuss it in detail later. It need only be noted at this point that for certain skew distributions, the mean does not exist, which places a restriction on the results stated so far.

We can, however, replace Theorem 9 by a more general result in one sense. Let $e_{ij} = 1$ if i exerts intellectual influence over j and 0 if not. Then δ_i, defined as $\sum_j e_{ij}$, is the exact number of disciples of i, and μ_j, defined as $\sum_i e_{ij}$, is the exact number of mentors of j.

THEOREM 10. $$\sum_i \delta_i = \sum_j \mu_j$$

Proof: The theorems about averages follow by dividing both sides of the equation in Theorem 10 by the ranges of i and j, respectively; both are $P(t)$ in this case. These are not averages in the sense of expectations of random variables. Theorem 10 holds only if the incidence matrix (e_{ij}) is known, which is seldom the case for large communities. Instead, only the distributions of I and I^{-1} may be known, and Theorem 9 applies, if the means exist.

Documents have an official birthdate: when they are submitted for publication. The date at which an agent entered a particular population requires greater specification of the population. A birth certificate documents the arrival of a person in the community of all people; the publication of the first document he authored documents his entry into the community of authors; the signing out of his first document from a library could document his entry into the community of users.

Our subsequent concern with authors and users as information-processors makes it useful to model them as automata. In a certain sense computers can also be said to generate documents, such as statistical reports, accounting statements, and even "documentation" of the languages and programs necessary to run the computers. Most of us would, however, be reluctant to say that the date a computer is installed marks its entry into the community of authors. It is the computer's programmers that *intend* and *plan* for it to publish a document. It was suggested by R. Tagliacozzo (private communication, June 1973) that it is this *intention* that makes the difference. It is the programmer, not the computer, which bears the intellectual responsibility.

While a document cannot cite another document *published* later than itself, a person can be a disciple of another who entered the community of authors later than himself. A plausible hypothesis which is empirically testable (after *exerts intellectual influence on* is suitably operationalized) is the following. Suppose P is a disciple of P'. Let $A^{-1}(P)$ be the set of all documents authored by P, and let $R(d)$ be the topic-profile of any document d in $A^{-1}(P)$. Form the union $\cup_{d \in A^{-1}(P)} R(d)$ and call it $R(P)$, the topic profile of P. We hypothesize that $\delta(P,P') = |R(P) \cap R(P')|/|R(P) \cup R(P')|$ is close to 1. To refine this, the individual topic-descriptors in $R(P)$ could be weighted by the number of P's documents that they pertain to. Even further, if we can operationalize and measure the *degree* of P's intellectual influence on P', we expect it to be proportional to $\delta(P,P')$.

In a similar way, P can be assigned a citation-profile by $\cup_{d \in A^{-1}(P)} C^*(d)$. Call this $C^*(P)$ and define

$$\delta^*(P,P') = \frac{|C^*(P) \cap C^*(P')|}{|C^*(P) \cup C^*(P')|}$$

It follows that if the hypotheses in the section on document–topic coupling are verified, then the degree of P's intellectual influence on P' should also be proportional to $\delta^*(P,P')$.

Another important difference between citation and intellectual influence is that the latter can be reciprocal. If document d cites d', d' cannot cite d; but if $e_{ij} = 1$, then c_{ji} can be 1 also. Such a symmetry in intellectual influence among authors should be paralleled in a symmetry among their citation profiles, in $\delta^*(P,P')$, which can happen.

A community (cluster or clique) of people, each of whom exerts intellectual influence upon the others in the clique, forms a *school*, perhaps several competing schools. Being intellectually influenced by P does not mean agreeing with P', but it does mean communication about the disagreement. They may form one or more professional societies, found one or more journals, and systematically train disciples. Two topic-profiles could be associated with such a community C. The first is $\cap_{P \in C} \cup_{d \in A^{-1}(P)} R(d)$. Call it $R^*(C)$, the outer or maximal topic-profile. The second is $\cup_{P \in C} \cap_{d \in A^{-1}(P)} R(d)$. Call it $R_*(C)$, the inner or minimal topic-profile. It is the set of topic-descriptors all members share. In the most tightly knit community possible, $R^*(C) = R^*(C)$. This does not mean cohesiveness, for even though each member is concerned with the same topics, they may have opposing views. The tightness of C may be indicated by $|R^*(C) - R_*(C)|/|R^*(C)|$.

The very important concept of an *invisible college* (Price and Beaver, 1966), has opened up one of the most interesting and vigorous areas of research at the heart of the information sciences. It is a group of people each of whom is regarded by most others in the group to be an important contributor to a topic and who is in communication with every other person in the group who is also so regarded. We defer discussion of this to another chapter where *importance* and *intellectual influence* are dealt with at length, in more detail and depth. No discussion of a community can omit reference to this notion. An invisible college is part of a community in the above sense. If it is viable, it becomes visible in time as a professional society, a university department, a research center, or some other institutions which can set up, operate, exert quality control over IR systems. For example, the first "Invisible College" turned into the Royal Society of London, which made one of the first attempts at creating an IR system.

A reasonable way to specify $P(t)$ is by topic-descriptors. Suppose a topic such as *mast-cells* is chosen (Goffman, 1966). Let $P(t)$ be the set of all authors who have published a document pertaining to mast cells prior to time t. Goffman operationalized this by using a reasonably complete 2282-document bibliography on mast cells by Selye, which went up to $t = 1963$. This topic had a clearly identifiable birth date, 1877, when the first paper on mast cells, by Ehrlich, was published. Here we assume $P(1963) = U(1963) = A(1963)$; it was the case that $P(1963) = 2195$ authors. An author is said to *enter* the pool Q of active contributors in the year his first paper on mast cells (in the Selye bibliography) was published; he is said to *leave* Q one year after the publication of his last paper in the bibliography.

Let $A_a(t)$ be the number of authors who entered Q at time t or before, and who left at a time later than t; it is the number of *actively* contributing authors. Let $A_s(t)$ be the number of authors who entered Q after t; it is the number of authors susceptible to the intellectual influence of the active contributors, those already in Q. Let $A_r(t)$ be the number of authors who left P at time t or before. Regard both these as continuous and continuously differentiable functions of t for all $t \leq 1963$.

Intellectual influence is analogous to infection. It results in the entry of authors not yet in Q. It is transmitted by the documents produced by authors already in Q. The documents serve as vectors, carriers, or vehicles of the intellectual influence.

Three plausible assumptions, borrowed from epidemiology, are

$$\frac{dA_a(t)}{dt} = k_1 A_a(t) \cdot A_s(t) - k_2 A_a(t) + k_3$$

$$\frac{dA_s(t)}{dt} = -k_1 A_a(t) A_s(t)$$

$$\frac{dA_r(t)}{dt} = k_2 A_a(t)$$

The first differential equation says that the rate at which authors enter Q is proportional to both the number already in Q and the number yet to enter; if we doubled the number of active contributors, already in Q and capable of influencing those outside, while the number of those to be influenced stays the same, then twice as many authors per year should enter Q. Similarly, if A_a stays fixed, and we doubled the number of potential contributors, there are twice as many people to be influenced, and the number entering per year should double. Hence the (first) product term, in which k_1 denotes the rate at which intellectual influence is spread, has to be estimated from the data. The term $-k_2 A_a$ in the first equation expresses the assumption that a fraction k_2 of the active contributors ceases to be active each year, perhaps due to age, shifting to another topic, etc. The term k_3 is the number of new people entering Q each year.

The second equation states that the contribution to the growth of Q made by authors not yet in Q is the rate at which $A_s(t)$ must decrease.

The third equation restates that the rate at which authors are removed from Q is just $k_2 A_a$.

No people are assumed to be removed from those waiting to enter Q, and no new people enter that waiting group.

These nonlinear differential equations cannot be solved in simple closed form in general. It is, however, possible to deduce from them interesting properties about the growth of the populations (Daley and Kendall, 1965; Goffman, 1970; Siegfried, 1965). Numerous fruitful theoretical and empirical investigations could use them as a point of departure.

A complete characterization of all possible ways that agents, documents, and topics could be coupled would call for two more sections in this chapter: agent–topic coupling and topic–topic coupling. It is more appropriate to discuss these at length in Chapter Six.

The next three chapters discuss the concepts of topic, document, and agent by themselves, in more depth. Chapter Three gets at the notion of a topic by an analysis of the development of a theory of knowledge helpful for understanding information retrieval. This theme is taken up again in Chapter Six, where the relations among topics and those between topics and agents are explored.

Chapter Three

Information and Representation in Topics

Our aim in this chapter is primarily to conceptualize *information* so we can use it in a formal theory of knowledge and IR systems. This requires an attempt to extend the basis for moving from communication theory to knowledge theory. Our main purpose with this theory is to provide a more rational basis underlying the design of IR systems that are to help people recognize and cope with problems of importance to them. Hopefully, it can also shed light on the basic principles governing storage and retrieval of information in nature.

As steps toward a theoretical basis of information in IR, we begin by conceptualizing what is intended by *recorded data*, and proceed to distinguish between this and *documents* as items to be retrieved. We then examine the *information* concept as developed in communication theory and used to characterize storage, transmission, and file organizations. Next we distinguish between information, knowledge, understanding, and wisdom.

The key point of the chapter is an explication of *topic*, denoted by triangles in Figure 1.1, as an aggregation of units of organized knowledge and understanding. This is done in Section 3.8.

3.1 RECORDED DATA

We begin with a proposal for how to use the term *data* with precision. This is a synthesis of usage in logic (Mendelson, 1964) and psychology (Coombs, 1967). We accept the view (Hanson, 1958) that observations, facts, data, and measurements are inferences and that our knowledge is the result of theory. Man, as a knowing organism, is first and foremost a theory-using animal.

To get at the meaning of *data*, imagine an observer who specifies a set D

called a universe of discourse. For example, D may be the set of human beings or the set of natural numbers, specified by the observer in just these phrases. Or D may be a multidimensional *psychological space* in which a stimulus, such as *peanut brittle*, is a point and an individual is represented in such a space by his most preferred stimulus point.

An n-place *relation* on D is generally understood to be a subset of D^n. For example, if D is the set of natural numbers, then $R_2 = \{(1,2),(1,3),(2,3),\ldots\}$ and $R_1 = \{2,4,6,\ldots\}$ illustrate a two-place and a one-place relation, respectively. The 2-place relation is a subset of $D \times D$, the set of all ordered pairs.

By an *interpretation* of a predicate-name such as "$<$" or "is even" is meant a D together with an assignment of a relation on D to that predicate-name. This is now used to interpret, for example, "four is even" or "two $<$ three." The interpretation also assigns to the names *two* and *three* the elements 2 and 3 of D, and allows us to check whether these well-formed statements are true—that is, whether they hold in the interpretation. If $4 \in R_1$ and $(2,3) \in R_2$, then "four is even" and "two $<$ three" are *data*.

For Coombs, data consists of two pairs of points of D, plus a statement about whether the points of one pair are nearer to one another than the points of the other pair. This is a special case of the more general notion of data as an interpreted statement in a language. The points in psychological space or in physical space are not data any more than are the stars, the view of a slide under a microscope, a chest x ray, or the heart rate of a person. What makes a telescopic or satellite-telemetered photograph of a quasar data are statements, explicit or implicit, about the light blotches on a dark background.

These statements are made in a language built of (terminal) symbols that can be recorded, transmitted, stored, and displayed. Recorded data, then, consists of well-formed statements (wffs) in *such a language which are true in some interpretation and which have been registered in a more-or-less permanent store where they are preserved for subsequent display*.

In a model for how data can be represented in a natural cognitive learning system, such as a person, a similar conceptualization is used (Kochen, 1971; Kochen and Badre, 1974). This conceptualization is to be viewed as a first, tentative step rather than as definitive.

Hayes has pointed out that some real-life files contain items that are not well-formed statements. Insofar as such items can be used in communication between an author and a user, and insofar as the notion of well-formedness is regarded as central to explaining how communication works, even such items could probably be regarded as well-formed. The rules may specify well-formedness for entire portions of text or records in a file rather than for single sentences. We would probably have to search hard for the rules according to which it could have been generated and parsed, but it is plausible that such rules could be found.

Many data files do not contain facts, but some files contain errors of fact and inconsistencies. Hayes rightly regards the really important problems to be those of how to use *such* files for decision-making and for acquiring knowledge. Explaining how people do in fact succeed with large files containing inconsistencies and errors is a difficult and important research problem outside the scope of this book. So is the problem of devising algorithms that describe how to do it cost-effectively. Confining the concept of data to well-formed sentences seems, however, to be valid both for our purpose and as a starting point for this more ambitious task.

3.2   WHAT IS TO BE RETRIEVED

In analyzing or designing an information retrieval system, it is natural to try to clarify what is meant and what is not meant by information. The document–topic coupling table illustrated in Chapter Two characterizes what has traditionally been called a *document*-retrieval system. Remember that its purpose was to respond to a user who requests all *documents* (for example, articles in periodicals or issued patents) which report, for example, measurements of the size of the cubic lattice of Zn–As. Two of the best known examples of such document-retrieval systems are *Chemical Abstracts Service* (Baker, 1966) and the U.S. National Library of Medicine's *Medical Literature Analysis and Retrieval System* (Lancaster, 1968).

By contrast, an *information*-retrieval system is intended to respond to a user who requests, not documents, but the actual best measurements of the cube in the Zn–As crystal. Such systems are also called data or fact retrieval systems (Kasher, 1967). The most common example of such a system is a handbook. To get the lattice constants of NiAs, for example, we would search the index of, say, the *American Institute of Physics Handbook* (Gray, 1957) for a suitable entry. We may decide that "crystal systems, lattice constants for," is the closest entry in the index. This will lead us to several tables in which NiAs appears as an entry. If the request could not be met by a handbook, an information center might help, and a directory to information centers (e.g., Kruzas, 1968) may help us locate one.

An entry in a table is, implicitly, a sentence. The entry of 8 in row 2, column 4 of a multiplication table is "two times four is equal to 8." The entire table may itself be an entry in a book of tables. We can retrieve the sentence by retrieving the book of tables. But we can also retrieve the sentence directly. Or we can retrieve a program which generates the sentence.[†] We can even consider retrieving and activating a program that generates such a program.

[†]Such a system for data retrieval was proposed by J. Belzer (private communication, 1970).

The question as to what is to be retrieved should be answered in three of its many ambiguous senses. In the first sense, something must now be retrieved if it is needed at a certain time and place, but it is not now there. To retrieve it is to bring it there. The *it* to be retrieved may be a physical object with an individual name, such as the serial number of an item in inventory, or the material contents of a storage location with a specified address. *It* can also be *information* (to be discussed in Section 3.4).

In the second sense, it is a response to an expressed need for recorded data that is to be retrieved. The central problem of information retrieval is to produce an appropriate response to a need for information. This means chiefly recognizing a need when it is expressed. Then that element in the set of all *possible* responses is selected which fits best.

In the third sense, it refers to how much or what unit is to be retrieved. For a simple request, say for the lattice constants of Zn–As, just one or two sentences representing the recorded data will do, but an entire handbook may be the smallest unit that will be retrieved. This is, of course, related to picking the best response; the extreme case of retrieving everything that is stored is an inappropriate response. Part of specifying an IR system is imposing constraints on the set of all possible responses to package them for retrieval.

3.3   STORAGE AND TRANSFER

What is to be retrieved is stored, either explicitly in the form in which it will be displayed or implicitly as a program that will *generate* the display when so instructed. If what is stored is a function $f(x)$ for a large range of values of x, and this function can be simply described and generated by a program—for example, to get $f(x)$, multiply x by itself—then it is obviously more efficient to store the program rather than a table. Whether the storage is in the form of a program or directly, we need a deeper conceptualization of storage.†

The symbols of which sentences that represent data are composed are usually configurations or states of a physical system capable of two or more stable states. The molecules in a glass of water are a physical system, but they are normally in only one stable state. An ordinary wall switch can easily be in one of two stable states, on and off. We can describe it as a physical system by plotting the potential energy in its spring against the distance it is moved by a finger in pressing it. Its plot will have a shape as shown in Figure 3.1. In the middle position, it is in an unstable state; if we succeed in getting it to stay (at equilibrium) between the off and on position, the slightest disturbance (thermal

---

†This circumvents, to some extent, the process–structure controversy in discussions of memory among educational psychologists.

motion) will cause it to fall into the well on either side. To get from one stable state to the other is to supply enough energy (to apply the force of a finger pushing the switch through distance d) to overcome the barrier of height e.

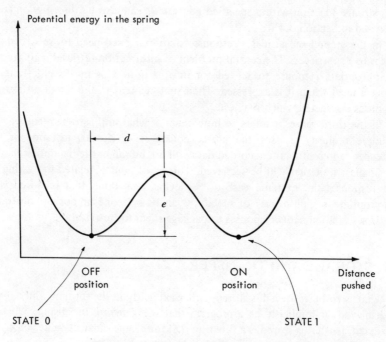

Figure 3.1. Energy diagram for storage.

Once such a physical system is set into one of the two (or more) simple, stable physical states, it stays there until such energy e is supplied. This is best captured by a logical feedback circuit with a delay, as shown in Figure 3.2. For large arrays of such switches, enormously many combinations of simple states are possible. To retrieve means to sense or to determine the state of the store, which can represent data *or* a program to generate data. Again this can mean reading $f(x)$, given x, or reading the contents of a portion of the store specified by an address known to contain the needed response.

To read a storage system is to test the states of its components. For example, to find out by touch if a wall switch is off or on, we would try to press it on; if it responds and clicks, it *was* off; if it does not, it must have been on. We have also changed the state with this test, and should turn it back off if it was. The result of such tests can cause packets of energy to be released in the form of signals. These signals can be transmitted to where they are needed to generate a display responding to the need.

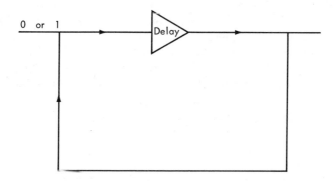

Figure 3.2. Logical feedback circuit.

We must not forget that the signals embody symbolic sentences that may represent data through an interpretation. The sentences may be false, in which case they do not represent data, according to our proposed definition. We will reserve the term *messages* to denote sentences whose sender had an intention in forming them, as distinct from sentences representing data.

To get into storage, sentences must have been transferred into the system by a process opposite that of reading them out. Which sentences to enter and when to do so is a second fundamental problem.

3.4. THE INFORMATION CONCEPT

If the signals embodying a sentence are transmitted from a source to a destination, where the sentence is displayed, and the receiver knew with certainty that this sentence would be displayed, then the communication of this sentence has conveyed no information to him. If all the receiver ever gets and expects is one of two equally frequent sentences, and the sender knows this, then the sender might as well use only two symbols. A source with only two stable states, capable of generating two different signals, would do.

Transfer of information is that property of a communication system (source, channel, receiver) which removes the receiver's uncertainty about what sentence is sent. In communication theory, information itself is measured in bits; if the receiver knows that one of n equally probable sentences is being sent, his uncertainty about which of these n will be sent next is $\log_2 n$ bits.[†] If the n sentences are sent with probabilities $p_1, \ldots, p_n$, then his uncertainty is, on the average, $-\Sigma_{i=1}^n p_i \log_2 p_i$ bits. If receiving a sentence leaves a residual uncertainty U (possibly because of transmission noise), then $-\Sigma p_i \log_2 p_i - U$ bits of uncertainty are removed by receipt of the communication; that is the amount of the information conveyed.

Bits are the units used to measure the amount of storage. They also measure transmission rates (bits/sec) and channel capacities. In storage, a bit corresponds to a physical system, such as a switch, with two easily reachable stable states.

This notion of information has been very fruitful in communication, control, and computer engineering. It has also had a pervasive influence on nearly every science. The temptation to extend the definition of *information* with its rich associations[*] in everyday speech beyond its narrow use as a precise technical term was great.

Despite warnings from its founders (Shannon and Weaver, 1949), behavioral, social, and biological scientists and many others tried to extend this notion to these associated uses, but without success. By about 1960 information theory became a "normal" science with its own puzzles. The paradigm underlying it is a body of coding theorems, which are all related to the first basic result of Shannon. He demonstrated the existence of a method to encode a source of messages so that they can be deciphered with arbitrarily high probability and

---

[†]A bit is a digit, similar to a decimal digit in the ones, tens, or hundreds position of a number, except that it takes only the values 0 or 1. With a one-bit number or code (analogous to a one-digit number), two items can be represented, while there are four two-bit codes: 00, 01, 10, 11 (analogous to the 100 two-digit numbers, 00,01, . . . , 09,10,11, . . . ,99). There are 2^k k-bit numbers; hence if $n = 2^k$, then k bits suffice to identify any one of n numbers, and $k = \log_2 n$.

The above meaning of *bit* is commonly used in computer science, as a symbol in a two-symbol alphabet. In information theory, *bit* has another meaning as a unit of information measuring the reduction of uncertainty by receiving a noiseless signal indicating which of two equiprobable events took place. To distinguish between these two meanings, Tukey proposed the term *binit* for the element of a two-symbol alphabet, leaving Shannon's term *bit* unchanged.

[*]Roget uses *information* in at least seven diverse senses: computer data, knowledge, enlightenment, news, instruction, arraignment, and accusation. With each of these are listed several synonym-groups, adding up to a total of over 100 associated words. Many of these various meanings have been studied, with varying degrees of success. Some were recently brought together by D. Nauta in *The Meaning of Information* (Mouton, The Hague, 1972). Though that compilation is quite comprehensive, it omitted the connection with IR suggested by Paisley and Parker and used by Heilprin (in Proceedings of the ADI *Symposium on Information Science*; see Goodman and Heilprin, 1965), who suggested that IR is a "receiver-controlled communication system," and that the content of messages sent is critical for deciding where they are sent.

transmitted through an imperfect communication channel with limited capacity at a rate which can be arbitrarily close to an upper limit (the channel capacity) that is determined by the channel.

Communication engineers, however, are not concerned with the *meaning* of the messages people transmit to one another by telephone or other channels. Information theory, which tells them how close to the natural limits their designs are performing, has therefore been called a theory of selective information. It deals with information as a synonym for selection, as an answer only to the question as to which alternative was chosen by a sender.

The user of an IR system needs more. If the alternatives are documents, he needs an answer to the question, "which alternative or documents should be chosen to help me with . . . ," or "what must I know if I am to do the following . . . ." He cannot specify a priori a set of *n* possible messages, one of which will help him.

3.5. REPRESENTATIONS IN AN IR SYSTEM

There is, however, a transition from the thinking used by communication theorists to the kind of knowledge theory we need. One way of looking at an IR system is to treat it as a file organized for use. The mathematical essence of a file is that of a function. Consider a collection of sentences or just strings of letters, such as {BROWN,SMITH,JONES}. If the alphabet consisted of only two letters, 0 and 1, the collection might by {01110,11011,10110}. Imagine these three five-bit "words" to represent numbers,[†] say 14, 27, 22. Suppose, now, that we order the items in the collection alphabetically: {BROWN, JONES,SMITH} or {01110,10110,11011} = {14, 22, 27}. Next, number the "words" in the alphabetized order:

Word number:	1	2	3
Its value:	14	22	27

The numbers in the second row may be stock numbers of parts in an inventory or identification numbers of records in a file. In an inventory, there may be duplicates, as in a table such as

1	2	3
1	22	22

[†]For example, we interpret 01110 to be $0 \cdot 2^4 + 1 \cdot 2^3 + 1 \cdot 2^2 + 1 \cdot 2^1 + 0 \cdot 2^0 = 8 + 4 + 2 = 14$, but many other interpretations are possible.

A *file* is a table (Elias, 1973) in which no such duplicates occur; the more general case is called an *inventory*.

Any file, such as $\{$BROWN,JONES,SMITH$\}$, can be *represented* as a string of bits. For example, we could encode each character into some six-bit code (including commas and spaces) and represent the above file by a string of $5 \times 6 + 2 + 5 \times 6 + 2 + 5 \times 6 = 96$ bits. We also need a special code to indicate start and end of file.

To design a file system is to select and specify (*a*) a representation, (*b*) a retrieval algorithm, and (*c*) an updating algorithm. Two design criteria have been proposed and investigated (Elias, 1973; Minsky and Papert, 1969): (*a*) the total number of bits of memory needed to store the representation and (*b*) the average number of those bits which must be accessed by the retrieval algorithm to answer a retrieval question. This ignores the efficiency of the updating algorithm, which is equally important in real file systems, but it is a good place to begin.

There are four types of retrieval questions for simple files:

1. *Direct Archival:*   List the entire file. (Print: BROWN, JONES, SMITH.)
2. *Direct:*   What is the jth value in the file? (Ans: JONES, for $j = 2$.)
3. *Inverse:*   How many words in the file come before a given word, for example, JONES? (Ans: 1, just BROWN.)
4. *Inverse Archival:*   What is the canonical or standard representation of the file?

Elias has found lower bounds to minimax measures of bits stored and of bits accessed for each of these four retrieval questions, and constructed both representations and algorithms which come close to attaining all five bounds at once. Extending these results to take updating into account and to apply to less simple files is just now being done. Yet these results on file organization are enormous advances, using the methodology of communication theory.

In many literature search and information retrieval applications, users rarely know enough about the file to ask questions corresponding to any of the four rather precise retrieval questions. The direct and inverse archival questions are asked usually by computer programmers, librarians who want an inventory, or users who want their entire file in book or hard copy form. The direct or inverse retrieval question is asked most commonly in known-item searches. It is subject-searching which presents the greatest challenge to a theory of IR systems, and this is not dealt with by the above, information-theoretic notion of representation. We need a revision of the concept that takes account of meaning and knowledge. Some steps towards this are in the next three sections, especially Section 3.8.

3.6.   KNOWLEDGE VERSUS INFORMATION

We suggest that an agent knows a topic if he is able to recognize and generate useful answers to questions in that topic that enable him to act purposively. Certain IR systems are needed to provide such answers, either indirectly by supplying documents or directly by providing data.

A file, such as discussed in the previous section, contains sentences. Some of the sentences are true in some interpretation, hence represent data or facts. Some may be information-bearing, depending on the uncertainty of the user for whom they are retrieved. None represent knowledge. That is in the user, not in the file.

Consider the difference between the following two questions. $Q1$: Did this coin you tossed land heads or tails? $Q2$: Was this coin you tossed true? Disregarding semantic difficulties, such as how to recognize heads and tails for any coin or what, exactly, *true* means, we could say that with $Q1$ we ask for one bit of information, *if* we believe the answer to $Q2$ to be Yes. If we believed the answer to $Q2$ to be No, then we must think that, perhaps, the coin is double-headed. If we think that, then the conditional probability with which we expect $Q1$ to be answered Yes is 1. Our initial uncertainty about the outcome of a toss will be $-1 \log_2 1 - 0 \log_2 0$, which is 0, given our belief that it is double-headed. The a posteriori uncertainty is also 0. Since no uncertainty is removed, no information is conveyed by the toss. To receive information, we must change our belief.

The notion of selective information does not seem applicable to $Q2$. If the questioner were to ask $Q1$ repeatedly, and get a Yes answer closer and closer to half the time, he should believe a Yes answer to $Q2$ with more and more weight. If he *assumed* a Yes answer to $Q2$, it would take infinitely many bits in answers to $Q1$ repeated before he could be absolutely *certain* his assumption was right. But only then could he be said, with certainty, to be receiving one bit with $Q1$.

Knowledge is not a collection of recorded symbols organized into well-formed formulas that satisfy semantic tests, and which can be retrieved by query and search (Churchman, 1971, p. 9). This would characterize information, in its technical sense, in the sense of computer data. Knowledge, suggests Churchman, is a potential for a certain type of action; it resides in the user, not in the collection of information. For example, a library does not store knowledge of how to drive a car with a standard transmission; a person wishing to learn must ask questions,[†] such as how to coordinate the actions of depressing the clutch, shifting gears, and depressing the accelerator; he may retrieve information which

---

[†]Another kind of inquiry is in order, if *question* is interpreted narrowly as an interrogative sentence intended to elicit a verbal response. We interpret *question* more broadly, conceptualizing it as representable by a sentence in an internal language *intended* to resolve a defect in an internal map or programs for using it.

he must not only interpret, *with his point of view*, but he must internalize it so he can apply it under unpredictably varying driving conditions. Note that his point of view differs from that of, say, an automobile design engineer or a psychologist who studies factors causing accidents. The *information* in the library, retrieved by a questioner in answer to a question, and processed by him with a point of view, becomes *knowledge*.

In this sense, a person can acquire knowledge from a file which does not contain recorded data as we defined it. Items in the file which are not obviously well-formed formulas could serve as cues to help a file user interpret other items in the file. As stated previously, there probably are some rules to explain how such cues were generated and how they function. The search for such rules is important for theory construction.

The sentences, $S1 =$ "47 is a prime" and $S2 =$ "The set of primes is infinite," can be coded into bits (or other symbols) and stored in a computer or printed in a book. We do not say the computer or the book knows or does not know $S1$ and $S2$. We can test whether a person knows this by asking him if $S1$ and $S2$ are true or asking him to tell us all he knows about primes. We could feed the nonlinear differential equations for the growth of the number of active contributors to a topic derived in Chapter Two into a computer, together with a program for solving them. After the program is run, the person interested in the solution knows the solution when he sees the printout. We say that the computer stores rather than knows the solution before it prints it out but after it ran the program; if we used *knows*, we would have to admit that the computer "knew" the solution even before the program was run, but the user could not know it then because no printout would be possible. Has the computer generated information? It has transformed some bit-strings into others, but the total number of bits has not changed. A computer or Turing machine does not generate information (in the technical sense) (Brillouin, 1952). It records, reads, stores, transfers, and transforms it; it uses it to control, and to refer (point or name). It, together with a user, can generate knowledge.

We could perhaps design a machine which drives (or learns to drive) a car with a standard transmission. We might not say this machine knows how to drive. It has no options for action. Every driving contingency has to be anticipated by its designer and planned for. There are no questions for it to ask, for it could not behave differently than it does. There are no possible points of view other than the one of a driver. There is no ambiguity, no imcompleteness in its blueprint; the information in that blueprint is frozen into the machine's structure and specifies it, represents it to within tolerable errors of technology.†

---

†Designing a control system to park (or drive) a car, in a "natural," elegant way is one of the challenges used to justify the utility of fuzzy set thoery (Zadeh, 1965). The central idea of that theory is to replace the sharp boundaries in the concept of a set—its characteristic function taking only the values 0 or 1—by a grade of membership which lies in [0,1]. This

To *know* arithmetic, in our proposed technical sense, is to know true sentences of arithmetic, such as $S1$ and $S2$. This means being able to answer questions related to $S1$ and $S2$. A question-answering machine capable of representing information as action-programs—that answers questions like: $S3 =$ "Can you lift the largest pyramid in this stack of blocks, pyramids, and cones and put it on top of the largest block which sits on top of another block" by conversing about it and doing it—can perhaps be said to know where the pyramid and the largest block on top of another block are located; also how to move it (Winograd, 1972).

In the standard analysis of knowledge (Ayer, 1956), a person P is said to know a proposition S if (a) S is true, (b) P is sure of S, and (c) P has a right to be sure of S. Thus to ascertain P's claims to know $S1$, that 47 is a prime, we should first check that 47 is a prime and then check that P says he is sure and believes unhesitatingly in asserting $S1$ by offering a proof or citing a reliable authority such as a published table of primes. He must be able to correctly answer the question "Are you sure that $S1$ is true and, if so, what makes you sure?" The same thing applies to $S2$ and $S3$. Winograd's program could probably be enabled to process the word *sure* so that it can pass this test.

To answer "Are you sure '47 is a prime' is true," an agent (person or program) must know precisely what *is prime* means; also what 47 means. This, in turn, requires the agent to know what terms such as *divisibility* and *number* mean. As a one-place logical predicate, the term *is prime* can be concatenated, according to rules of formation, with any natural number-expression such as 47. Its interpretation or denotation is a one-place relation in the universe of discourse, which is the natural numbers in this case. This one-place relation is the particular infinite subset of the natural numbers $2,3,5,7,11,13,\ldots$, or the extension of the concept *prime*. The intension of the concept is a logical expression built of other predicates, such as "is not divisible by any natural number other than 1 or itself." There may be several expressions corresponding to the same extension. The set of all the intensions and extensions together constitutes the *concept* which the term *is prime* denotes.

The core extension of a concept, at any time, is the finite subset of the extension that is known and documented. This may be the largest table of all known primes. The core intension (Bunge, 1967) of the concept is a minimal intension that is necessary and sufficient to generate the extension. Together, the core extension and core intension constitute the *meaning* of the term.

Note that a term such as *divisible* refers to an operator, *division*. This can sometimes be applied to a pair of natural numbers to generate a third. To know whether 8 is divisible by 2 is to be able to apply, or to imagine applying, that

concept may play an important role in the future development of knowledge theories (Negoita, 1970). A similar notion was tried in IR with probabilistic indexing (Maron and Kuhns, 1961).

operator to 8 and 2 to generate 4. Similarly, to know whether $S3$ is true is to lift, or to imagine lifting, the largest pyramid, etc.

An IR system helps its user acquire knowledge if he asks it questions that it can answer. To cope with problems, the user must *know* rather than merely *process* information in the technical sense, though we use that term to include utilization of knowledge as well.

3.7. UNDERSTANDING VERSUS KNOWLEDGE

We suggest that an agent understands a topic if he can generate deep questions and recognize good questions by virtue of their relations with other questions. Certain kinds of IR systems are needed to help people realize what they need to, but do not, know to help them ask better questions.

To be justifiably sure that 47 is prime and that the set of primes is infinite is to know some arithmetic; to know 10^6 such sentences is to know a lot of arithmetic. It is not necessarily *understanding* arithmetic. The answer to "What makes you sure $S1$, $S2$, . . . are true" could in each case be by reliance on authority. Even if proofs could be supplied, they could simply be retrieved from memory rather than generated. And even if a proof were generated for some theorems such as $S2$, which could be done by a computer program (Fikes and Nilsson, 1971; Robinson, 1967) we would still be quite unwilling to say the theorems are *understood* and *comprehended* by the agent (computer and therefore also a person).

In the attempt to explicate[†] *understanding* (Kochen, MacKay, Maron, Scriven, and Uhr, 1967) in its narrow sense as a technical term, it seems useful to identify *knows what a term means* with *understands a term* in the sense that *meaning* was discussed above. To understand a term, such as "is prime," is to know its core extension and its core intension or to be able to potentially answer correctly any question of the form "Are you sure that X is or is not prime and what makes you sure" and "Are you sure you can specify an algorithm for determining whether X is or is not prime and what makes you sure?"

In analogy to the extension of a concept, consider for any well-formed formula S the union $H(S)$ of all sets of wffs from which S is provable:[‡] $H(S) \vdash$

[†]The practical importance of recognizing the distinction between *scientific information* and an *understanding* of science lies in shaping current policies for enhancing understanding of science by the general public (Etzioni, 1972). To understand science, says Etzioni, "one must acquire a taste, or at least a tolerance, for the beauty of mathematical models . . . , to appreciate the value, validity, and vitality of an empirical–logical approach to the world."

[‡]This means that there is a sequence S_1, . . . S_n, of wffs with $S = S_n$ such that for each i, A_i is either an axiom, or A_i is in $H(S)$ or A_i is a direct consequence by some rule of inference of some of the preceding wffs in the sequence (Mendelson, 1964, p. 30).

S. Consider also the set $G(S)$ of all sentences S' and sets $F(S)$ which include S such that S' is provable from $F(S)$: $G(S) = \{S': F(S) \vdash S'\}$. Now define $E(S)$, as something like the extension of S, as $G(S) \cup H(S)$. It is the set of all wffs which are logically (by implication) connected with S. An analogy to the core extension would be the finite subset of $E(S)$ which has actually been used and is recorded in the literature.

An analogy to the intension of a concept, applicable to wffs, might be an algorithm for generating $E(S)$. This does not, of course, exist for every wff. Even if it exists, only a small number of proofs of S and proofs of other theorems that use S may be known. That would constitute the core intension.

To complete the analogy, then, an *idea* (in place of *concept*, at least within logic) expressed by a wff S is specified by $E(S)$ together with the algorithms that generate $E(S)$. The *significance* of an idea (in place of *meaning*) is specified by the core of $E(S)$ and the core of the algorithms generating $E(S)$. To *understand* an idea (in place of *know*) is to know its significance.

It follows that, in principle, a computer program together with its user who asks it questions can be said to understand ideas in this sense. The test of knowing the answers to such questions as "Are you sure that $H(S)$ and S are both true and what makes you sure" must be passed as a prerequisite to understanding. And, as suggested earlier, knowing is a potential for action or answering such questions. Understanding goes beyond knowing in that to understand, such questions must not only be answered by the comprehender but asked as well. The comprehender must know that he knows or does not know. If *knowing means question-answering, understanding is question-asking*.

An IR system helps its user understand if it helps him formulate or revise his questions. The range of problems a user can cope with, utilizing knowledge alone, is less than what he can cope with if he has some understanding as well. IR systems that stimulate question-improvement have to be conversational, and allow for query negotiation (Simmons, 1967; Taylor, 1968).

3.8. REPRESENTATIONS REVISITED: THEORIES AND TOPICS

To be rigorous, the symbol $\vdash$ (read: "has as a consequence" or "entails") should be written $\vdash_T$, where T is a specified *formal theory* (Mendelson, 1964). A formal theory is specified by: (*a*) a denumerable set or *terminal vocabulary* VT (of symbols)—such as x_1, x_2, x_3, $=$, t, $($, $)$, $\sim$, $\wedge$, A, E—and the various possible strings of finite length that can be formed from these—for example, x_1, $x_2, x_1 = x_2$, $x+ = x_3$, etc.; (*b*) a subset of these strings called wffs, specified by a finite set VA of auxiliary symbols such as WFF, EXP, and REL; (*c*) a set RF of formation, or rewrite rules—for example, $WF \to (\text{EXP})(\text{REL})(\text{EXP})$, EXP $\to$ (VAR) (OP) (VAR), VAR $\to x_1$, OP $\to +$, REL $\to =$, and EXP $\to$ VAR; (*d*) a set

RT of transformation rules; and (*e*) a specially designated auxiliary symbol such as *WF* used to design well-formedness. A wff is any string that can be generated by these rules beginning with *WF*, for example; substituting (EXP) (REL) (EXP) for it, by formation rule 1; substituting (VAR) (OP) (VAR) for the first EXP by rule 2, = for REL by rule 5, and VAR for the second EXP by rule 6; and getting (VAR) (OP) (VAR) = VAR in place of *WF*. One more application of rules 3, 4, 3, and 3 replaces all the auxiliary symbols in the above by *only* the symbols specified in (*a*) to generate the wff "$x_1 + x_1 = x_1$." A formal theory is also specified by (*f*) a special set *AX* of wffs called axioms and (*g*) a finite set *RI* of relations among the wffs called rules of inference—for example, "modus ponens" or "if *a* and *b* are wffs and $a \supset b$ is a wff, then *b* is a direct consequence of *a* and $a \supset b$"—which generate wffs as *direct consequences* of other wffs. A *proof in T* is a finite sequence $S_1, S_2, \ldots, S_n$ of wffs such that for each *i*, $i = 1, \ldots, n$, either S_i is a member of *AX* or a direct consequence of preceding wffs in the sequence through the application of a rule in *RI*; a *theorem* is a wff, S_n, which is the last one in a proof.

A formal theory is *decidable* if there is an effective algorithm (one which can be executed in a finite number of steps) for determining for each wff whether or not it is a theorem.

A formal theory *T*, decidable or undecidable, is thus specified by the seven-tuple of sets $\{VT, VA, RF, RT, WF, AX, RI\}$.

We propose that *theory*(as distinct from formal theory) is a formal theory together with an *interpretation* of the elements of *VT* (the symbols). This is a set of mappings *IM(D)* of a set $\cup_i D^i$ into a *VT*; *D* is called the *domain of the interpretation*, and it is the range of the *variables*, such as x_1, x_2, x_3 in *VT*. A theory is called first-order if its predicates and function-symbols are not applied to arguments which are themselves predicates or function-symbols, but only to variables ranging over *D* or to constants in *D*.

A wff is *true* if it holds in the interpretation. This has been made rigorous, but it is rather technical (Tarski, 1936). For example, the wff $(Ax_1)(Ax_2)(x_1 + x_2 = x_2 + x_1)$ is true because whenever there is a triple such as (0,1;1) or (2,3;5) in the relation within D^3 that corresponds to +, there is a corresponding triple such as (1,0;1) and (3,2;5) in that relation also. Logicians use the term *model for a set W of wffs* to mean an interpretation (in the above sense) for which every wff in *W* is true; and if a wff is true in that interpretation, that wff is in *W*.

Group theory is an example of a formal first-order theory. *AX* includes five (logical) axioms which specify any predicate calculus [for example, "if S_1, S_2 are wffs, $S_1 \supset (S_2 \supset S_1)$"], four (proper) axioms for = [for example, $(Ax_1)(x_1 = x_1)$], and three (proper) axioms (sometimes called postulates) for group theory [for example, $(Ax_1)(Ex_2)(x_2 + x_1 = 0)$]. The elements of *RI* are just the two rules of inference for predicate calculus: if S_1 and S_2 are wffs, (*a*) S_2

follows from S_1 and $S_1 \supset S_2$; (b) $(Ax_i) S_1$ follows from S_1. Groups are models for group theory.

This notion of theory applies as an ideal to certain sciences. In mathematical sciences, as distinct from mathematics, the domain of an interpretation corresponds to data,† and truth is determined by observations. Models, for a theory, are states of nature and relations among them. Thus the motion of planets is a model for gravitational theory. (Often, in science, the term *model* is used for a mathematical structure to describe a natural phenomenon, contrary to the use of the term by logicians.) There is always some kind of idealization, or abstraction to focus on only the most essential few variables, and to separate the fundamental and central from the less important and peripheral.

A theory, such as group theory, would be a topic, except that in specifying a topic we must take account of the state of development of both the theory and its models. At any time t, there will have been proved a set $TS(t)$ of theorems in the theory; not all of these will have been found true. By time t, there will also have been established a corpus of data in $\cup_D \cup_k D^k$, where D is some domain of interpretation, which corresponds to observed truths. For each domain D there may be a different mapping $IM(D)$. Let IM denote the set of all these mappings together. For example, the infinite set of triples $\{(0,1;1)\ (2,3;5)\ (3,4;7)\ldots\}$ *denotes* the relation which gives the function $+$ its meaning. It is what is checked to verify the truth of "$(Ax_1)(Ax_2)(x_1 + x_2 = x_2 + x_1)$." *In principle. In fact*, this set of triples is finite; only finitely many triples will have actually been recorded at any time, though this set may grow with t.

Let us denote by $FS(t)$ the finite subset of all possible domains of interpretations $\cup_{k=0}^{\infty} D^k$ which is recorded at time t (mnemonic for facts). Moreover, there will be a set of propositions and facts which are recorded only as questions; they represent what is known to be unknown. This includes such unproved conjectures as "Every even number is the sum of two primes," undecidable propositions (not the theorem that they are undecidable), impossible problems such as paradoxical questions (not the theorem that they are impossible, but, for example, "Can the catalog of all catalogs which do not list themselves refer to itself?"), and as-yet-unverified or unverifiable factual questions such as "Is $(10^{25} - 2^{24})^{18} - 3$ a prime?". Let us call this set of questions $QS(t)$.

Finally, there are connections among questions that enable experts to call some questions deep and fundamental and others less profound or trivial.* We will try to make this more precise in the next section. For now, we call the set of

---

†Which, as suggested in Section 3.1, is wffs in a formal language with an interpretation of their own.

*There is a small but interesting literature on the analysis of questions (Harrah, 1963; MacKay, 1961; Polish Academy of Science , 1970).

relations among questions $CS(t)$ (mnemonic for connections). This enables us to propose the following 12-tuple as one way to characterize a topic[†] as time t:

$$\left\{ VT, VA, RF, RT, WF, AX, RI, TS(t), IM, FS(t), QS(t),\ CS(t) \right\} = TP_1(t)$$

Example: As a formal theory, group theory is specified by the first seven sets of this 12-tuple. As a topic, group theory is continually growing. At time t, $TS(t)$ contains such theorems as "the subgroups which are invariant under each inner automorphism are the normal divisors of the group;" $FS(t)$ contains all the known groups, such as the symmetric group S_4; $QS(1972)$ contains such as-yet-unsolved problems as the word problem for the group associated with knots. Finally, $CS(t)$ is the set of rich relations of the questions (answered or open) of group theory to one another or to questions in other branches of science: the Lorenz group is such a connection with physics; the automorphisms of a group G are themselves a group; and some of its properties reflect the deeper properties of G.

We can now imagine another way of characterizing "the same topic," $TP_2(t)$. For example, $TP_2(t)$ might differ from $TP_1(t)$ in that some of the axioms and theorems are interchanged, but $TP_1(t)$ was proved to be logically equivalent to $TP_2(t)$. We will call $TP_1(t)$ and $TP_2(t)$ two *representations* of the same topic, and view a topic as that abstraction which is invariant under shift of representation. A translation of, say, $TP_1(t)$ into some natural language L gives yet another representation, say, $TP_1^2(t)$, and $TP_1(t)$ is that abstraction which is invariant under all such translations (into English, French, etc.). The problem of deciding whether TP_1^E is equivalent to TP_1^L is, in general, even more difficult than the problem of deciding whether TP_1 and TP_2 are logically equivalent.

The notion designated by $CS(t)$ is as important as it is difficult to explicate. It could be defined precisely as a two-place relation on questions (Kochen, 1974) such that if the relation holds for Q and Q', then the answer to Q is known to imply the answer to Q'. For example, the answer to "Is there a largest prime?" implies the answer to "Is the set of primes infinite?". By analogy, the answer to "Is there a largest pair of twin primes [for example, $(3,5),(5,7),(11,13),\ldots$] ?" implies the answer to the still-open question "Is the

---

[†]This may begin to capture an aspect of what Kuhn intended by "paradigm" (Kuhn, 1962). To characterize a topic more fully than can be done by specifying these twelve sets, we should also describe how many paradigms, if any, there are. In describing a paradigm with less mathematical precision than implied in this section we should use the original sense of paradigm as a prototypical example for other explorers of the topic to follow. This includes a description of the state-of-the-art of thinking about the topic from a particular viewpoint, a history of how that state was reached, and an assessment of current trends and their projection. The latter may be indicated by what the leading institutions and investigators are working on, their rate of publication, of being cited, and of success by other measures. If there are several paradigms in a field, the relations between them should be indicated.

set of twin primes infinite?". The analogy between these question-pairs has, however, been of no value: Euclid's technique used to prove that there is no largest prime does not seem to work with twin primes. Other analogies, such as that between finding the number of ways of changing a dollar and finding the mean of a probability distribution, are most useful.

This way of specifying $CS(t)$ would interconnect only questions in the topic; it is purely internal. The external connections—to questions outside the topic— are at least as important as the internal ones. For even the internal questions, we cannot expect that just one relation such as implication can account for how some questions play a more central, fundamental role than others. The techniques of analysis available at the time, the priorities, and the fashions with which they are likely to be used on various problem classes must also be taken into account. For the external connections, the situation is even more complex.

Few topics have the logical precision of mathematics, which exemplified our development so far. Even within mathematics, it is impossible to tell the boundaries of a topic at any time; to try charting with any precision where group theory (as a topic) ends and field theory begins is as hopeless as it is unimportant. Because of the considerable overlap in the vocabulary VT and the formation rules RF of two similar topics, there is even greater overlap in the well-formed formulas (possible propositions). For field theory, for example, we would have to adjoin to VT for group theory a new function symbol $\times$. We could not simply index field theory by the conjunction of the symbols $+$ and $\times$, for that would also pertain to ring theory; one must look further into the specific axioms.

Nor can we expect, with profit, to define a distance function on topics that will, for example, identify field theory as being closer to Galois theory than to group theory. Again, methods of research play a key role, and topics which were intuitively remote (such as combinatorics and complex variables) become intimately close.

Even mathematical theories are not often stated in the completely precise logical language beginning with VT of the kind we illustrated above. They are stated in some subset of natural language which includes the formal 12-tuples we defined here. Nonmathematical topics are even harder to delineate, circumscribe, specify, and relate to one another with any degree of precision. This makes it quite futile to look for a rationale underlying decisions about classifying books by topics.

3.9. UNDERSTANDING VERSUS WISDOM

"Wisdom is the right use of knowledge" said Spurgeon. Holmes characterized it as the "abstract of the past," and Hutchison as "pursuing of the best ends by the best means." We propose that it is recognizing, choosing, and coping with or solving, by acceptable methods, the right problems at the right time.

We are at all times surrounded by problems.[†] We exist in a task-generating environment. To some extent we help shape this environment. Some of the tasks it presents to us can be traced to the actions of our ancestors. The tasks are either opportunities or traps. By making the appropriate moves, we can bring about beneficial consequences or avoid disastrous ones.

To cope, we must first recognize some of the key problems facing us. This means selecting, from all the problems we face at one time, those requiring our attention with top priority. How well we can do this depends on both our formal and informal representation or way of looking at the world. It depends on how well we have learned from the past to judge, to sense, to feel what matters most and when. It also depends on our understanding of the problem in the sense of Section 3.7.

Selecting the right problem at the right time is the first half of wisdom. Perhaps there is an element of luck in this. The genius may be lucky in his choice of problems and appear wise in retrospect. But, as Pasteur observed, chance favors the prepared mind. We all may be equally lucky in being surrounded by unusual opportunities (or traps), but some of us, by virtue of a more developed representation of the world, recognize these opportunities, while others do not. Even among those who recognize opportunities only a few seize them; the rest waver, hesitate, seek certainty, and let opportunities slip through. This is where wisdom plays its role.

Utilizing the options available for problem-solving is the other half of wisdom. Options resemble opportunities. Knowledge and understanding of alternate methods for coping with or solving a problem are necessary, but not sufficient. They must actually be tried, at the right time. Wisdom drives the supervisory program, the conductor of the orchestra, which actually causes the moves to be made. Great knowledge and understanding alone do not guarantee success in coping unless the implicit actions are made at the right time and place. Knowledge and understanding provide the potential. Wisdom realizes it, and provides the sufficient conditions for successful coping.

What role does an IR system play in the use of wisdom? Wisdom can be constantly acquired and exercised. An IR system can help in both. An important source of wisdom is experience. An IR system can direct its user to experiences less likely to be encountered without it. For example, an IR system can suggest to its user that he converse with a certain person, read a certain book, or

---

[†]Note that the use of *problem*, as in "he has problems," is in sharp contrast to the sense widely used in the problem-solving literature. It is our thesis that the decision-maker's first responsibility is to recognize problems in our sense; only secondarily does he solve problems posed by others. By a *problem* we mean a difficult situation, an undesirable state of affairs, a trouble to be overcome, or an opportunity to be seized.

participate in certain physical activities. If he follows the suggestion, he may emerge wiser after this experience.

An IR system can also help in the exercise of wisdom. Frequently, picking a problem or a method to solve it can be helped by "jogging" or "shaking up" the thought process. (That is the etymology of the word *cognition*.) This can be viewed, in its more extreme forms, as stimulating a shift of representation. Certain stimuli generated by an IR system can be instrumental for this purpose. This leads to the design of a special class of IR systems to help with ill-defined problems, and they must be coupled effectively with the internal representations of a variety of individuals (Badre, 1973).

This is where the ambiguity of words and phrases in natural language plays an important role. Words that have one, well-defined meaning are likely to trigger unusual associations only if they occur in an unusual context. Words with many meanings, used appropriately, can stimulate the imagination greatly. Both poetry and humor (especially puns) capitalize on this.

The case for language design—that is, specifying a formal language which users must learn and adjust to—is strong for what we call *mechanizable fields* in Chapter Six. This is analogous to the use of the telephone or typewriter. Most of us probably prefer learning and adjusting to the constraints of keyboards or dials to paying the cost of systems that automatically read our (natural) handwriting or recognize our unconstrained speech. Phonemes have an ambiguity analogous to that of words.

Decision-makers who use IR systems in mechanizable fields do not have to exercise wisdom to the extent that decision-makers working in *explorable fields* (Chapter Six) must. An executive, legislator, or judge uses "judgment" to a greater extent than does a scientific analyst. Such judgment—for example, in the use of intelligence data, drafting of laws, or interpretation of laws—requires transscientific considerations (Weinberg, 1972). For that reason, IR systems to help them should not be denuded of all ambiguity. The ambiguities in the U.S. and other constitutions, and even more so the Ten Commandments, may contribute to the great flexibility and long, useful age of these law codes through a great variety of social changes.

SUMMARY

The notion of *information* in its broader sense is viewed as having five key aspects: recorded data, information in the sense of communication theory, knowledge, understanding, and wisdom (Figure 3.3). IR systems to help people recognize and cope with problems deal primarily with the last column. This conceptualization is useful in the search for conditions under which IR systems contribute to the healthy growth of knowledge.

Figure 3.3. The notion of information.

Information as a generic term

Recorded data	*Information in the sense of mathematical communication theory*	*Knowledge in the sense of theory of knowledge*	*Understanding*	*Wisdom*
A well-formed statement in a formal language, which is true in some interpretation and registered in some store	A property of a collection of transmittable, coded messages which reduces receiver's uncertainty about which message is sent	A mental state enabling a person to answer a question he posed as an actor who finds the answer necessary for some action	A mental condition enabling a person to ask a question as a knower who realizes what he does not know and needs to know and how this question relates to other questions	A mental state enabling a person to take a useful action at an appropriate time based on all his available understanding and knowledge
Generated by:				
Experimenters	Sources (telephone callers; telegram senders)	Applied scientists	Theorists	Men of experience and intuitive insight
Used by:				
Analysts	Destinations (telegram receivers)	Professionals	Theorists Experimenters	Men of action
Notion useful for:				
Computer scientists Social scientists	Communications engineers	Philosophers	Commentators Appreciators	Decision scientists

Chapter Four

Documentation

In this chapter we delve more deeply into the second of the three ingredients of an IR system's environment that we discussed in Chapter Two: documents. These are also the basic constituents of an IR system. The central idea is to identify documenthood with authenticity and reliability, and to explore the relations of documents to people and to themselves. To develop this idea, we first discuss the distinction between retrieval of recorded data and retrieval of documents. We start with an analysis of the function of a library. We then analyze the dynamics of document development, prior to discussing document–document coupling and document–person coupling in greater depth.

4.1 LIBRARIES AND BIBLIOGRAPHY

Books, whether in the form of clay tablets, parchment scrolls, or bound pages, are among the most ancient examples of documents. The concept of a book is central to the analysis of IR systems, if only as an important source of input. The notion of a library appears not only as the collection of books everyone knows, but as a collection of computer programs or subroutines as well. Principles underlying its function may also apply to how a person retrieves information with his own memory.

Bibliography, as a term, originated from the post-classical Greek word for book-writing. Until about the middle of the eighteenth century, a person who wrote or copied books was called a bibliographer. In 1763 (Chandler, 1963, p. 8), bibliography began to refer only to writing *about* books. Today, it still means the description and listing of books and other physical items collected by libraries. The primary use of bibliography is still to trace such items in order to find out something.

The term *document* is used in many ways. None is of the precision necessary for use in theory-building. Its most widespread use among practitioners in the information arts and sciences is in reference to the physical medium which contains information that a library user might wish to retrieve. This does not, in our view, capture the essence of the concept of *document*. Document-retrieval, in practice, refers quite often to ascertaining the existence and location of, and to the physical transport of, information-bearing objects or the transmission of information-bearing signals. In this broad, popular usage, documents include books; articles in encyclopedias, handbooks, and journals; serials; newspapers; maps and prints; films; tapes; and documents in the more narrow sense of librarianship.

In this somewhat technical sense, documents are publications which are outside of the open-market monograph-serial literature because of insufficient demand, but which contain information that the issuing body wants to make known anyway. Government publications, patents, pamphlets by international agencies, reports by commercial firms, and privately produced manuscripts are examples. The number and growth of such documents greatly exceeds the number of books.

In its broader, popular sense, the notion of document is best exemplified by the physical form of a book, whether in the form of clay tablets, a scroll, a set of bound pages, a micrograph, or a tape. A document in this sense is a thing, a physical object, which contains reliable information. A "collection of books organized for use" is the traditional definition of a library. It is also traditional to regard a library as performing three main substantive functions: (*a*) book selection (input), (*b*) bibliographic control, and (*c*) reference (output). In this classical framework, a library exerts bibliographic control over its collection to the extent that it can efficiently establish the existence and location of any unit in that collection at any time. The units are primarily books and serials, to be specified by author, title, publisher, date, etc. Providing such bibliographic control is bibliography, which includes cataloging and classification.

More recently, this time-honored way of looking at the functions of a library and of bibliography has been reexamined. One modern view † (Egan, 1956) is that a library's function is "to maximize the effective social utilization of the graphic records of civilization." Note the replacement of "books" by "graphic records of civilization," and "use" by "maximization of effective social utilization."

Librarianship and bibliography can supply some of the necessary but by no means all of the sufficient ingredients required for maximizing the effective social utilization of records. It can identify and locate a record, but it cannot coerce someone who needs this record to want it or use it, much less ensure that

---

†Other views are readily available (Kemeny, 1966; Kilgour, 1967; King, Edmundson, Flood, Kochen, Swanson, and Wylly, 1963; Licklider, 1965; Lipetz, 1966; Morse, 1968; Overhage, 1966; Rawski, 1973).

he uses it to the benefit of society. Moreover, not all records need be graphic; audio tapes may serve also. *What is required, however, is that the records be authentic, validated.* We propose the following as the primary function of a library: *To maximize the greatest potentially attainable, effective, and efficient social utilization of documented knowledge, understanding, and wisdom.*

This shifts the burden on bibliographic control from keeping track of physical objects to intelligence. The "really unique, gut problem of any library or information service," said Swank (1970), is devising schemes for the *intellectual organization* of the information resources of the library. The modern catalog is to serve as a directory to resources with a high potential for social utilization, to couple the challenges of our time with our accumulated capabilities to respond.

Perhaps the most important aspect of the above statement for the function of a library is the term *documented*. It is nearly synonymous with *authenticated, validated, proven.* This appears to capture the criterion for what a useful IR system is to store more directly than does either the broad, popular conception of a document as any information-bearing physical object or record, or the narrower conception of a publication outside the marketplace for monographs and serials. Not every scrap of paper † or record which some library may collect should be called a document if that term is to serve us in designing IR systems. We need to explicate *documentation*∗ and *document* as scientific concepts.

4.2 DOCUMENT-RETRIEVAL VERSUS FACT-RETRIEVAL

In Section 3.1 we defined recorded data as well-formed statements, (or their equivalent in tables or diagrams) in some formal language, which are true in some interpretation, and which have been registered and preserved in a store.

---

†The average company in the U.S. creates over 3,000 pieces of paper a year for every person on its payroll (Barcam, 1964). The average government agency creates 12,000 pieces of paper per year for every person on its payroll. The total is about 3.85×10^{11} records/year generated in the U.S. The American Paper Institute estimates that the U.S. uses about 500 pounds of paper/person/year, compared with 300 for Sweden and Canada, 42 for USSR, and for China, where it began in the first century, only 6 pounds (*New York Times*, 1/17/1966, p. 58).

∗Defined in *Documentation in Action* (Shera, Kent, and Perry, 1956) as the group of techniques necessary for the ordered presentation, organization, and communication of recorded, specialized knowledge, in order to give maximum accessibility and utility of the information contained.

Documentation is elaborated, to delineate the field, and as a kind of consensus of prior literature (Henderson, Moats, and Stevens, 1966) to consist of six processes: (*a*) communication of recorded basic data, primary publications, tables, abstracts, indexes, etc.; (*b*) routing; (*c*) acquisition; (*d*) storing; (*e*) searching; and (*f*) retrieving. These include organization for search and storage, systematization such as vocabulary control, analysis in descriptive and subject cateloging, publication, presentation, reproduction, and dissemination.

The statements may be displayed directly as responses to expressed needs, or they may steer a computer to generate responses to requests. Fact-retrieval is a procedure for analyzing requests to ascertain the needs they express and then producing responses, based on statements in this store, most likely to meet the needs.

To distinguish between fact-retrieval and question-answering systems (Kochen, 1969), we will use fact-retrieval to mean answering questions that do not require inference. A map which gives the average driving time between major U.S. cities can be used for fact-retrieval if it is asked for the time from Los Angeles to San Francisco; it is used as a question-answering system if it is asked for the time from Los Angeles to Portland, Oregon, even if the map shows only the time from Los Angeles to San Francisco, and from San Francisco to Portland, because the time from Los Angeles to Portland has to be deduced. Similarly, a chart which shows that in a certain month there were more motorcycle accidents in a certain town than car accidents can be used for fact-retrieval if it is asked for that data; if it asked whether motorcyclists have a significantly higher accident rate than car drivers in that town, a statistical inference is called for, and a question-answering system is needed.

In line with Section 3.6, we must admit that such a question-answering system together with the user *knows* or stores and processes knowledge if it can answer enough questions in an appropriate way. A fact-retrieval system stores and makes available information.

In Section 3.2 we called attention to the difference between documents in a collection and recorded data. Bar-Hillel was one of the first to stress the distinction between information-retrieval and literature-search. He defined information as we do: production of a list of declarative sentences in response to interrogative sentences. Literature-search produces a list of references in response to a topic description. This is also called *document retrieval* by some. The difference is only one of directness. Literature-search retrieves references to units likely to contain the sentences that information-retrieval would display directly.

But what are the items a literature-search is to produce? They can be in the *form* of physical objects, such as clay tablets with inscribed symbols, scrolls or books with ink on paper or parchment, microphotographic transparencies with tiny spots of silver or sections of magnetic tape, or discs on which patterns of domains with different magnetic orientation are recorded. Just as a sentence is an abstraction from the various physical forms in which it is sensed—phonetic, printed, Braille, etc.—or stored, so a document is an abstraction from all the various forms in which it can be stored, transmitted, and displayed. We must distinguish the abstract concept—for which we propose to use the term *document*—from the generic concept for the class of physical objects that includes book copies, individual articles, or patent reprints. The concept of a book (or work, as librarians call it) does not denote any particular copy a library or owner may possess, but what is common to all copies, revisions, translations, etc.

The distinction between document- and fact-retrieval is summarized in Figure 4.1.

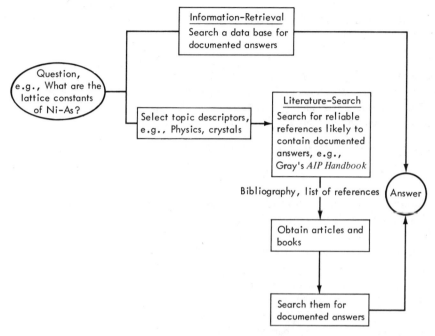

Figure 4.1. Literature-search versus fact-retrieval.

4.3 THE DOCUMENT CONCEPT

We propose the following definition for purposes of a formal theory. A document is a nonempty set of wffs in one or more languages which has the following properties:

1. It has at least one name by which it can be referred to.
2. It is assigned to at least one author who bears intellectual responsibility for it.
3. It cites prior documents.
4. It legitimizes or regulates certain actions.†
5. It is validated by an authorizing agency.

---

†For example, making decisions in designing a bridge based on data in a text on strength of materials; arriving at a legal opinion on the basis of a sociological study report.

The following examples justify the plausibility of these assumptions.†

Example 1:   Consider a *patent*. One of its names is the patent number. One author is a person or corporation to whom it is assigned. It refers to other patents to show novelty. It legitimizes the inventor to build the patented device and requires anyone else building it to pay him royalties. It is validated by the patent office.

Example 2:   A *passport* has a number. Its author is probably its bearer, who supplied most of the data in it. It implicitly cites his birth certificate or a naturalization certificate. It establishes his identity and citizenship with the privileges and duties thereof. It is validated by an arm of his government.

Example 3:   The name of a *book* can be its call number in a library or its citation as it appears in a bibliography. Authorship and references are clear. It entitles any reader to cite it or its contents. It is validated by a publisher.

Example 4:   A *birth certificate* is a document. The name is that of the newborn. The authors are the parents and the authorizing agency is a hospital, church, or other institution which affixes its validating stamp or signature. It can be thought of as containing a formal sentence documenting the birth of a person to specified parents at a specified time and place. It cites, implicitly, the birth certificates of the parents of the newborn; it can similarly be used to authenticate the birth certificates of offspring, or to authorize citizenship by providing proof about place of birth. This is necessary in certain disputes over inheritance, citizenship, religion, and marriage. This example illustrates the distinction between an implicit and an explicit citation.

Example 5:   In the sense used by historians, documents sometimes include *poetry, sermons, folk-lore, letters, coins, paintings, and buildings*. Commager, in his compilation *Documents of American History*, defined the notion of document more narrowly by requiring that they be of an "official" character. Thus he includes presidential addresses, judicial decisions, treaties, acts, plans, and letters; he would also have included church records, school reports, minutes of fraternal orders, and records of labor organizations as documents of the undercurrents of social life, had they been available in the form of documents. It is easy to verify that all the documents in Commager's book satisfy, though not rigidly, our criteria for documenthood.

Example 6:   A *published article* in a scientific periodical is a document. It always has at least one author who bears intellectual responsibility. If it is a

---

†A sixth plausible assumption we might add is that it be of long duration (Goodman and Heilprin, 1965), but that applies to recorded data, too, to some extent.

scientific article, for example, it should not violate the conventions of scientific methodology—of logical and statistical inference and valid observation—which are implicitly adhered to by members of the scientific community. As a rule, the elaborate system of refereeing and editing ensures conformity to those conventions. The scientific paper almost always explicitly cites prior documents; it may itself be cited by future documents; and sometimes a scientific article is used by engineers as an authoritative source on which to base technological decisions.

Example 7: A *mathematical theorem and its proof*, in the abstract, constitute a document. There is at least one author, the one who created the document and who must be able to defend it against all doubts. The proof follows very precise rules of inference, and each step follows syntactic rules for well-formedness. Very few proofs use axioms as their base, for proofs would be inordinately long and impossible to follow if that were done in all cases. Most proofs begin from previously proved theorems. Many theorems are, in turn, used in the proofs of further theorems. That is how mathematics grows. Some theorems are used by scientists, for example, to authorize certain procedures, to carry out certain methodological operations, and to predict testable statements about events in nature. While the proof of a theorem might contain a statement such as "this step follows from the Riesz–Fisher theorem," that citation is not the same as the direct citation of one published article by another. Sometimes the theorem used to justify a step in a proof is so well-known, elementary, obvious, or all three, that it is not even mentioned (for example, the Pythagorean theorem). This is an implicit citation. There exist, of course, documents to which explicit reference might be made, but this would be superfluous.

The last example illustrates what would happen if, say, the rules of inference had been violated, and a nontheorem were introduced as a document. A propagation of errors would result that might not be detected for some time. Eventually it would be detected [†] because of the contradictory implications which would appear. The source of such error propagation would be quickly traced, and the responsible author would suffer discredit, making it less likely that he would propagate further errors. In this way the social process of generating and using documents is self-correcting. Deviations from the ideal document remain automatically under control.

A preprint or privately circulated report is not a document if no one may cite it or use if for any purpose other than commenting to the author. Manuscripts with an unknown author, no references, or without validation by some

---

[†]A person *using* a result may be at least as likely to detect the error as another author who wants to build on it. Certainly, the nonauthor user, even if he does not detect the error, will not contribute to its propagation. This supports the statements made in Chapter Two that it is undesirable for the only users of an IR system to be the authors.

authorizing agency are not full documents in our sense, though we may call them partial documents of special kinds.†

What we hope to capture with this definition is not only what publishers produce and libraries catalog, but also what computer programmers produce when they document a program, the paper work that controls movement of cargo in trade (also called documentation: for example, bills of lading, letters of credit, suppliers' invoices, and truckers' receipts), as well as historical documents, passports, birth certificates, licenses, etc. The wffs in a document can be in several languages in the same document—for example, English, graphics, tables, and formulas. Some wffs, such as entries in a table, can be implicit. The names are generally part ‡ of the document, implicitly recognized as such by a wff, such as its position and format in the document. This is also the case for criteria (2), (3), and (5). Actions by its users that the document permits or regulates may not be explicitly stated in the document but in other documents that refer to it.

The purpose of creating a document is to enable its users to act in ways that will help them to cope with their problems. To take certain actions, such as creating another document, adding to knowledge, using knowledge to make a decision, going to a foreign country, or running a computer program, a person needs some document to give him needed authorization or information. The most important requirement, however, is that it be *valid*. Validity is to a document as truth is to a wff or sentence. We distinguish between a valid document, corresponding to a datum, and an invalid document, corresponding to an unverified or false sentence.

A document serves to legitimize certain actions because most people have faith in its authenticity and validity. This faith is implicit agreement by social convention. It derives from the reliability people impute to the source issuing from documents as well as that of the validating agency.

Yet there must be stabilizing mechanisms to guarantee that even though a few documents are not valid, the effect of these few will not propagate through the system as a whole and affect it adversely. One such mechanism is to assign intellectual responsibility to someone for the authenticity of a document and to hold him accountable for any breach.

Human authors occasionally fail to meet that intellectual responsibility. The authenticity of a document must be more reliable than the author. To help ensure this, various checking procedures are used. A validating agency, such as a

---

†Scratch paper and rough drafts used by a researcher to help him think and notebooks in which he records data are also partial documents. Even though unreliable, segments of such records have to be retrieved also. Several IR systems serve as such personalized, electronic notebooks.

‡This is developed in more detail in Chapter Seven.

publisher, has to approve it before it is valid. Referees, acting on behalf of the validating agency, check a candidate document for relevance to the agency's mission, significance[†] for its clients, validity, novelty or authenticity, clarity, and conformity to rules.

If the item is a collection of sentences, then conventions of style, syntax, length, and so on, must be followed. If the item reports a logical inference, conventions for valid logical inference must not be violated. If the item reports material truths, observed facts, or findings, conventions of accepted methodology and reporting must not be violated. These conventions are not always very precise or explicit and require interpretation. In the case of published articles in science, this is done by the leading practitioners of a scientific community adhering to a paradigm. It is judged and enforced by editors and referees of journals.

If a "document" explicitly violates such conventions, not only will it decrease in reliability, but its author and validating agency may suffer loss of reliability, and the "document" as well as others generated by that author may be removed from circulation as a document.

The validating agency derives its authority from its responsibility to the various document users. A publisher is accountable to its readers and to an extent its authors, critics, and intellectual leaders as well. The referees acting on its behalf are to be a representative sample of both the users and the leadership.

There are always enough deviant documents to ensure the possibility of genuine innovation and scientific revolution, but not so many as to disintegrate the entire system.

4.4 LIFE CYCLE OF A DOCUMENT

A document is conceived, officially published, and usable for solving problems which help us cope or which add to knowledge. With age, it gradually ceases to function as a document because knowledge has grown or the environment has changed. Thus U.S. patents expire in 17 years. A document conventionally betokens authorization to use the information it contains. It can also serve as a carrier of "infection," an agent for the spread of ideas. If thus helps generate more documents. It is therefore useful and not unreasonable to associate some life-like properties with it.

[†]The process of referee-selection and these criteria by which referees are to judge manuscripts submitted to a journal, as a means of improving quality, are explicated in more detail elsewhere (Kochen, 1970). A new measure of the importance of a scientific paper was also developed recently (Virgo, 1971).

It is important, once more, to distinguish between the concrete, physical tokens which embody a document and the abstract notion of a document itself. In practice, the physical token of the symbol is far more important than the abstraction. Depending upon the physical medium, it decays or dies. Therefore special care must be taken to preserve the physical form of ancient documents, for example. Should they vanish, however, what they symbolize would not also disappear. The traveler who loses his passport may have difficulties with authorities, but he can still, despite difficulties, claim and substantiate all that this document authorized.

The birth of a document occurs when its author submits it to a validator. He does this with an implicit agreement that, unless the validator rejects it, the contents of the submitted manuscript will be public property. Furthermore, the author has been assigned and has accepted intellectual responsibility that, to the best of his ability, all the properties a document should possess have been incorporated. The time of birth is established by a secondary document, a letter from the publisher acknowledging the manuscript's receipt. This can be used as legal evidence in priority disputes.†

During the prebirth period, the searcher-author must:

1. Formulate the main message to be documented and formulate the query to be resolved, the goal of his labors.
2. Clarify issues; logically structure his message; and formulate subgoals to be met.
3. Search and study the past and current literature.
4. Compose his message and supply additional material to be included, if needed.
5. Form and style the document, edit, and rewrite to conform to conventions.

After the birth of a document comes publication. Documents did not originate with the printing press.‡ Type composition has been a manual process for centuries. The publication process has not been greatly automated. Recent developments in type-composition by computer, with by-products such as automated error-correction and hyphenation, are big strides toward more complete automation. The great benefit of automation has always been decreasing the

---

†If the document is not accepted by that journal, but submitted to other journals in one of which it is eventually accepted, this is still a reasonable time of birth. If it is never published, we may call it stillborn. It should be citable as a document.

‡The printing press can be viewed as an example of an invention which was more expressive of the inventor's need for creativity than of a latent public demand. Nor was the full potential of this invention for automating the publication process by decreasing time lags, increasing volume, and lowering cost, fully realized at that time.

cost-to-performance ratio, of providing more and higher-quality goods and services per unit cost. Photo-offset printing (resulting in paperback books) and other inexpensive printing methods have already increased this ratio very far, and new photocomposition methods coupled to computer-based typesetting can be expected to increase it further, but only to a point of diminishing returns. At that point, the automation process becomes uncoupled from human beings and is likely to be replaced by the notion of man—machine interaction and time sharing, both of which are now under vigorous development.

The average time lag between submission of a manuscript to a journal and its first appearance in print varies greatly from field to field and from publication to publication (great lags have been reported by psychologists and short ones by logicians). It is only 3 months before publication for a letter to *Physical Review*, and 2–3 weeks for a letter to *Physical Review Letters*, but it may take 1–2 years for a full-length article in a major popular journal (for example, one sent to all dues-paying members of a professional society). Because it costs a publisher about $20/published page, and this cost is going up, it is somewhat surprising that about three new journals are being founded every day. This may be less surprising when we estimate that, at 7%/year, about 100,000 people are joining the ranks of educated Americans each day. The predictably increased use of automation in publishing will decrease these costs and time lag, but will very probably not affect the number of people reached; the demand curve for a journal may show price as a relatively constant function of the quantity demanded; but this requires empirical study. More important, however, the role of publisher will mesh more closely with that of the sponsor, the indexer, the reviewer, and all other elements involved in the period between conception and birth of a document.

A newborn document need not and should not cite documents with a date of birth later than its own. It is quite difficult to conduct a good literature search for documents which have been born and which ought to be cited, up to the time the manuscript is submitted for publication. This would leave only the time period between manuscript submission and casting of the document into its final, printed, unchangeable form for such searches, and this time is hardly ever so used. If an author is "scooped" by another while his paper is in press, both are generally credited with independently reaching the same result. It is analogous to a tie in a race. To be obligated to cite articles in press would put a great burden on IR systems to help with such searches. Pending patents are an example of the difficulties encountered.

Furthermore, documents in this early infancy—after birth but before imprint date—should also be available for citation, and this is never the case. This is a serious defect in the present system because the early infancy period of a document is, from the point of view of use, the most important. Automation could remedy this, even though it would reduce the early infancy, in that it would be easier to add references at any time after birth because the manuscript would be available in digital electronic storage rather than matrices of type metal.

4.5   CITATION NETS REVISITED

The most significant way that documents are coupled to one another is by means of explicit citations (Tukey, 1962). Though often understood to be references at the end of a scholarly paper, the notion of citation is more general and quite important. Consider first *explicit citations*.

Given a pair of documents, how can we decide whether or not one ought to cite the other? If one document contains information that can be found nowhere else, and this information is used in an essential way in a second document so that it could not exist without this information, the second document should cite the first. Such conditions are the exception rather than the rule. Generally, no *single* item of information is critically essential to a document. Documents other than the one to be cited frequently contain nearly the same information. The question, however, has many subtleties buried in the phrase *same information*. This is often a concept or an idea. Sometimes it is vague; the phraseology used by one author may not resemble that of another expressing the same idea, and the idea itself may have escaped everyone.

With these difficulties it is not surprising that there is a great deal of arbitrariness in the way authors select references for their bibliographies. Undoubtedly, many documents which should have been cited are missed; and many documents which the author does cite are only slightly relevant. Measuring the extent of such misses is an interesting topic of experimental investigation. To some extent, such misses reflect (and cause) ineffective retrieval. There may even be cases where authors consciously or unconsciously fail to cite documents they know to be relevant.

The number of older documents referred to by a given document is a random variable. On what should the nature of its distribution depend? The probability that a document cites very many prior documents should be small if the field of knowledge to which the document pertains is very novel, very uncrowded, or unexplored, or if the choice of problem and method of solution is highly original; it would also be small if the information retrieval system used to find relevant prior documents produced only a small fraction of the documents it should have found. To make these notions precise, a number of variables must be introduced.

When an author generates a new document, he has posed a query, recognized a need which his document is designed to meet. Corresponding to this need is a query topic. Suppose that the author, now a querist, is using a retrospective search system to find prior documents relevant to his query topic. We call a prior document relevant if the querist, upon seeing it, would judge it relevant. (We will later try to replace this by a less subjective, more querist-independent criterion.) By presenting the querist with samples of documents chosen at random from the document collection of his system, we can estimate the a priori probability that a document is relevant. Call this p.

Consider now the conditional probability C that the document to be generated will cite a randomly chosen prior document, given that the latter is relevant to the query topic. We define c as the conditional probability that a document is retrieved, given that it is relevant to the query topic. It seems reasonable to suppose that the number of documents actually used and cited in the generation of a new document will be a fixed fraction of the number of documents retrieved. That is, $C = \mu c$, where μ is the fixed fraction. Furthermore, c is equal to the hit or recall rate h, which measures the extent to which a retrieval system retrieves all relevant documents.

We now consider the conditional probability C' that the document to be generated will cite a randomly chosen prior document, given that the latter is *not* relevant to the query topic. This, too, is taken to be μ times c', the conditional probability of retrieval, given irrelevance. The acceptance rate† a, which measures the extent to which a retrieval system does not retrieve irrelevant documents, is related to c by

$$a = \frac{cp}{cp + (1-p)c'}$$

The probability q that the document to be generated will cite a randomly chosen document is simply $pC + (1-p)C'$, or

$$q = \mu \left[\frac{ph + ph\,(1-a)}{a} \right] = \frac{\mu ph}{a}$$

The probability that exactly r documents from a collection of D documents are cited by the newly generated document is given by the binomial distribution

$$\binom{D}{r} q^r (1-q)^{D-r}$$

or its Poisson approximation

$$e^{-Dq} (Dq)^r / r!$$

---

† Usually called precision ratio.

A reasonable side condition is that $1 > c > p > c' > 0$. From this it follows that $ph/a < 1$ and that the mean number of references per document, $\mu Dph/a$, is finite and a reasonable number. The distribution itself is such that the probability of r references decreases approximately exponentially with r, after having reached a peak near the mean number.

If we think of the number of prior documents cited as a function of t, it would seem reasonable to suppose that this is a stationary stochastic process; the distribution should not change with t if the retrieval system and μ do not. This stochastic process may, however, be considered an integral of a stochastic process for the number (random variable) of prior documents generated T time units before the birth of the newly generated document which cites them. The integral ranges from $T = 0$ to t, the age of the document collection over which retrieval occurs. Thus the assumption of stationarity is not strictly correct because of the finite age of the document collection. The distribution of the number of prior documents cited will depend on t for t small, but this dependence will vanish rapidly as t increases. Derivations for the distribution of the number of cited documents generated T time units ago as a function of T depend on the growth of the number of fields of knowledge and related matters.

Consider now some elementary properties of a citation net. First, no link can be bidirectional. If Doc_1 cites Doc_2, then Doc_2 cannot cite Doc_1 because Doc_2 was generated before Doc_1; the relation *cites* is usually antisymmetric. It is also irreflexive: no document can cite itself. The citation net contains no circuits in the sense of graph theory (Berge, 1964). If Doc_1 cites Doc_2 and Doc_2 cites Doc_3, then obviously Doc_3 cannot cite Doc_1 because Doc_3 was generated before Doc_1. Nor is the relation Cit transitive: $Cit(Doc_1 Doc_2)$ and $Cit(Doc_2,Doc_3)$ does not imply $Cit(Doc_1,Doc_3)$, although the latter statement should be more probable if the former two are given, than if they are not; clearly, Doc_3 has some indirect debt to the influence of Doc_1 even though it does not cite it, because it is one generation removed. There can be one edge at most between any two nodes since a given document cannot cite another given document more than once.

In graph theory (Harary, Cartwright, and Norman, 1965, Saaty and Busacker, 1965), such graphs are called trees or digraphs (oriented graphs) without circuits. Most of the existing theorems about such trees are of more value for other branches of mathematics than for citation nets. The real question is how the graph can be "decomposed" into subgraphs. These subgraphs are to have the property that each node within a subgraph is linked to a greater or equal number of nodes in the same subgraph than it is linked to nodes outside that subgraph. These subgraphs are also to have the largest number of nodes with such properties and be other than the entire graph itself.

Figure 4.2 illustrates what we mean. If we extract from this graph two subgraphs, one with nodes I = (A, B, C, d, e, f), one with (D, E, F, j, k, l) = II, it

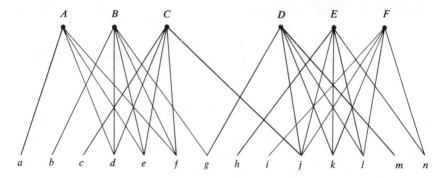

Figure 4.2. Clustering in a citation net.

will be seen that for each upper node of I, there are three links to points outside A (A, B, and C each go to d, e, f), but only two links outside. This is also true for subgraph II. We might adjoin a, b, c, g to I and h, i, m, n to II, thus effecting a decomposition of the graph into subgraphs I$'$ and II$'$, with one link from I$'$ to II$'$ (C,j) and one link from II$'$ to I$'$ (D,g). Had we adjoined g to II rather than I, then there would have been two links from I$'$ to II$'$.

4.6 GROWTH OF THE NUMBER OF DOCUMENTS

Documentation involves the organization of recorded knowledge. This becomes more difficult if the number of documents increases. The growth of the function $D(t)$, the number of documents in a collection at time t, is an important function. A theory should shed some light on its mathematical form under various assumptions about the mechanisms underlying growth.

Over the sample space of all institutions[†] of the same age t, $D(t)$ is a random variable; its distribution depends on such factors as the budget allotted by the institutions to their information system and the library subsystem in particular, on the specific goals and policies with regard to acquisition—that is, whether to collect comprehensively in all fields to serve research scholars as the Library of Congress does, or whether to aim for complete coverage in a special field as the FBI fingerprint file—and so on.

For a particular institution, $D(t)$ is not a random variable. One plausible collection policy for an institution starting a document collection at $t = t_0$ is to collect current literature at a documents/year and build up its historical collection at b documents/year so that T_0 years after time t_0, it will hold and con-

---

[†]Estimating $D(t)$, even at one time t, is a large and difficult topic in applied statistics, which we do not go into (Barr, 1967).

tinue to hold a fixed fraction a of the world's published literature in specified fields of knowledge. It might be more realistic to replace the above-mentioned single fixed fraction by a sequence of fractions, the sum of which is equal to the fixed fraction; each fraction in the sequence specifies which part of the world's literature should be held in each field of knowledge. However, this would be more complex and would obscure the main issue of the type of growth. The world total of documents, originated since the beginning of man's effort to collect documented records, would then have to be treated as a sum of subtotals for the various fields of knowledge. These, of course, have continually changed throughout history. For simplicity, we shall here assume that all these subtotals have grown according to the same law as the total itself.

In brief, we assume that $D'(t)$, the rate at which an institution adds to its document collection, is determined by:

1. Acquisition of currently generated documents, starting with $t = 0$, equalling the same fixed fraction of the world literature it eventually wants to hold. Here $t = 0$ is the time at which the institution began its library. The number of pertinent currently generated documents is proportional to the number of authors multiplied by the average number of documents generated per author per unit time; the number of authors, in turn, grows proportionally to the number of educated people; at present, that number seems to grow exponentially (geometrically) at a rate of about 7% per year, or doubling in a decade.

2. Collection of literature generated prior to $t = 0$ at a constant rate into the past, so that at $t = T_0$, it will have the desired fraction a of the older literature as well. In other words, T_0 years after the library is founded, it will have acquired bT_0 items published prior to the library's founding at the rate of b/week, plus a fixed fraction of all the documents published subsequent to the library's founding. (In many cases, $b = 0$, especially if $D(0)$ is substantial.)

It follows, by integration, that if the rate at which the world total of currently generated documents increases exponentially with t, because of proportionality to the number of educated people, then the cumulative total of documents generated up to time t will also increase exponentially with t. The exponential form of $D(t)$ follows from the assumption that the number of authors grows exponentially (at least now). It could also follow from an assumption that the rate at which the number of documents increases is proportional to the number of documents present at that time. Each document stimulates the creation of a fixed fraction of new documents per year. This is, however, conjectural. Yet it is attractive both as a testable hypothesis and for the other interesting implications it may have.

Suppose that the literature in a certain field doubles (for a few decades) every λ years (e.g., $\lambda = 10$). Then the world literature in that field grows at the rate of $A2^{t/\lambda}$ documents per year, where A is the number added per year when that field was founded. The cumulated total number of documents by time t is $\int_0^t A2^{\tau/\lambda} d\tau = A\lambda \ln 2 (2^{t/\lambda} - 1)$.

If a library collects a constant fraction a of current literature in this field after $t = t_0$ plus a smaller fraction b per year of the $A\lambda \ln 2 (2^{t_0/\lambda} - 1)$ older documents that existed at $t = 0$, then

$$D'(t) = \begin{cases} aA \cdot 2^{t/\lambda} + bA\lambda \ln 2 (2^{t_0/\lambda} - 1) & t \leq T_0 \\ aA\, 2^{t/\lambda} & t > T_0 \end{cases}$$

Buildup of the historical collection proceeds until $bt = a$ or $t = T_0 = a/b$. Integrating with respect to t gives

$$D(t) = \begin{cases} aA\lambda \ln 2 (2^{t/\lambda} - 1) + bA\lambda t \ln 2 (2^{t_0/\lambda} - 1) & \text{for } t \leq a/b \\ aA\lambda \ln 2 (2^{a/b\lambda} - 1) + aA\lambda \ln 2 (2^{t_0/\lambda} - 1) \\ \quad + aA\lambda \ln 2 (2^{t/\lambda} - 2^{a/b\lambda}) \end{cases}$$

$$= \quad aA\lambda \ln 2 (2^{t/\lambda} + 2^{t_0/\lambda} - 2) \qquad\qquad \text{for } t > a/b$$

Consider the total expected number of future papers that will cite a given paper. That this be independent of t, the time the given document is generated, is a plausible assumption. It follows from the above assumption that this expected number of citations is finite. Since, however, the expected number is also proportional to $D(t)$, this constant number of "citations back to" is greater for more recently generated documents than for older documents.

Returning to the citation net—the graph in which documents are nodes and an edge directed from Doc_1 to Doc_2 stands for the sentence "Doc_1 cites Doc_2"—we can now give a partial description of its structure. With increasing t, the number of nodes in the graph increases. But the number of new edges terminating at an old node born at t_0 decreases as $e^{-k}(t - t_0)$. The number of edges terminating on a new node is an increasing function of the number of nodes.

4.7   STRUCTURE WITHIN A DOCUMENT COLLECTION

This is only a partial description of an actual citation net, because not all sets of r nodes to which edges could be directed from a given node are equiprobable.

That is, the citation net shows stratification, local aggregation, and clustering in that some subsets of the nodes are more strongly interconnected within themselves than are other subsets. It is intuitively clear that a document pertaining to the design of heat shields in spacecraft, for example, is far less likely to refer to some *r* documents about biochemical reactions in the kidney then to some *r* documents about high-temperature metallurgy.

One might be tempted to speculate that most of the documents citing a given document pertain to the same field of knowledge as the cited document, that citation nets decompose into tightly knit, reasonably separable clusters. This may not correspond to fact. A small sampling of the citation net for computer patents, for example (Reisner, 1965), showed that only about half of the citing patents are in the same "class" as the cited patent. The numerical values of such empirical studies depend greatly on how documents (for example, patents) are classified, as well as on the sample size. But the general conclusion that there is considerable overlap in the citation net among documents on different topics is very likely to hold up. If all the documents about the same field of knowledge formed a tightly knit cluster in the citation net, cross-fertilization of fields would be much rarer than it is.

This notion of *clustering* apparently appeared in the literature of a variety of fields, such as astronomy, economics, psychology, sociology, and taxonomy. One of the early results dealt with *cliques* (Luce, 1950), which were the most tightly knit clusters possible. They were complete graphs, with each mode connected to every other. This is too rigid a criterion. At the other extreme is the notion of decomposing a graph into components. This is too weak. Somewhat more germane concepts from the graph-theoretic literature are those of leaves and lobes (Abraham, 1965; Ore. 1962), which are based on the notion of accessibility, rather than adjacency. If *a* and *b* are two nodes, then *b* is said to be accessible from *a* if there is a directed path of edges from *a* to *b*, regardless of length. A citation net is likely to be a single tree if we discount all documents which cite no prior documents whatever, except one. In that case, each node is accessible from this bottom node.

Although numerous ideas have been published about how to find clusters in such graphs, there is not yet an adequate concept of stratification. The distribution of clusters in a large graph is very difficult to determine even by computer (Garner, 1967; Taulbee, 1968). The recent formation of the Classification Society, which has begun to stimulate an energetic and creative interdisciplinary approach to this problem, is a promising sign.

Perhaps the most realistic approach to description of structure in citation nets is to empirically study the properties of large citation nets more thoroughly. Such empirical studies will become feasible in the near future because of increasingly widespread interest and availability of citation indexes. These indexes may be thought of simply as an ordered list of documents, each followed by a list of documents which cite it. To use such an index in the search for all documents pertaining to the same topic as a given document, one might proceed as follows: look up, under the given document, the list of more recent documents which cite it; at the same time, from the document given we copy all the references believed to be on the same topic, and repeat this procedure with them. Before iterating the procedure, we examine each document for relevance to the topic. Only those which are selected can survive as ancestors in a geneological document tree. At one point, documents cited before will be cited again. When that happens often, to several documents, we can approach the "boundaries" of the topic in question. Strictly, there are no sharp boundaries or edges to a topic. It is very likely that the graph corresponding to the citation net of the world's literature is connected, and cannot be decomposed into disconnected components. Many documents belong to several fields.

Citation indexes have long been used in law (for example, Shepard's). Recently, several major and significant efforts for the construction of large-scale citation indexes in science have been started (Garfield, 1955; 1963; 1964). Although these include millions of document citations, this is not a large sample for studying the properties of a comprehensive citation net. It is important to remember that almost half of all the citations to a document probably come from fields different from that of the cited document. Thus a citation index with source documents in genetics will soon cover documents in chemistry, biology, statistics, and mathematics; one with source documents in statistics will lead to documents in all fields using statistics, to which there are very few exceptions.

A hopeful approach to detecting the clusters in a citation net may be to count how frequently various nodes are cited recurrently, in tracing forward and backward from a given node. Another possibility is to trace backward only, and to observe the confluence of two genealogical document trees, calling two documents close if they are terminals of very recent branches; clustering may show up in concentrations of branches, much as it does on real trees. From a practical point of view, a searcher interested in one of two documents would be interested in both these two documents, in which the lists of documents they cite or which cite them have many elements in common.

Critics of citation indexes have pointed to the dangers of "inbreeding," possible misuses, and unreliability of explicit citations as indicative of significant connections, as well as the danger that many significant documents (for example, Mendel's paper) might remain in obscurity because they are not cited or do not cite.

There are, however, other problems as well. First, it should be recognized that a citation index is not likely to be the *sole* bibliographic search tool. By his resourcefulness and ability to cope with unique situations, the human searcher can always be expected to originate numerous and unexpected clues that aid search. A discovery in the literature is not fundamentally different from any other discovery as far as human processes are concerned. The deviations by authors from conventions in the generation of documents—though kept under control by social mechanisms—are also balanced by searchers' deviations from conventional search procedures in retrieving items. Often this leads to failure in searching, but sometimes it leads to discoveries. Adherence to conventions guarantees that the vast majority of situations at neither extreme will result in a stable system (one which automatically tends to remain under control) for the generation and use of published documents.

Thus the author who does not cite properly generates a deviant document. No matter how good it is in other respects, it does not serve its function as a document as well as it should. As a member of a class of similar deviant documents, it is potentially dangerous as an error propagator that does not facilitate tracing to the source of error. If a few such deviant documents become irretrievable because they are difficult to reach through a citation net, the number of deviant documents can be kept below the level at which instability results. The security of the entire system is bought at the price of losing a few possibly valuable, but deviant, documents.

Is this likely to create conformity to conventions? While eliminating the deleterious effects of deviant documents, such citing rules might also eliminate the possibility of discovering treasures in the literature. Some of the most significant pioneering efforts might well be deviant if only because they are so original that there is no previous literature to cite. Even worse, it might create a bandwagon effect whereby authors who wish their document to be used will cite, and try to get cited by, the most popular documents. This would be an aberration, a disease of the information system.

The fundamental purpose of generating a new document is to answer queries which have not been answered. If too many queries congest a field of knowledge and nobody asks the outlandish, unpopular questions, then the crowded fields will soon be overwhelmed by redundant and insignificant questions. Competition will force some authors to seek greener pastures, more virgin and unexplored areas of knowledge. It is not that the congested popular fields are such that there are no more questions to be asked; it is rather that the speed at which questions are being asked and answered is beginning to exceed the capacities of individual human agents to create new queries and answers.

A very plausible yet far-reaching thesis is that the answer to every question generates new questions in some of the readers' minds in such a way that the ratio of what we know to what we know we do not know remains the same throughout history. This may be an important constant of genetic epistemology (Piaget, 1971), related to limitations on man's cognitive information-processing capacities. Answers about questions concerning the velocity of light stimulated questions about simultaneity, space, and time, which people may not have thought of asking before in just the way they did. They did not all at once ask more questions than they could answer, nor fewer than were stimulated by the answers of Michelson and Morley.

Aspects of the structure of a citation net, insofar as it shows inbreeding, can be obtained through attempts to rank documents according to a popularity index, w_i for document i, $i = 1 \ldots, D$. Documents which are cited by many other documents are popular. They are even more popular if they are cited by many documents which are themselves popular. That is, w_i should be proportional to the number of documents citing i weighted by the w_j for each document j that cites i. Denoting the citation net by a node-by-node incidence matrix $(c_{ij}) = C$, where $c_{ij} = 1$ if $\mathrm{Cit}(\mathrm{Doc}_i,\mathrm{Doc}_j)$, and if not, then $w_i = 1/\lambda \sum_{j=1}^{D} w_j c_{ij}$, where λ is a constant of proportionality. This equation has solutions for the vector $(w_1,\ldots,w_D)$, however, only when λ is equal to one of the eigenvalues of the matrix C: when it is a solution to the polynomial equation, Determinant$(C - \lambda I)$ $= 0$, where I is the identity matrix. The matrix C is of order D, hence the polynomial will be of degree D; barring the case where the rank of C is less than D, and where the characteristic equation has multiple roots, λ will have D distinct values. There will be a different characteristic vector for each such value. But D is an enormous number, and the matrix C cannot be specified except in terms of statistical properties such as the distributions of the row and column sums of the number of zeroes in the bit-by-bit mod 2 sum of any two, three, four,... rows of C. In terms of such statistics, the distribution of the eigenvalues can sometimes be specified. This would give some indication of at least the types and number of popularity classes present.

Documents can be usefully classified according to their position in the citation net. There are documents—such as birth certificates, affidavits, or items admissible as evidence in a court—which are based on other documents of the same class. Scientific articles form another class, citing for the most part other scientific articles. Patents, on the other hand, cite both other patents and scientific articles and books. And books and articles should not be in the same class.

Books and articles are distinguished from documents such as patents in that they cite both more and a greater diversity of documents of all sorts. Survey articles could be classed either with books or articles, depending on length and purpose. Reports cannot always be considered mature documents, although they frequently have all properties required of documents; it depends on whether the author makes it public property by allowing citation and accepting intellectual responsibility. If this is done, then reports, which account for a large fraction of the literature, should be classed with articles available as separates, reprints, and so on. Republication of reports in a journal should be treated in the same category of problems as republication of any document.

A good case has been made (Passman, 1969) that journal editors should authorize reference to some of the report literature.

Books, handbooks, encyclopedia articles, and other documents representing efforts to synthesize and integrate the documented literature into a coherent whole are articulation points in the citation net. They interconnect otherwise isolated document clusters. They form bridges between fields which may lead to new fields of knowledge. Such documents are key items in the document collection: if the nodes corresponding to them were removed from the citation net, the latter might fragment into much more isolated clusters. The presence of such documents shortens the paths in the citation net and facilitates retrieval. Critical review articles share many properties with the documents just considered, but they do not occupy the same role in the citation net.

4.8   AUTHORSHIP

To be an author, a person must have official, intellectual responsibility for at least one document. In general, the birthdate of the document will occur during the productive period of the author's life, say between the ages 20 and 70; many famous documents were submitted for publication posthumously, however. Nonetheless, the date of conception obviously must occur during the author's productive lifetime. During this lifetime, the number of documents generated by an author may vary from one to over 600, as for Lord Kelvin.

That some authors generate documents at a higher rate than others is not surprising. The productivity of an author depends on numerous factors, such as energy, ambition, and ability. The distribution of the number of articles/author could be expected to be similar to that of income. A formula based on estimates from a small sample of authors at the IBM Research Center in 1963 showed that the number of authors who generate k documents in a given time period decreased as a power of k, rather than exponentially with k. This means that though authors who generate very many papers, such as Kelvin, are extremely rare, there are quite a number of them.

To derive a distribution for the total number of documents generated by an author, let d_t be the number he has authored by age t (in years). Call this the size of his authorship. Its growth is due to the action of numerous mutually independent causes acting in an ordered sequence throughout his life. Let X_{t+1} denote the effect of a cause acting on the author at age $t + 1$, so that the growth in his authorship, due to that cause, is proportional to both X_{t+1} and a function f of the size d_t of his authorship at t. That is,

$$d_{t+1} = d_t + X_{t+1} f(d_t) \qquad (4.1)$$

If $f(d_t) = d_t$, then X_{t+1} represents the number of new documents generated at $(t + 1)$ as the fraction of papers authored up to t (which are added due to the cause acting at $t = 1$). The cause might be exposure to a particularly stimulating event or document. We assume these causes, and thus the random variables $X_1, \ldots, X_{t+1}$, to be mutually independent from $t = 0$ to $t - 1$.

From (4.1) it follows, by summation, that

$$\sum_{t=0}^{t-1} \frac{d_{i+1} - d_i}{f(d_i)} = X_1 + \ldots + X_t$$

Approximate the sum by an integral:

$$\sum_{i=1}^{t} X_i = \int_{d_0}^{d_t} \frac{dy}{f(y)}$$

The causes denote events or experiences which influence the author's productivity; it does not seem unreasonable to assume that they satisfy the general conditions of the central limit theorem. ($X_1, \ldots, X_n$ independent, identically distributed, with finite means and variance). If that is so, then as $t \to \infty$, the random variable $\sum_{i=1}^{t} X_i$ is normally distributed. If $f(y) = y$, $\int_1^{d_t} dy/y = \ln d_t$ so that $\ln d_t$ is normally distributed also. The resulting distribution for d_t, $\ln d_t$ in this special case for $f(y) = y$, is the log-normal:

$$\lim_{t \to \infty} P\ (x \le d_t < x + dx) = \frac{1}{\sqrt{2\pi}\ \sigma x}\ e^{-(\log x - \mu)^2/2\sigma^2}\ dx$$

where μ and σ^2 are the mean and variance of $\sum_{i=1}^{t} X_i$, but are best viewed as two parameters to be estimated, in order to get a good fit to data.

Some data has been compiled (Davis, 1941) to show that the number of authors, in a sample of authors who have written r papers, fits a Yule-type distribution. It is asserted (Learnes, 1953), for example, that the number of authors who published exactly r papers in *Econometrica* over a 20-year period is approximately $a r^{-k}$. From a 20-author sample (by the author of this book) at the IBM Research Center, we found that the number of people who authored exactly r papers during a given time period varied approximately as $a(r + 0.55)^{-3.5}$. A general form for these skew distributions is

$$A(r + b)^{-(1 + \alpha)}$$

It states that while relatively few highly productive authors create, say, half of the literature, the remaining half is due to very many less productive authors.

Much has been written about this type of distribution and the variety of different phenomena (Mandelbrot, 1959; Zipf, 1949) which it seems to fit. In our case of author distribution over a specified number of papers, while the fit to data is neither very poor nor very good, there is no acceptable substantive rationale for accepting the distribution (Horvath, 1959). The log-normal distribution, on the other hand, gives a better fit than the Yule distribution to the data shown in Table 4.1.

TABLE 4.1

r	1	2	3	4	5	6	7	8	9	10	11
Number of authors contributing r papers to the Chicago Section of American Math Society over 25-year period	133	43	24	12	11	14	5	3	9	1	23
Number of authors contributing r papers to *Econometrica* over 20-year period	824	217	94	50	30	20	14	10	8	6	52

Let us now consider, instead of d_t, a more precisely defined stochastic process, $CIT(t,T)$, the number of documents generated at time $t + T$ by an author born at time t. If we consider that the productive lifetime of an author does not generally begin until he is about $T = 20$ years old—and it may last until $T = 70$—then the random variable $\sum_{t=1}^{T} X_i$, which was used in the derivation of the log-normal distribution, should be normally distributed to a high degree of approximation. It seems reasonable to assume that the mean of the log-normal distribution in this application grows roughly linearly with T for T between 20 and 80, being 0 at $T = 20$ and a constant which may be in the neighborhood of 10 for $T = 70$. (The mean number of papers per author in the above table, for the 20–25-year period in a single publication, is about 3.)

It is also reasonable to assume the above stochastic process to be stationary. This asserts that the productivity of an author does not depend on when he is born. Barring major technological or evolutionary changes, which affect the creativity and productivity of people as a whole, this assertion seems plausible.

The coupling between documents and authors is concretely represented by an author catalog. Its function, besides providing a tool to aid in recall and search, is that of bringing together all documents generated by the same author. This may be regarded as a table of listings, just like a citation index. Each list or entry in the table is headed by some identification number for the author instead of a document. This list consists of documents by that author. As in the case of document–document coupling, this table also determines a directed graph, this time with two types of vertices: those corresponding to authors and those corresponding to documents.

To derive some properties about the stochastic process $CIT(t,T)$, let $A'(t)$ be the number of (potential) authors born at time (in the year) t. Then Exp $CIT(t,T)$ $A'(t)$ denotes the average number of Author-links from $t + T$ to t, where Exp denotes Expectation.

If we let Exp $Au(tT)$ denote the average number of authors born at t who co-author a paper generated at $t + T$, then the mean number of Au-links from $t + T$ back to t is also given by the product of the above quantity and $D'(t + T)$.

We would not expect the stochastic process $Au(t,T)$ to be stationary. The average number of co-authors per paper in the twentieth century may be greater—especially in experimental fields—than it was is previous centuries; it often takes a team effort to attack today's problems in science, whereas a solitary individual with only string and sealing wax may have been able to acomplish significant feats in previous years.

Now $P(Au(t,T) = k)$ is the probability that a given paper generated at $t + T$ was co-authored by k people of the same age of T (years). Evidently, this quantity is close to 1 for $k = 1$ and decreases very rapidly with k thereafter. If the probability of k such co-authors were large, adding yet another co-author would greatly decrease this probability to the probability of $k + 1$ co-authors. This decrease would be greater with larger k. Thus it may be reasonable to suppose, considering P to be a continuous function of k as a real variable, that $dP/dk = - aPk$. The solution to this differential equation is $P = Ae^{-Bk^2}$, where A and B are constants. The total number of co-authors per paper generated at $t + T$, regardless of the authors' ages at generation time, is the sum, over T, of $Au(t,T)$. If we think of this sum as a sum of independent random variables (about 50, the number of productive years of an author), the characteristic function of the sum is the product of the characteristic functions of the above distributions. In this case, the characteristic function is the Laplace transformation. Using these methods, it is possible to relate the mean number of co-authors per paper generated at $t + T$ to the mean number of co-authors born in one year prior to $t + T$. The mean can easily be estimated by sampling the literature. Such sampling shows that the average number of co-authors per paper is about 1.1 for papers in pure mathematics, about 1.4 for papers in psychology and in applied mathematics, and 1.8 for papers in the *Journal of Applied Physics*. While the rapidly decreasing exponential functions might give an adequate fit to the number of co-authors per paper for pure science fields, the distribution is more probably log-normal or Yule-type for professional fields and for applied science and technology.

There is, of course, a connection between the number of papers generated by an author, the number of backward citations (references) per paper, and retrieval. There is a maximum number of documents a potential author can read, even if he were to spend all his nonwriting time on reading. Depending on how much time he spends in generating a new document, this determines an upper limit to the number of references in that document. If that maximum number is large—if he has written a book or comprehensive survey article, for example—then he could not have generated very many such documents during his lifetime.

Information technology has reached an advanced stage of development. Powerful computer-based IR systems such as SPIRES, developed by a group led by E. Parker and T. Nelson at Stanford University, and the system developed by Engelbart at the Stanford Research Institute (available over the ARPA-net) are demonstrating their potential for cost-effective, practical application. They are no longer laboratory curiosities or playthings for the computer science community, although difficult problems of organization, economics, and documentation are widespread, and cost-effective use of such systems over a network has yet to be worked out. The SPIRES system, for example, has been adapted by Veaner of the Stanford library into a system which, with the MARC data base from the Library of Congress as part of its input, librarians use daily to prepare purchase orders, to catalog, and to search catalogs.

To ensure that such powerful systems will not be counterproductive, it has been suggested that not only access to the data base but permission to update it be widely distributed. The only requirement for certifying such updating entries would be that the author publicly accept intellectual responsibility. This may change existing conceptions and practices.

An entry would become a document, by our proposed definition, when it has passed the test of time and no one has faulted it. If few used it during an initial period, even fewer will use it in the subsequent period, and it may not matter whether the item is authenticated. Here we see a final tradeoff between too much control of what qualifies as a document at birth and the risk of error and clutter.

Chapter Five

Users and Uses

In this chapter we probe more deeply into the first[†] of the three ingredients of a knowledge system analyzed in Chapter Two: people who use and add to knowledge. The primary function of an IR system is to meet the information needs of its users. Principles underlying the design of IR systems should take account of the needs and practices of users and various classes of use. Beyond this, users have their own internal IR systems which must be coupled with those designed by technologists. Moreover, we are deeply interested in such principles as may apply to both the IR systems designed by technologists and those evolved in nature.

The main thrust of this chapter is, therefore, how people use information. We restrict our analysis to the notions of information explicated in Chapters Three and Four, namely, documents or recorded data likely to help them cope with important problems. This is to lead to a classification of users and uses to be taken into account in designing or analyzing IR systems.

It is not likely that a single kind of IR system will serve all users equally well for all purposes. Nor is it likely that all individuals remember in exactly the same way. Yet we do not expect to have to design an IR system custom-tailored for each user without being able to transfer some key design features of an IR system that meets the needs of other users. Between a single universal IR system and as many individualized IR systems as there are users may be a small number of IR system *types*, which correspond to classes of users and classes of use.

In the search for fundamental principles, however, we hope to find only a few rather general ones that apply to all classes.

[†]This corresponds to the rectangles of Figure 1.1. We reversed the order and discussed *topics*—the triangles of Figure 1.1 and the third of the three ingredients—in Chapter Three, and the second ingredient (the circles of Figure 1.1), in Chapter Four because this is a better way to build up the logical sequence of the ideas.

We start our analysis with an idealized model of people as information processors in order to get at the essence of *information use*. We then extend this model to account for people as problem-solvers and particularly as users of "wisdom" to *cope* with ill-structured, real problems.

5.1.   USERS AS INFORMATION-PROCESSORS

Modeling man as an information-processing organism has been popular for the past two decades (Newell and Simon, 1972; Simon, 1957). Attempts to account for how a person thinks, even in just his role as a problem-solver, by constructing computer programs has always been suspected as too simplistic. Yet this has the considerable merit of laying bare all the assumptions, separating them from facts and implications, and making quite clear what was left out and which variables and assumptions are most essential. Just as the 12-tuple presented in Chapter Three is an idealized, yet helpful, oversimplification of the concept of a topic, representing information users by an algorithm is an idealized, yet helpful, oversimplification of what an information user does.

The benefits of such oversimplification are primarily a charting out of the "ball park," an exploration of its logical extremes and limits. This provides insights into what users of IR systems cannot do and what IR systems cannot be expected to do. This benefit is bought at the price of distorting reality, but the net result is positive if the insights thus gained are sufficiently robust to hold despite the imperfect fidelity of the model. We can only make this plausible. To prove it would require developing a more realistic model and showing that basic results are insensitive to the differences between the more and the less over-simplified models. This has yet to be done.

The primary function of users in their role as information processors is to *use* knowledge in coping with problems. Their secondary function is to *add* to knowledge. They perform this second function by examining a topic, picking and solving a problem. In terms of the 12-tuple of Chapter Three, a user picks an element of $QS(t)$, the set of questions or unsolved problems recognized as such at time t; by the time he has solved the problem, he deletes it from $QS(t)$ and adds it to TS, the set of theorems, or to FS, the set of facts (recorded data). The set CS of connections among questions will also be modified. In this way, he contributes to the growth of a topic. Documents—for example, scientific papers—serve as the vehicles or carriers of this growth.

An information-processor consists of five essential organs: an input device for accepting information; an output device for sending information and control signals; a memory for storing information and programs for time periods ranging from microseconds to years; a processor for transforming input or stored information; and a control unit to decide which unit should perform which operation on what information at what time. It is completely steered by a program that is put in and stored and which may modify itself in a prepro-grammed way. An information-processor implements a computable function f, where x is the input and $f(x)$ the output; f may be viewed as a description, in a finite number of words, of how $f(x)$ is obtained from x for any possible input x.

An information-processor cannot compute every conceivable function. We could order all possible computable functions by arranging the descriptions ac-cording to increasing number of letters and alphabetically in case of ties. Denote the resulting sequence of computable functions by $f_1, f_2, \ldots, f_n, \ldots$. Now let

$$f(g(n)) = \begin{cases} 1 \text{ if } g(n) \text{ is computable, or in the above list.} \\ 0 \text{ if } g(n) \text{ is not in the above list.} \end{cases}$$

The function $f(g(n))$ is not computable if we let $g = f_n(n)$. The reason for this is that the computability of g is undecidable, if the metamathematical statement "the nth function in the sequence of all computable functions $f_1, f_2, \ldots, f_n, \ldots$ evaluated at n has the value k" is translated into a pure arithmetic sentence, one which the information processor can process. If this translation is not made, a paradox[†] results: $g = f_n$ is computable; and so is $h = f_n(n) + 1$. Yet it is not computable because it differs from $f_1(x)$ when $x = 1$ from $f_2(x)$ when $x = 2$, etc. The point of this rather profound example is that information-processors, regarded as devices which compute computable functions, have inherent limits on what they can do. They can generate an output, such as $h(n)$, for some n without being able to anticipate that output for every possible n. In a sense, an information-processor cannot know everything about the way its own outputs are generated. This is one limit on what an information-processor can know and do.

If we could model, with the help of this notion of information-processor, how a user reads and how he assimilates and utilizes what he reads, then we could specify limits on capacities, and the implications of these limits for the growth of knowledge. As the number of documents, potential users, and topics all increase together, what stay constant are the users' information-processing capacities. Even if the growth of people, documents, and topics should stabilize, the number of questions and wisdom may continue to grow indefinitely. Yet information-processing limits of people are not likely to change,[‡] though they may be amplified by technology.

[†] This is a variant of Richard's paradox (Kac and Ulam, 1969, p. 126).

[‡] On an evolutionary time scale they may, of course, change. Man's cognitive capacities 1000 years from now may exceed his capacities of today by as much as those of contemporary man exceed the capacities of his ancestors of 10,000 years ago. This may happen even sooner if such biomedical technologies as cloning, for example, are allowed to shape indi-viduals with specified characteristics. The price for allowing this, however—in the moral, ethical, social, and theological problems thus raised—may be greater than what we are willing to pay.

It is the central thesis of this book that if people are to cope with their problems at least as well as they have been coping, then their abilities to utilize the resources in documents and topics must stay constant or improve. To help make this possible is the ultimate purpose and proper role of IR systems.

5.2. COPING VERSUS PROBLEM-SOLVING

We are concerned with people who use or add to knowledge primarily for the purpose of improving their lives. Some knowledge-users are concerned exclusively with their own lot over the next few days. Others make decisions on behalf of many others, with effects lasting for decades. Yet others pursue academic activities of enriching the literature. Presumably this, too, will improve the lives of people who use the literature at unspecified future times.

When a person succeeds with a well-defined problem statement, we say that he *solved* it. When he succeeds with a problem that does not appear to him as a well-defined problem-statement, we say that he *coped* with it. Both solvers and copers are users of IR systems, but the kind of IR system that best helps a person in coping differs greatly from an IR system that best helps a person in solving a well-defined problem-statement.

We are using "problem" as in "he has a problem." A problem is either a difficult situation, a trouble to be overcome, an undesirable state of affairs, *or* an opportunity to be seized. A decision-maker's first responsibility is to recognize problems in this sense. An important class of IR systems is to help him do this. In this discussion of problems and problem-solving, we are not referring to the problems faced by a library scientist or problems arising in the design or operation of information systems. Rather, we regard the information and library sciences as the study of how to bring knowledge to bear on helping all people cope with whatever problems they face.

A well-defined problem-statement, as it is understood in much of the literature on problem-solving, has the following three properties:

1. It specifies the set of possible solutions.
2. It specifies the properties a solution should have.
3. It specifies methods and facts necessary to find a solution.

Example: "What is the speed of light in miles/hour, in vacuum, to six significant figures, measured by interferometry" is a well-defined problem-statement. The set of possible solutions are all positive numbers. The properties a solution should have are that it be the speed of light, that it be expressed in miles/hour, and that it be accurate to six figures. The method to be used in determining it is interferometry.

Had the method not been specified, it might still be called a well-defined problem-statement, but not as well-defined as the one given. Few problems encountered by people in daily life are wholly or even partially well-defined. Engineers and scientists have, through professional experience, learned to create well-defined problem-statements for problems they are concerned with. They know better than others that this cannot be done for all the problems of interest to them.

In Figure 5.1 we sketch an information-processing model that relates problem-solving and coping in terms of the major steps involved in both processes. The purpose of showing this relation in Figure 5.1 is to exhibit the various places where IR systems can contribute. Use of an IR system is shown by a box with a double frame. If used to help in coping, the double frame is filled with dots; if used for solving, it is filled in solidly; if used for either, it is left blank.

To read the flow diagram of Figure 5.1, trace the fate of an illustrative problem faced by a hypothetical user. Imagine the user to be a single person, of average education, in whom, quite unsuspected by him, a malignant tumor has started to grow. This is but one of a variety of problems he "has" at any time. For example, he may also carry several deleterious genetic traits. At the same time he has potential access to a great variety of IR systems and services available to help him. Yet he may not be an active user of any of these, nor may he even sense any of his problems.

The first stage in any successful process of dealing with problems is problem-recognition (boxes IS1, D1, IS2, D2, D3, D4). This involves sensing the existence of a problem, grossly sorting it, at least by severity, and deciding whether to attend to it. Figure 5.1 shows seven information systems, labeled IS1 to IS7. Each includes an IR system. IS1 is one which aims to inform the potential user about existence and availability of services (such as IS2) which aim to inform him about the existence of problems as soon as they arise. IS1 is more active, less passive, than IS2. An example of IS1 is the use of mass media to broadcast to all potential users of IS2 (*actual* users of the mass media for a mix of many uses) about the services offered by cancer-prevention clinics, the desirability of using them for annual medical checks, and advice about self-diagnosis from the American Cancer Society. IS2 can be anything from a clinic to a roving health van with books and pamphlets on cancer and a systematic procedure for self-examination.

Success in the problem-recognition phase means attending to a serious problem when there is one (for example, cancer) and not attending to a condition that is not a problem or a potential problem. Performance of IS1 and IS2 is measured by the extent to which they help decrease those errors of omission and commission and the time for accurate recognition.

The next stage in dealing with problems is formulation. There is no sharp boundary between recognition and formulation. Sensing the existence of a problem, such as being troubled by painful symptoms, already allows a crude formulation in terms of symptom-removal. Judging the problem to be severe enough to consult a doctor is another stage, with formulation in terms of which doctor to

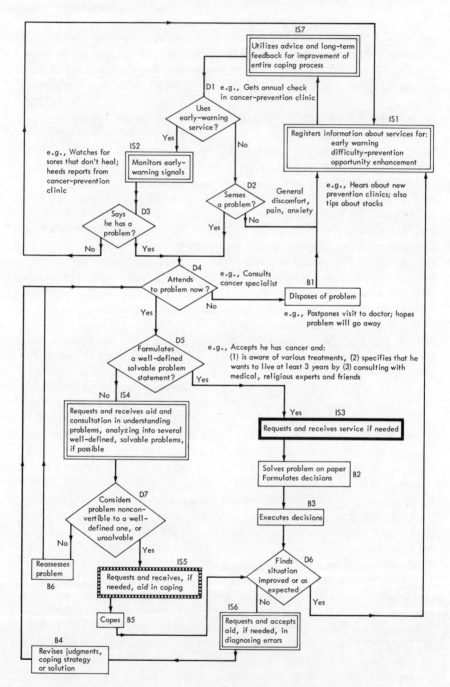

Figure 5.1. Information systems in problem-solving and coping.

see, when, and what to present to him. The process of problem-formulation is one of forming and revising a *problem-statement* so that it is increasingly well-defined, up to a limit. That limit is determined by both the user and the problem. For some problems, well-defined problem-statements with the three criteria listed earlier cannot in principle be formed with the present state of knowledge (or perhaps ever). Choosing a career or a mate are examples of such problems. For some problems, such as certain kinds of curable cancers, well-defined problem-statements can be formed, but not by the user himself; an experienced cancer specialist may have to do it. We consider him part of IS4.

Success in problem-formulation means the creation of a problem-statement that leads to a solution—that is, reducing a problem to a problem-solving or solution-searching exercise, when that is possible, and if that is not possible, recognizing this to be the case. Performance of IS4 is measured by the amount it decreases the expected time for an accurate decision of either kind.

It is at D7 that problems are sorted into well-defined problem-statements to be solved or situations to be coped with. IS5 is to help a user cope. We outline design principles for such an IR system in Chapter Seven. IS3 and IS6 are to help a user either to cope or to solve. In both cases, the user is to take actions—execute decisions—that change his situation, his state, for the better. Success is measured by this improvement in the user's problem-state.

If the problem-state resembles an avoidance task, success consists of avoiding actions that worsen the current state, such as avoidance of falling into a trap. If the problem-state is an opportunity, such as a large return on the right investment, then success is finding and choosing that investment. If the problem-state is an undesirable condition, such as cancer, success is best possible improvement of that condition or at least minimizing deterioration by either avoiding or choosing certain actions.

In coping, the user makes decisions and judgments without explicit awareness of using any methods or facts, without clear-cut criteria for comparing a future state with a goal state or a definite course to reaching a goal-state. In solving, there is an explicit reason for each decision, a clearly prearticulated goal-state, operational criteria for its attainment, and an algorithm for reaching it. The performance of IS3 and IS6 is measured by the average time it saves the user in finding a solution and the extent to which that solution is optimal. This time may be the time it takes to converge to a solution because it may require many passes with feedback from the outside world. The performance of IS5 corresponds to the time saved in leaving D6 at the "Yes" exit sooner.

5.3. PROBLEM-SOLVING IN SCIENCE: TOWARD A SCIENCE OF SCIENCE

We now examine users-as-problem-solvers in more depth. The best examples of problem-solvers are pure and applied scientists. One way to characterize the distinction between them is to say that pure scientists add to knowledge, applied scientists use it. The growth of science, pure and applied, is one of man's greatest successes. Insights into the dynamics of that growth may enlighten our understanding of the growth of knowledge more generally. Such insights may advance the study of what we have called epistemodynamics. (Kochen, 1969b). This is the area in which the basic principles of information retrieval are likely to be found.

Shera (Montgomery, 1968, p. 7) has called this needed new epistemological discipline "social epistemology." He points out that advances in the philosophy, history, and sociology of knowledge have led to some understanding of how scientific knowledge is accumulated and transmitted from one generation to the next (e.g., Barber and Hirsch, 1962; Polanyi, 1958; Popper, 1959, 1962; Storer, 1966). But the study of how knowledge is integrated and applied is only now beginning to emerge. There is an increasing volume of high-quality work on the relation between science and public policy (Brooks, 1973; Price, 1962, 1965; Teich, 1972). From this emerges a focus on two central questions about the organization and administration of science and perhaps organized knowledge more generally. The first is how to organize, staff, and direct the serach for knowledge so as to maximize the rate of progress for a given investment. The search for basic new knowledge is often seen as the creation of diffuse, general-purpose knowledge which requires investment of public resources. By contrast, production and development work signals its social value, and is likely to be supported by investments from private sources who see the benefits to them.

The second question is how to couple existing knowledge, as well as the search for new knowledge, to existing, identified needs for policy or action. It is to the second question that the study of information retrieval principles is more closely connected.

The study of learning and the growth of knowledge in individuals has long been a field of interest to psychologists and others (e.g., Boring, 1950). So has the study of organizations devoted to the growth of knowledge (Carr-Sanders and Wilson, 1933; Himsworth, 1970; Machlup, 1962). If we examine all these fields of study which relate to the growth of knowledge, or more specifically to the growth of science, in their totality, we begin to see the emergence of a science of science (Himsworth, 1966). This includes nearly all the sciences, such as the biology, chemistry, and physics of knowledge; the philosophy, history, and policy science aspects of knowledge; the psychology and sociology of knowledge; and the economics of knowledge (Boulding, 1966; Marschak, 1968, 1971, 1972, 1973; Lamberton, 1971; Polish Academy of Science, 1970).

One of the great, still outstanding, mysteries that challenge a science of science is this. Here is a man, a scientist, who is in one sense a vast assembly of macromolecules. Like any other such molecular aggregate, he is part of nature, subject to its laws. Among these laws must be some that enabled properties to emerge that correspond to question-asking, information-processing. The macro-molecular assemblies with these emergent properties called scientists are nature's way of knowing about nature, about science, and about scientists themselves.

Scientists generally work exclusively on problems for which they can create well-defined problem-statements. These problems have, of necessity, become more specialized. The sciences have, on emerging from philosophy, split into a plurality of specialties, each with aims, techniques, and paradigms of its own. "Every discipline is whittled down and pulverized to the point where no man of science can pretend to grasp more than a small branch of even his own branch of knowledge" (Rostand, 1960, p. 125). Actual progress, says Rostand, depends on specialized, differentiated units, whether in the development of cells from the embryo or in the evolution of species and societies. Potential progress, on the other hand, "is possible only by virtue of nondifferentiation" (Rostand, 1960, p. 130), by general-purpose (jack-of-all-trade) units, whether in the developing organism (for example, germ cells, responsible for reproduction, as distinct from the somatic cells which become liver cells, blood cells, etc.) or in a community of scientists.

This dichotomy has been further interpreted as one between specialization linked with automatism on the one hand and nondifferentiation linked with invention on the other. Scientists also invent.

Some scientists are predominantly inventive, while others are predominantly problem-solvers. Normal science (Kuhn, 1962) is an activity carried out mostly by problem solvers. Kuhn has used the term puzzle-solvers, to which Popper objects on the ground that puzzle-solving connotes something more frivolous than the serious investigations of a scientist (Lakatos and Musgrave, 1970). Scientists engaged in normal science in a specialized topic are guided by a paradigm which characterizes that topic. One of the ingredients in the specification of some paradigms is the 12-tuple introduced in the section *Theories and Topics*. Another is the style of communication, publishing; yet others are the laboratory procedures, tastes, work-habits, and priorities used by practitioners of that scientific discipline, acquired from their mentors, and passed on to their disciples.

Normal science is a process by which a scientific community pushes back the frontiers of both what is known and of what is known to be unknown. This process has been described to pass through three stages. The first is one in which the paradigm is explored and developed at a vigorous rate. There is reasonable consensus about what constitutes the significant problems, the most valid methods, the most prestigious journals, and the intellectual leaders. The community of practitioners sets up contingencies of positive reinforcement to those who pick and solve problems according to these norms. On the whole, its members behave in conformity with the norms, and those who deviate do not attain great visibility or influence. Thus a scientist in this stage picks a problem in the course of reading a few articles in a few prestigious journals in his specialty, such as topological algebra, or as a result of stimulating communication with a key practitioner in this area who exerted intellectual influence on him. Reading a paper, listening to a lecture, or participating in a seminar or discussion often triggers an idea for how an existing result might be generalized, how two contradictory findings could be reconciled, how a gap which suddenly became evident might be filled, or how a method used to obtain a result might be applied to another problem. The question posed and answered by one author leads another author to pose—and perhaps answer—another question no one had thought of asking before. When the scientist is competent, he will pick problems matched to his problem-solving capability. If his performance deviates from his competence, it is because his judgment about the nature of the problem or about his ability to solve it, or about both, was in error. From such mistakes he can learn. In time, he may become successful and pick only problems he can solve, and these may become more significant and difficult as his experience and specialized expertise grow.

The solution to the problem he picked is likely to be published in one of the same few journals which inspired him to pick it, intended for the same few fellow-specialists who communicate and exert intellectual influence on one another. Associated with fragmentation and differentiation of topics in numerous narrower specialties is fragmentation and differentiation of the scientific community into numerous, small, special-interest groups. The specific, solvable problem which results in a research publication is one that usually is solved in one to several months. It may be analyzed into simpler subproblems that can be solved in a few days. It is usually also part of a larger problem or problem class in which the author maintains interest for several years. Let us call the problem-classes at these three levels month-problems, week-problems, and year-problems. There are still lower and higher levels, and IR systems can help with each class, but the requirements differ.

In the second stage of normal science, scientists begin to tidy up their discipline. The main activity has shifted from ground-breaking and cream-skimming to filling in cracks, resolving minor discrepancies, completing and verifying. Anomalies or such discrepancies as cannot be resolved are put aside while foundations are strengthened and the entire paradigm is consolidated. Standards for quality increase; the problems get harder. There is more conservatism and defense of the paradigm. Problem-solving is for experts and established specialists only. Newcomers to the specialty must spend at least a year familiarizing themselves with the paradigm and catching up with progress.

The third stage is one of crisis. Some anomalies that have been set aside and successfully ignored turn into major paradoxes and threaten the paradigm seriously. The foundations of the discipline are being questioned. Practitioners feel more insecure. Some switch to other specialties. The flow of scientists entering the specialty slows down. Scientists have difficulty picking good problems and agreeing on the criteria for significance, relevance, validity, novelty, and good style. Generally, morale drops.

The fourth stage is no longer normal science. It is revolutionary science. It is an activity carried out mostly by inventive minds. The total intensity of problem-solving activity wanes, to be replaced by increased activity in shaping a new paradigm which has grown side by side with the old one and which has begun to assume the dominant position of challenger. A few inventive individuals play a greater role in this stage than in any of the stages of normal science, during which the combined effort of a social community of problem-solvers accounts for progress. These leading individuals may be helped by IR systems of quite a different kind, classified more according to who the people are than the characteristics of the problems they are to help solve.

One of the most significant current developments in information science is the vigorous study of the social system of science, of the phenomenon Price called an "invisible college." These empirical studies emanate from what is in itself an invisible college (Crane, 1969; Crawford, 1971a, 1971b; Griffith and Mullins, 1972; Mullins, 1968; Price, 1966). The findings support the following general propositions:

1. The more productive a scientist is, the more he exerts intellectual influence on several specialties as measured by others who named him as an object of contact.

2. Any scientist in a community of specialists is likely to have continuing person-to-person contact with any lay specialist in that community or, if not, with a specialist in the community who does have such contact with this key specialist; only in 5% of the cases would it take more than one such intermediary contact. Through this study, the experimental and theoretical work on contact nets (Milgram, 1967; Pool and Kochen, 1958; White, 1970) can be brought to bear.

3. Communication is most intense and organizational structure is greatest in social specialty groups which are about to shape a new paradigm; they are in stage 4, in revolutionary science. Such groups usually have (a) one or more acknowledged intellectual leaders (for example, Hilbert and Minkowski for the "Algebraists" studied by Griffith; the term "Algebraists" in this context is due to Griffith); (b) one or more organizational leaders (for example, F. Klein for the Algebraists); (c) a geographic center (Göttingen); and (d) a specific life span during which activity is very intense (for example, 1896–1910 for this group of Algebraists; typically, 10–15 years).

4. Groups without disciples or students wither.

5. Central to a group's operation is frequently a single, definitive program statement, a seminal document.

6. A coherent group continues only if there are sufficient resources to maintain the group at a critical size at the geographic center for a decade or so.

The above-mentioned findings apply primarily to revolutionary rather than to normal science. Groups engaged in these intensely inventive activities do not generally need IR systems. Most of the information needed by these creative scientists shaping a new paradigm they can readily supply from their own memories or through their intimate informal communication network. The results of their activities, however, are critical input to the IR systems which are needed by scientists engaged in stages 1 and 2 of normal science.

Work on stages 1 and 2 of normal science is predominantly problem-solving. The Popper-Kuhn debates (Lakatos and Musgrave, 1970) stimulate an image where normal and revolutionary science are opposed as extremes. Normal science involves routine problem-solving of a kind that some artificial intelligence projects aim to specify by a computer program. Revolutionary science is creative and advances by intuitive leaps. Popper would say scientific thought in all stages is essentially creative, and the revolutionary stage is the normal stage of science. Kuhn would say that the revolutionary stage is exceptional and rare. Most probably, both normal and revolutionary science involve both logical-deductive, systematic analysis and inventive-inductive leaps in different mixes. Kuhn's term, "puzzle-solving," for the activity of normal science actually suggests the image of a scientist at play, motivated by the sense of wonder; the serious, determined, routinely systematic and perhaps mechanizable search for a solution is tempered by occasional lapses in which the imagination romps freely, a precondition for creative thought and inductive leaps.

Nonetheless, problem-solving is a good part of the scientific method. It is taught to and practiced not by scientists alone but by engineers, operations analysts, and planners in increasingly more problem-areas. Much of problem-solving is information-processing. If a problem is specified by (a) a set of possible solutions, (b) the properties a solution should have, and (c) a well-structured data base of knowledge and methods necessary to find the solution—all in a system of representation—then solving it, without shifting the representation, is indeed a systematic search for which a computer-implementable algorithm can be specified. In normal science or in mission-oriented applied science, problem-solving is often carried out by a team or otherwise coordinated group of problem-solvers.

To help users with well-defined problem statements, such as scientists, IR systems should be classified according to uses because most users follow a few similar patterns of use, employing scientific method. That is, two users with the same well-defined problem-statement are not likely to require vastly different IR systems. The same options among methods of statistical inference or deduction should be available to both.

5.4. CLASSIFICATION OF USES AND PROBLEMS

The most obvious use of an IR system for problem-solving is checking whether the very problem-statement has already been solved with a solution readily available for the asking. Let US1 denote this first class of uses. There are two subclasses: US1.1 and US1.2. In the first are uses where the searcher knows that it has been solved and recalls only some clues, such as the name of the person who solved it, or the year, or the place he heard about it. In the second class are the uses where the searcher is not sure that it has been solved before, but thinks it is likely.

In a second class of uses, US2, the searcher does not consider it likely that his exact problem has been solved, but he can specify other problems which are such that if he could see a solution to any one of them, he would know how to solve his problem. He is specifying a more generic problem which subsumes an entire set of more specific ones. For example, his specific problem might be to find, within five minutes, two integers x, y such that $214x + 19y = 1$. He has seen an *algorithm* before. If he can find it, preferably illustrated on some other example, he would be able to solve this right away. He has not seen this particular equation solved before. Hence it is not in US1.1. Nor does he think it likely that it has been solved. So it is not in US1.2. But he has seen $ax + by = 1$ solved for some a, b, though he does not recall which a, b; he does recall that the solution procedure was explained. We could again designate a problem of this kind as subclass US2.1, as distinct from one where he has never seen a solution of $ax + by = 1$ for any a, b but feels sure a solution for some a, b must exist. That would be a problem of subclass US2.2.

Designing an IR system to help *any* user with such a well-defined problem is a very difficult task. A system to help a high-school student with this question—a person who has never heard of diophantine equations—is entirely different from the IR system that could help a user who recognizes it as a diophantine equation. Thus, even for well-defined problems, user-classes as well as use-classes must be taken into account in selecting an appropriate IR system.

Consider next the class of uses, US3, where the user does not believe a solution to his problem or one like it exists, but, because the problem is well-defined, he knows exactly what knowledge and methods he needs to solve it. In the above example he knew that he needed the Chinese remainder algorithm—though he may not recall or know its name—for solving a diophantine equation—though he may not recall or know that name either, and he knew or surely felt it to exist. Now he has not seen the needed facts or methods and is not sure that they exist. This may apply to the problem itself. As an example, consider the question: "Is it possible to partition a square into a finite number of squares, all of different size?" Up to a certain year, the answer was not known. Now it is.

Consider next the class, US4, of uses where the user cannot solve a well-defined problem as he has stated it. He has to analyze it and restate it as a set of problems he can solve, and such that he can synthesize a solution to his original problem from the solutions of these simpler ones. An IR system is to help him with this analysis, restatement, and synthesis. Suppose that it can be done without shifting representations. An example is the following problem: "Of 13 coins at most one has a false weight. Using weights, show how to ascertain in three weighings, (a) whether there is a false coin; if so, (b) which one, (c) how much it weighs, and (d) the true weight". To solve the problem, it can be analyzed into 13 problems, one for each coin. One version of the restated problem is: "If the first coin is false, find its weight y and the weight of a proper coin x such that $8x + y = a$, $4x - y = b$, $y = c$, with $a:b:c = 9:3:1$; a is a weight to be placed in the right-hand pan of a scale if coins 1, 2, 4, 5, 7, 10, 11, 12, 13 are in the left pan to get balance; b is what must be added to coins 1, 11, 12 in the right pan when 2, 3, 6, 7, 9, 10 are in the left; and c is what must be joined with coins 2, 9, 11, 13 on the right if 1, 5, 6, 7, 8 are on the left."

An even more complex class, US5, of uses is to help the user with a problem which must be restated and requires a shift of representation. Having to solve the missionary and cannibals problem in a time less than it takes to do it by trial and error is an example. Another is the tennis tournament problem—finding the number of no-tie tennis matches that have to be played, if the winner of each match plays the winner of another, until a single winner emerges—in less time than it takes to look at combinatorial possibilities. The IR system is to help the user restate the problems so that he asks for the number of losers.

Consider next several classes of real problems which are well-defined or at least readily transformable into well-defined problems. An evident criterion for classifying problems—hence uses of IR systems to help solve them—is urgency. If the decision-maker recognizes himself to be in a problem-state and the possibility of reaching a goal-state vanishes if the appropriate moves are not made by a certain deadline, then he must recognize and solve the problem within a time limit. This imposes response-time constants on an IR system to serve such decision-makers. A shopper who wishes to verify the total he must pay, as it appears on the sales slip produced by a cash register operator at a long checkout line in a supermarket should be able to (a) retrieve the prices of all items purchased and (b) check the addition within the few minutes he is at the register. A price retrieval system would help him (the addition could, in principle, be checked by retrieval if a table of all possible sums were stored, but this would be impossibly hard to maintain and use). We do not label this class of uses separately because the criterion of having a deadline can be crossed with all the others.

Another important criterion for classifying uses is significance of the real problem. If the stakes are high and the problem is solvable, solution efforts are assigned correspondingly high priority. Significance differs from urgency. It is related to utility. To the diabetic detained in a foreign country without an adequate supply of insulin, knowing where to get more is highly significant; it may not be urgent if his supply still lasts for some time. But he should be willing to pay quite a bit for information about where to get insulin.

Currency is another important criterion for a class of questions such as about the time and place of scheduled events, reservations, prices, and natural, economic, social, and political indicators that are continuously monitored. An inquiry for the departure time of a scheduled flight is of no value unless the information is current. If the schedules are changed every 3 months, information based on the new schedules can be available even before the new schedule goes into effect. To forecast the weather, data about pressure, temperature, and wind velocity at various points is read every hour or so. An ideal IR system recording such data should, if used at a certain time, be able to supply the readings taken within a half hour or so, on the average.

The language and formats in which questions must be posed to an IR system and in which outputs are displayed is another set of criteria for classifying uses such as computer-assisted instruction.

Accuracy and completeness of the data base in an IR system are twin criteria which are critical for such uses as computer-aided diagnosis and other aids in health care.

Last but not least is cost. There are uses, such as credit card or similar transactions, for which the cost must be low for people to bother at all. Other uses, such as military intelligence based on formatted files—for example, monitoring, tracking, and identifying high-speed missiles to check for and counter a surprise attack—are of necessity costly if the costs for errors of commission and omission are intolerably high and if only the very best available system is ordered. This is not to say that credit card transactions are insignificant, only that there are many alternate ways of meeting the need, and a new method must be competitive.

Another way of classifying problem-statements for the purpose of classifying IR systems is whether solutions involve adding to or using knowledge. The former are often at the frontiers of a narrowly specialized topic. IR systems to help users with such problems need extensive coverage of advances in that specialty, with great currency and depth. The latter tend to draw on several disciplines. IR systems to help users with such problems are discussed in the next chapter.

Table 5.1 gives a classification of problems from a logical point of view. This will be useful in a subsequent classification of IR systems.

TABLE 5.1. Logical Classification of Problems

Class of problems	Example	Example of IR system likely to help
A Unrecognized	Unsuspected malignant tumor	Directory to prevention and screening services
B False	Suspicion of cancer when absent	Aids to diagnosis
C Vaguely sensed	Loneliness, anxiety, depression	Aids to diagnosis
D Neglected	Worn brake linings	Aids to preventive maintenance
E Ill-structured	Judge a defendant	Directory to precedents
F Well-defined	Find speed of light in vacuum	Handbook via Index
G Impossible	Word problem for general groups	Aids to advisor
H Crackpot	"Proofs" for squaring circle	Aids to advisor
I Incompletely specified	Given three angles of triangle, find area	Aids to advisor
J Contradictory	Given $x + y = 3$, $2x + 2y = 7$, find x, y	Aids to advisor
K Premature	Is there life on Mars?	Current awareness service
L Overly laborious	Add 10^6 random numbers in 1 hour	Aids to advisor
M Overly complex	Divide two 10-digit numbers with 1 square inch of scratch paper	Aids to advisor
N Solvable	Find x such that $x \log_2 x = 50$	Handbook via Index

5.5 RECOGNIZING PROBLEMS AND PROBLEM-STATEMENTS

When a user has formulated a well-defined problem-statement and needs help from an IR system, he can enter such a statement as input. The IR system must first recognize this input. This is similar to what a problem-solver does at first when he poses well-defined problems to himself and then acts as his own IR system or as an inferential processor. Recognition is also important in updating. An IR system or its users must recognize[†] inputs that are sentences, true

---

[†]This differs from recognizing a problem. Some experimental work on problem-recognition and formulation by children was started recently (Kochen, Badre, and Badre, 1973). It was found that fourth and fifth grade children could be trained to significantly improve their ability for recognizing and formulating "real" problems similar to the pre-formulated mathematical problems to which they were exposed in school and which they find at the ends of chapters or throughout their texts. Testing for the ability to recognize and formulate problems involved a new experimental technique based on requiring the children to ask questions, and measuring the time it took until they asked questions indicative of their having recognized a task that was set for them. The training procedure involved exposing the children to games such as "Twenty Questions" and other opportunities for shifting representations and employing different modes of inquiry.

sentences, and relevant sentences. Insights into the recognition phase of information processing of problems shed light on the nature of the agents in our knowledge system.

From automata theory we know that a sentencehood-recognizer is not well modeled by a *finite-state* automaton. It is not known what kind of automaton best models the various kinds of recognizers. But the notion of a hierarchy of recognition automata is useful for clarifying the way an environmental problem-state stimulates the generation of a problem-statement which is relevant to something known and stored in an IR system.

At the bottom of the hierarchy are elementary feature detectors. These classify at each instant an environmental stimulus at a particular site as one or another in the set VT. Thus VT might consist of elementary arcs such as $\subset$, $\supset$, $\cup$, $\cap$, or horizontal or vertical straight-line segments. A set of formation rules for two-dimensional concatenation, expressed with such predicates as "_____ does not intersect_____," "_____ intersects at the top with_____," "_____is above_____," "_____is to the left of_____," and "_____is inside _____" can then specify the subset A of all well-formed figures of the set $X = VT^*$ of all possible two-dimensional strings. The set A could represent all physically realizable "visual scenes" that a user in Figure 5.1 might encounter or all the alphabetic characters on a typewriter. A character-recognizer is an automaton recognizing A at this level.

At the next level is a word-recognizer. Here VT is the set A of all the well-formed strings within X. Let us call VT_1 the new VT to distinguish it from VT_0, the set of primitive features, with $VT_0 = A_0$, and $A_1 = VT_1 \subset VT_0^{**}$. The set of well-formed "words" A_1 is specified by a new set of formation rules—for instance, rules such as govern admissability of a new string of characters into an official dictionary.

At a higher level is a sentence-recognizer or its equivalent. The set A_2 of well-formed sentences is specified by formation rules such as constitute the syntax of certain programming languages or logics. Here $A_2 \subset A_1^*$. A sentence-recognizer is not necessarily at a level immediately above a word-recognizer; there may be many recognition automata at intervening levels.

Next consider a truth-recognizer. Here $VT_3 = A_2 \subset VT_2^*$. That is, its input consists only of strings of well-formed sentences or propositions, the set A_3 of strings of propositions which satisfy the definition of a proof. We should call such a machine a proof-checker; if it is given a proposition and an alleged proof, it will check if that proof is valid.

Lastly, consider a relevance-recognizer. Its inputs are strings of valid proofs A_3^*. The set A_4, a subset of A_3^*, is composed of all those proofs that "belong together"—for example, all proofs of the same proposition. Such an automaton might be presented with a pair of proofs and responds with whether or not they belong together according to criteria stated as replacement rules. A proof is a string of well-formed propositions. We may replace a proposition by a question and a proof sequence by a sequence of questions such that each is answerable by direct lookup or else its answer is implied by the answer to one or more previous questions in the sequence. Thus a relevance-recognition automaton could be presented with a valid question sequence and a valid proof and could decide the relevance of one for the other.

People use IR systems to cope with problems. In so doing, their functions transcend those of *automata*. How? In some respects, they function as automata. This can shed light on the question.

In one respect, a person U is a living physical object, which results from an unfolding of an embryo. It does not accept information from the environment, which merely causes the genetic instructions already in the DNA of the embryo to be carried out. As such, U functions in a rather specialized way according to its blueprint and wiring diagram; it is an automaton. Yet in another, "external" respect—the dual nature to which we have referred—U is a general-purpose algorithm. By virtue of his brain, which embodies this algorithm, U can accept information from the environment. The internal or endosomatic hereditary system is evolutionary in that genetic instructions in the DNA-chains are communicated from U to his offspring with changes—due to reassortment, etc.— which are systematic in the long run. Similarly, the external or exosomatic hereditary system is evolutionary. U can not only learn, but teach, contribute to the accumulation of tradition, and "record information and wisdom in books" (Medawar, 1960).

The difference between these two hereditary, evolutionary systems, however, is fundamental. While the environment cannot transfer genetic information to U, it can and does transfer nongenetic information. Coping with social problems for which U uses an IR system is not governed by laws that apply to the internal genetic evolution.

What kind of algorithm is it, though, which enables U to learn and to communicate in the exosomatic hereditary system? It is an algorithm which must form and use representations of its environment. This environment includes U in *both its aspects*. The simplest possible environment would be one consisting of an exact replica of U. The algorithm must then be capable of representing itself. This leads to a classical paradox, which is resolved by arithmetizing both the mathematical and the metamathematical aspects of the algorithm, thus replacing the paradox by an undecidability condition. In other words, U the algorithm builds representations of its environment, but these are necessarily incomplete: there is always at least one question about the environment which it cannot settle (Kochen, 1973b).

5.6 CLASSIFICATION OF USERS

Different users with the same well-defined problem can often, within limits, be served by the same IR system. Any person who wishes to verify the exactness of a quotation, a bibliographic reference, or a fact can use the same reference sources, such as an encyclopedia. He must, of course, be literate in the language of the reference source and somewhat experienced in looking things up. Any person with these broad qualifications should be able to use the same IR system for many well-defined problems.

We have already seen examples of well-defined problems, such as a person seeking the solution of a diophantine equation, for which one class of IR system would be necessary for the person who knows he is dealing with a diophantine equation, and another type of IR system is needed for the user who does not. Similar examples might occur with well-defined problems in linguistic syntax, and especially with computer-aided instruction. The IR system to serve a student who asks the well-defined question, "Why does ice float on water," and who already knows about molecular crystal lattices, differs from the IR system to help a student whose familiarity with atomic theory is nil and who has barely mastered the concept of density. We can, of course, envisage flexible IR systems which can be adjusted until they custom-fit their user, but in designing them, the range of capabilities over which the system is adjustable must still be specified.

In coping with genuinely ill-structured problems, such as choosing a job, career, course of study, or friend, an IR system can help, but it must be highly individualized and tailored to the particular characteristics of its user. A good IR system to help Mr. Smith choose a career may differ in some basic respects from a good system to help Mr. Jones, if Mr. Smith and Mr. Jones differ sufficiently in their levels of education, personality, etc. To specify IR systems that are to help with ill-structured problems, it seems more useful to classify them according to user classes than according to use classes.

Fortunately for the IR system designer, user classes are often coherent, visible, social groups. A professional society, such as the American Chemical Society, is a large class in which the members have enough common characteristics to be served by the same IR system, such as *Chemical Abstracts*. The industrial research chemist in search of a novel patentable process for synthesizing a material with specified properties may begin with an ill-structured problem; he may not be able to specify all he needs to know at the start. Interaction with the literature, via *Chemical Abstracts*, may stimulate him to ask appropriate questions. The articles most likely to stimulate him are more likely to stimulate another industrial research chemist than a nonchemist.

Differentiation and growth among professional societies closely parallel those trends among topics as well as among document clusters. Special interest

groups arise within a professional society. Each may begin to publish its own journal, specialized in the topic on which the special interest group is focused. As the membership grows along with the topic, the interests of the members begin to diverge and their publications begin to scatter. Just before extreme fragmentation sets in, the special interest group may have grown into a new professional society, with several journals and special interest groups of its own. Occasionally, members in a special interest group from one professional society may join with members in special interest groups of other societies to form a new society. Thus the Classification Society emerged as a union of biologists, statisticians, psychiatrists, astronomers, etc., all with a common interest in clustering phenomena.

The "Invisible College" is another way of grouping users. It is through these informal social organizations that intellectual influence is spread, news of discoveries are propagated, and the development of a topic is governed. These social structures have been studied primarily in the context of science, but something analogous is at work in the coupling between the scientific community and the world of decision-makers coping with ill-structured problems.

It has been shown (Havelock, 1971) that the transfer of knowledge from the scientific community to decision-makers who utilize such knowledge is mediated by opinion leaders. Decision-makers tend to rely on the advice of certain advisors who are also highly esteemed in their fields of knowledge and who shape the opinions of scientists and the public alike. Opinion leaders are often elder statesmen among scientists, authors of popular books, advisers to political leaders, or chief executives in industry. By and large, they remain informed by sifting the significant items from all that reaches them, and it is generally assumed that no significant new knowledge fails to reach them. Moreover, beyond sifting and recognizing the significant, they must interpret by applying "transcientific" criteria (Weinberg, 1972). IR systems customized according to these criteria could help them in this great task of screening, interpreting, evaluating, and synthesizing for presentation to a decision-maker.

Several bases for classifying users could be listed as follows:

1. Formal societies, such as professional societies, with a common field of interest, membership criteria, and identifying documents. Membership presumably helps to cope.
2. Invisible colleges. Members shape fields of knowledge.
3. Opinion leaders, classified according to values shared with the decision-makers they aid.
4. Partitions of parameter space, which are discussed next. We consider the parameters of the following users' characteristics.

Urgency.   Consider several users faced with the same deadline, say, handing in a term paper. Suppose we allowed each user the use of the same IR system for one

test request of greatest importance to him. We then ask each user how much he would be willing to pay for various response times. This is like the plot as shown by the solid or the dashed line in Figure 5.2. The user whose urgency profile is like the dashed line does not value rapid responses as much as the user with the solid curve. The average slope of the curve may be a useful parameter to characterize a user's urgency. If this parameter had a bimodal frequency distribution for all the users, we would divide them into two corresponding classes.

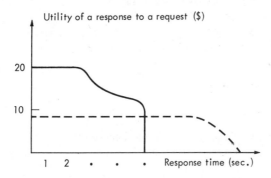

Figure 5.2. Shape of urgency profile of a user.

Scope.   Some users consistently cope with or solve problems that have a more long-term and more far-reaching effect than others. For example, a judge's sentence affects the defendant and his family for a longer time than the policeman's decision whether or not to issue a summons or make an arrest. Assuming that the effect of a decision decays exponentially, we could measure its half-life and parametrize the time-scope of a user by the average half-life for all his decisions. Again, if users distribute themselves over this *time-scope* according to a distribution with n nodes, we can specify n user classes by this criterion.

Another aspect of scope is the number of people and problems affected by a decision. Let us call a problem faced by a particular person at one time a problem-token or problem-encounter. The chief executive of an organization usually makes decisions which affect more problem-encounters than does a decision-maker at a lower level in the organization. Declaring war creates more problems for more people than the decision to join in a battle. Let us define the *PE-scope* of a user as the number of problem-encounters affected by the user's decisions, averaged over these decisions. Over various users this parameter is again a random variable.

Currency.   The currency profile of a user, analogous to his urgency profile, is a plot of utility of data age a as a function of a.

Diversity.   If few of the requests entering an IR system recur, then it might have a broad data base. Updating and storage costs will be great. If the resources available for the IR system are fixed, then either little effort can go into servicing each request, or the quality of servicing the more frequently recurring requests can be traded against the quality of service for the rarer ones. It is, however, important to characterize a user according to whether he asks only the same question over and over (for example, the temperature, pressure, and wind speed at a given airport, daily at 1 PM) or whether he is broad-gauged. To do this, plot against f the number of request-classes $r(f)$ that the user poses at least f times per year. If this is a skew distribution similar to new acquaintances or word use, the shape of the curve resembles one described by $r(f) = \alpha f^{-(1+\alpha)}$. The one parameter α can then characterize a user's diversity; if near 0, he is broad-gauged, while if it is near 1, he is narrow and repetitive.

Dedication. By this we mean how long a user with low diversity expects an IR system to be dedicated to his particular use or few uses. An example is continual recording of, analyzing, and making available electrocardiograms of a group of patients. A special-purpose, low-cost, microcomputer might serve as well as a more powerful computer that could be used to run a vastly different program every few minutes.

Quality. By a user's quality profile we mean a plot, against q, the quality of service, of the number of request-classes for which the user requires a quality of at least q. This may resemble the skew distribution for diversity. For the discerning and demanding user, it will be flat with small α. For the easy-to-please user, it will be steeper, with larger α. If both a demanding and an easy-to-please user were to use the same IR system, it would have to contain resources for the former. The cost would have to be borne by the easy-to-please user as well, and he may be burdened with details he does not need.

Location. An obvious way to classify users for the purpose of allocating them to IR systems is on the basis of where they work or live. There are conjectures that if a library is within 20 feet or so of a user's location, he is much more likely to use it than if it is further away. Despite the promise that telecommunications will make geographic distance between the location of a user and the IR system a less important factor, it is still important. Such conditions as availability of nearby parking, a stop of a public transport system, and safety of the neighborhood are not unimportant determinants of use. Of course, different users differ in their tolerance of the level of exertion required for a given use. This can be combined with a user's actual distance from the IR system to give as a parameter the *effective radius* within which people will be drawn to use it in person.

Jurisdiction. Political criteria, such as citizenship of a certain ward or taxpayer status in a certain political division, is another obvious basis for classifying users. This is relevant if the IR system has a tax or other political support base.

Socioeconomic and Educational Status. IR systems to serve users who pose more enlightened requests or who can accept a greater variety of responses certainly differ from IR systems which have to interpret their inputs and simplify their outputs. Socioeconomic status and level of educational attainment are correlated. Moreover, in private IR systems with a financial base derived from users' payments, users who pay more expect higher-quality service. Socioeconomic status and educational level are two more important parameters for classifying users.

Psychological Profile. This includes tolerance to ambiguity, inconsistency, vagueness, and overload, which differ from user to user. At least four parameters are included here.

All these parameters are discussed in more detail elsewhere. Altogether we have listed 15 parameters. Assuming that, as random variables over the users, they are all statistically independent, we have a 15-dimensional parameter space. Actually, they are not independent. There is, for example, an important constraint between quality and response-time. The response-time to attain a given quality grows rapidly with quality. Moreover, some of the parameters, such as quality, are really composites of several parameters. The quality of an IR system's response, for example, could be taken as a function of recall and precision ratio. In any case, parameter space has many dimensions, and the distribution of users over points in it is a plausible basis for classifying them.

To illustrate, let us take just three parameters: urgency, time-scope, and currency. Dichotomizing the users according to whether they fall on the high or low end of each parameter's range, we get eight categories of users, shown in Table 5.2.

TABLE 5.2. Illustrating a User Classification

Example of a user class	*Urgency: immediate response preferred to delayed response*	*Time-scope: decisions have long-term effects*	*Currency: new information greatly preferred to old*
Military intelligence analysts in war	Yes	Yes	Yes
Suicide preventors	Yes	Yes	No
Stock market speculators	Yes	No	Yes
Impatient people	Yes	No	No
Scientists	No	Yes	Yes
Counselors, judges	No	Yes	No
Reporters	No	No	Yes
Novelists (most)	No	No	No

Chapter Six

Topics and Directories

In Chapter Two, we introduced agents, documents, and topics as the key ingredients of a model for our knowledge system, the environment in which IR systems must perform. We also analyzed document–document, document–topic, document–agent, and agent–agent couplings. In Chapters Three, Four and Five we examined the notions of topic, document, and agent (user), respectively, in more depth. To complete the analysis, we now analyze topic–topic and topic–agent coupling.

In our search for principles and for more clearly explicated concepts related to information and its uses in IR, we now turn to *how* an IR system can help or hinder the normal growth of the knowledge system in which it is embedded. We have assumed that the knowledge system's growth is healthy if its people can recognize and cope with or solve an increasing variety of problems at least as well as up to now. We now examine more closely how an IR system affects a person's ability to recognize and cope with problems. Problems are part of topics. The connections among problems, which enable us to sort them by significance, are reflected by relations among topics.

To show how IR systems help people cope with and solve problems, we start by classifying topics into those which are mechanizable, indexable, and explorable. We analyze the notion of a directory which is to orient a user in an explorable field. We then analyze classification and cataloging as means of coupling users and indexable topics. This leads to an analysis of cross-referencing. We then relate this to topic–topic coupling and thesauri, and also to topic–agent coupling with manpower registers.

The terms *topic* and *field* originated from meanings relating to place and area. Like an area on the earth's surface, a field of knowledge can be characterized by a great degree of organization or by chaos, by a great deal of bewildering detail or by a desert. To find one's way to a famous landmark in a big, chaotically organized city is harder than finding a tower in a desert. A map is most useful for the searcher in a city. Similarly, a map is most useful to a searcher in a complex, vast field of knowledge. If a map exists. Some fields are not as well charted as others. Though numerous explorers may have pushed back its fron tiers, none may as yet have paused to chart it. Then there are fields which are sufficiently amorphous to defy efforts at charting them. It is extremely difficult to chart a landscape in which rocks with nondistinctive features are randomly scattered.

A map with a gazeteer illustrates a directory. So does *Yellow Pages*, and to some extent an index or subject catalog. If a field is without a paradigm or without a theoretical foundation, it is difficult to anticipate questions users will pose to an IR system, because there are few well-defined problems to be solved. For such fields, IR systems with descriptors are inappropriate, because there are few generally accepted concepts and terms to express them. Moreover, the concepts are not defined with the necessary precision required for accurate indexing and searching. Thus "schizophrenia," and "amnesia," do not denote well-defined concepts. A question such as "How many schizophrenics were in Ohio hospitals in each year since 1965" is closer to ill-structured than to well-defined. An IR system capable of retrieving all patient records carrying the diagnosis of "schizophrenia" could, of course, be constructed, but such a system is equally suited to retrieving century-old inmate records carrying the label "possessed" or "demented." It might mislead more than help. If the intent behind such a seemingly well-defined question as the above is to *cope* with mentally ill patients or to help them cope by planning enough hospital facilities of a certain kind, then perhaps a totally different kind of IR system, not descriptor-based, is called for.

The practitioner in an ill-structured field may benefit most from anything which helps to orient him. A directory which tells him what there is to know, the various viewpoints, and how to explore them might be more welcome than answers to questions which were unnaturally specific and only seemingly well-defined. In a field consisting of a miscellany of isolated facts, creating a directory which can help people get oriented is structuring that field to some extent. A full-fledged theory in the sense of Section 3.8 structures a field to the greatest extent possible. A simple taxonomy, such as a naturalist might construct in organizing his observations in a notebook, structures a field to a lesser extent.

6.1. CLASSIFICATION OF TOPICS

Some fields can be represented by a data base that is so well-structured and a technical language that is sufficiently rich that direct information-retrieval or automatic question-answering is possible. We will illustrate such a system in Section 6.6. An example of such a field is mass spectrometry with data bases consisting of rules for inferring the topology of probable chemical structures of unknown molecules on the basis of mass spectrometric data (Lederberg, et al., 1968). Another example is a part of mathematical logic (Robinson, 1967). Let us call these fields *mechanizable*.

Other fields, such as chemistry and physics, have sufficient structure known to most experts that they do not need a directory to orient them, but can be adequately served by descriptor-type indexes. Let us call these *indexable* fields.

The remaining fields, which we shall call *explorable*, are those best served by a directory to help orient the users. Figure 6.1 sketches the differences among IR systems for these three types of fields. People in application areas, decision-makers, students, and nonspecialists should be considered to be in such a field even if the field they are concerned with is indexable or even mechanizable. Even experts in certain fields of medicine and the social sciences would be better served if their fields were viewed as explorable rather than indexable.

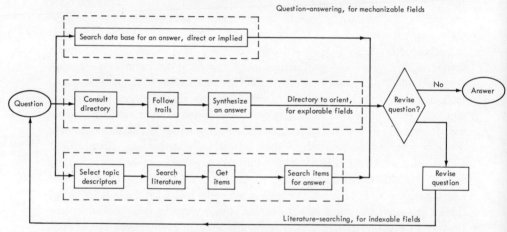

Figure 6.1. Mechanizable, indexable, explorable topics.

6.2. PROPERTIES OF A DIRECTORY

The primary function of a directory, as intended here, is to orient its users. This means that a user has a better overall perspective of a field (even his own, including how others see his work fit in) with the directory's help than without. Such a perspective helps him to ask deeper and more well-defined questions, and it may stimulate him to shift† from one representation to another.

To perform this function, a directory should have four properties. First it should be *sensitively selective*. This means that it stiumulates it user to acquire

---

†Human behavior in tasks requiring shifting has recently been investigated experimentally (Badre, 1973; Kochen and Badre, 1974).

just the knowledge, understanding, and wisdom which are of optimal help to him in coping.

Suppose, for example, that a city council member has to vote for or against a proposal for locating a new library at a certain site; and suppose that the main argument for this recommendation is based on the application of linear programming. He is aware of and understands many of the political pressures by interested parties—some for, some against the proposed site—but he has never heard of linear programming. He needs a few hours'—perhaps a few days'—worth of orientation about it in the context of its applicability to such land-use problems.

A mini-course which teaches him about convex sets, fixed-point theorems, and the simplex method in detail would be too much. A one-paragraph description from an existing encyclopedia may be too little for him. What may serve him best is following a trail of his own choosing through a network of packaged teachings. The first teaching might be a brief bird's-eye view of linear programming, analogous to the smallest-scale map of a region which gives the general outline of the whole, but which also orients him about which of several possible blown-up sections to turn to next. For example, the first packaged teaching might impart to him some knowledge, perhaps with examples, that linear programming is a general technique for finding the values of variables, such as where to locate a building so as to maximize a function of such variables as net utility, while at the same time satisfying constraints, such as the cost not exceeding a specified limit.

But this first package would also probe so that the user can ascertain whether he really understands concepts such as "function," "variable," and "utility" well enough for his purpose; if not, the package would point him to other packages that would help him acquire this understanding, and when he judges this to be the case (again on the basis of evaluative data from the directory), he returns to the first package. That first package also offers him options to go to packages which stimulate him to explore the assumptions about linearity, about the scales along which variables and coefficients are assumed to be measurable, about estimation, etc. The directory is selective in that it stimulates him to pursue a path of discovery which provides him with neither too much nor too little for him to cope optimally.

Second, such a directory should be *hierarchical*. This refers to scale in the map-analogy. Since the user's information intake capacity is limited, there is a tradeoff between scale and scope (aperture). Suppose the amount of detail the user can assimilate in one package is k details. Suppose also that details should be spread at a density of d per square inch for optimal utilization by the user (both locating one detail and seeing the entire pattern). If k and d are fixed, it should have an area of k/d square inches, and if this map has a scale of $S{:}1$, it maps a terrain of area $A = kS^2/d$ square inches. In other words, A/S^2 is a constant, k/d. If a user wants to see part of an area in a given map at double the scale, he must point to one of four subregions for which he receives a blow-up; the blow-up of a subregion is lower in the hierarchy than the given region he started with. The hierarchy may be viewed as continuous, and traversable with a zoom lens that can also be shifted to selected subregions. Several zoom lenses may be available for near-simultaneous use, so that a user can locate himself within the entire area at the same time that he pinpoints the detail he is exploring.

Third, a directory should be *interactive*. This means that it is highly responsive to its users. If the user is in a learning mode, it should provide immediate reinforcement as well as evaluative data to help him explore a topic. A self-guiding nature trail is a directory, but it is not very interactive, while a tour led by a ranger provides more opportunity for interaction. The directory should guide its user, by means of its packages, to three resources: people, documents, and facts or methods. Thus information packages contain not only statements about linear programming, tests for understanding, and pointers to packages with more detail, but pointers to passages in books and articles, and, above all, pointers to people with experience on problems similar to that faced by the user. The directory is to actually place a user in active contact and communication with another person, perhaps an ex-user. Such communication is three-way interactive; the directory is a third party which makes sure that there is a good match between the two parties it has brought together. In this way, the user may acquire some of the wisdom others are willing to share.

Fourth, the directory must be *dynamic*. This means that it is kept up-to-date in that no new item of knowledge is unavailable when needed. The way the information packages are interconnected reflects the structure of the field. This network topology of the directory must change as the organization of the field changes. In a rapidly maturing field, led by competent theoreticians, revision of the directory structure may lag behind the changes in the organization of knowledge, unless the intellectual leaders use the directory itself as their vehicle for representing the change. Being dynamic also means that the directory structure must accomodate to changes in the users.

A single directory is not likely to serve all users equally well. In place of a dynamic directory, we could imagine a growing set of directories, with some directories becoming obsolete as knowledge grows or gets reorganized, and others being added. Users, as they become better oriented through their guided explorations, switch from one directory to another. The entire set of directories could, however, be viewed as a single one at a higher level in the hierarchy.

The idea of a universal directory of this kind has been explored in some detail (Kochen, 1972a) and may someday become important as a major goal toward which the development of IR systems should be directed.

We proceed now to examine how IR systems can help a user with a problem in an indexable field. This is the role of indexes and classification systems.

6.3.   CLASSIFICATION AND CATALOGING†

Literature searches are generally conducted in a library. The primary tools for organizing the physical items in a library are the catalogs and their shelving according to a classification scheme. We suppose, as before, that a user enters this IR system because he senses a problem. If it is well-defined, he wants to solve it, and comes to the library with a fairly precise image of what he needs. If it is ill-structured, he wants to cope, and comes to the library with the intent of exploring, of becoming oriented. This is often stimulated by browsing.

Suppose that a user, with access to the shelves of the Library of Congress, had an ill-structured problem and wanted to browse through that set of books which are shelved next to each other because they pertained to turtles. He could try the subject-catalog, locate one book, go to that section of the stacks, and hope to find others among its neighbors. Or he could consult the book *Classification* by the Library of Congress Subject Cataloging Division. He should be led to, for example, "Chelonia" (Tortoises and turtles), and find the LC Class number QE862.C5. To locate this class name, however, the user must have known to look under, first, Geology (Class QE); within that, Paleozoology (701-996); within that, under Vertebrates; within that, under Reptiles; within that, under Systematic Divisions, A-Z (862). Had he started under Zoology (QL); then within that, under Vertebrates; then under Reptilia; then under Systematic Divisions, A-Z; then under Reptilia; and finally Chelonia, he would have found the class No. QL666.C5. The latter class might have been labeled, "Chelonia, zoological aspects"; the former, "Chelonia, paleozoological aspects."

Subject headings, as distinct from class names, are also representations of fields of knowledge in terms of linguistic phrases, but each document may be assigned to as many as it "belongs" to. A book such as the Library of Congress' list of Subject Headings is an authority list for phrases which may be used to represent such fields of knowledge. The subject catalog displays an alphabetized list of these subject headings, listing next to each the books to which these subject headings have been assigned during the cataloging process. Thus if "tortoises" and "Paleozoic" were subject headings, and the user sought a book pertaining to tortoises in the paleozoic period, he would first look under tortoises, and then look for all items listed there to see if it is also listed under Paleozoic.

---

†There is a large literature on this, particularly on various novel techniques of indexing (Foskett, 1970). There has been special concentration on automatic techniques for classification and indexing (Salton, 1968) with stress on linguistic aspects, both in its statistical and syntactic aspects (Borko, 1963; Doyle, 1965; Hays, 1967; Stevens et al., 1965). Because this diverts from our central theme, we do not discuss this here.

Such a list of subject headings is typical of other types of subject authority lists†, whether these be descriptors (numbers with special definitions), uniterms, keywords, etc., which are to be used for cataloging books, articles, reports, and other types of documents. The number of subject headings grows according to the function $S(t)$ defined in Section 2.3. This can be roughly estimated by the number of subject-headings in the Library of Congress' Subject Headings List. The first edition of the subject headings used in the dictionary catalogs of the Library of Congress has an estimated number of about 22,000 headings. This count* includes subdivisions which are not from divisions such as "Bibliography, Collections, Dictionaries, etc." It also includes cross-references, that is, headings that might be synonymous with established headings. There are, on the average, about 1.5 such synonyms per heading. The first edition appeared in 1914, when not all of the Library's collection had as yet been cataloged; hence we have only a crude estimate of $S(1914)$ as equal to 22,000. The corresponding counts for later years are: $S(1919) = 27,000$; $S(1928) = 31,000$; $S(1943) = 37,000$; $S(1948) = 42,000$; and $S(1953) = 62,000$. Based on different ways of estimating the number, these figures are within ±20% of the correct number.

In information centers where subject authority lists have been specially constructed for purposes of indexing reports and the serial literature, estimates of T are on the order of 10^4. Such lists are still too recent to observe any marked changes over time. In general, $T'(t)$, the rate of change of $T(t)$ with respect to time, is rather small. It could be expected to be greater for a subject authority list to be used for indexing serial literature than for one to catalog books. The former should include considerably more specialized topics than the latter. Nearly all the growth in the number of subject headings takes place at the most specialized level.

It should also be noted that the above count of subject headings for the Library of Congress did not include names of persons used as subjects (for example, in biographies), names of corporations, names of places, systematic names of lower divisions in biology, names of individual chemical compounds, names of ships, names of special prayers, or names of deities. Frequently, especially in indexing the serial literature, such proper names are of great value. Their number, of course, is proportional to population, and their growth could be assumed to be exponential. Furthermore, with each proper name must be included a large number of variants in spelling, phonetic transcription, and transliteration, as well as the numerous possibilities of error.

---

†The index terms found in the back of a book or in a concordance are not elements of an authority list. The index to the *Oxford Dictionary of Quotations*, for example, indexes the phrase "And He hardened Pharaoh's heart" (Exodus 1.12) under "hardened" and "Pharaoh," but not under "heart."

*These estimates were supplied by H. Dubester, then Information Systems Specialist at the Library of Congress.

Documents come in a great variety. Indexing criteria are quite dispersed and inconsistently enforced. This makes it difficult to derive a distribution for the number of subject-headings per document. To get some feeling for this, consider a collection of prose articles of about 2000 words each. Most of the proper nouns in a piece are good index terms. But the number of proper nouns varies greatly with the type of article. In news stories as many as 30% of the word-types may be proper nouns. In a technical article a correspondingly high proportion could be specialized technical terms.

If we suppose that all word-types except about 400 or so very common or general words are index terms, and that, on the average, each word together with one of its synonyms, or one of its morphological variants, has four occurrences in the text, then about 400 different word-types could be expected. While very few of these would, by themselves, serve to discriminate one document from all the others, the particular mix of the 400 is probably an identifying signature for the document. Thus the number of index terms per document could be, as an extreme, as large as 400.

In information centers where serial literature is indexed, the mean number of index terms per document is often in the vicinity of 10. If this is so, then, for a collection of 10^5 documents and 10^4 subject headings,

$$10 \times 10^5 = \overline{C}(d/s) \times 10^4$$

One hundred documents will, on the average, be posted on each subject heading. A document is usually indexed once for a given collection. No index terms are usually deleted or added to the number assigned by the indexer after he is done. There is a time lag between the birth of a document and its appearance in the catalog of a collection. This lag may typically be a year or even more, because several months elapse between birth and publication or imprint date; several more months elapse between publication date and acquisition and cataloging. With novel techniques, this serious lag may be greatly reduced, perhaps to days or weeks. It is both feasible and desirable that a document appear in the index prior to its publication date.

6.4. TOPIC–TOPIC COUPLING: THESAURI[†]

In a catalog, all documents, whether texts or other forms such as photographs from satellites, electrocardiograms, musical scores, and paintings, are described by linguistic surrogates built of phrases such as subject-headings and titles. Subject-headings designate fields. Relationships among various subfields

---

[†]A great deal of the literature on IR systems theory started here (Gardin, de Grolier, and Levery, 1964; Kochen and Tagliacozzo, 1968; Needham and Sparck-Jones, 1964; Reisner, 1965; Sparck-Jones and Jackson, 1967).

and fields should be reflected in relationships among corresponding subject-headings.

We will call the configuration consisting of all the subject-headings and their interrelations a thesaurus.

Different groups have different images of the world. Politicians have a different image of the geography of the U.S. than do meteorologists. For politicians, the image may be organized into voting blocks; for meteorologists, it may be organized into areas where certain atmospheric conditions consistently prevail. The subject-heading "Solid South" is as unlikely to appear in the vocabulary of a meteorologist (in his role as such) as is the subject-heading "low-pressure area" in the vocabulary of a politician. The names of states and cities, however, will occur in the vocabulary of both.

A good vehicle to illustrate the main ideas is U.S. geography. One aspect of the image of U.S. geography which is probably common to many people is how it appears on a map. This consists of an approximate outline of the coastlines and borders between the states, Canada, and Mexico. It includes some idea of the approximate location of the U.S. on the globe. For any two cities, most of us can probably say whether one is east or west, south or north of the second, whether they are in the same or in different states, whether one is bigger than the other, etc.

Our ability to store and use the image is greatly enhanced when we have first organized the country into states and then located the cities in the states rather than locating the cities directly in the entire country without proportioning into states.

The idea of organizing all images is akin to the idea of classifying the images into subimages, and the subimages into subsubimages, etc., all in particular relations to one another. There are many ways of classifying. The one which is chosen depends upon the role and interest of the classifier or of his social community.

A classification of an organized image has its counterpart in the linguistic representation of that image. By the linguistic representation of an image we mean a set of sentences from which the image could, in its essential features, be reconstructed. Consider the general public image of the U.S. sketched above as classified into states, cities, etc. There will be sentences about the U.S. as a whole. The sentences "The U.S. consists of 50 separate states" and "Every American is both a citizen of the U.S. and a citizen of some state" are two examples. They "belong together" in a certain sense. They both pertain to the *United States*. The term *United States* is a subject heading for the two sentences.

Now consider the sentences, "Texas is the largest state in the U.S." and "Texas has a coastline on the Gulf of Mexico." The set of these two sentences pertains to the subject-heading *Texas*. Indirectly, they also pertain to the subject-heading *U.S.* The first set of two sentences did not pertain to Texas, only to the U.S. In this sense, the subject-heading Texas falls under, is specific to, the more generic subject-heading *U.S.*

Actually, "U.S.:Texas" is not the ideal example of a generic-specific relation. The relations "Vertebrates:Reptiles:Chelonia," or "aircraft:jets," or "country: U.S." would be more illustrative of that. Nor does "U.S.:Texas" exemplify a pure whole:part relation as would "turtle:turtle-shell" or "jet:wing." It is a mix of both, typical of most real relations (Kochen and Tagliacozzo, 1968).

To proceed more formally, let s be a set of sentences which "belong together" in the sense that there exists a true metasentence of the form: "All the sentences of s pertain to S," where S is a subject-heading. Let us denote this relationship between s and S by $P(s,S)$, a *pertinence* predicate. Now consider another subject heading S'. We define a two-place relation $I(S,S')$, read as "S is included in S'," as follows.

$I(S,S')$ holds if and only if, for every s for which $P(s,S)$ holds, $P(s,S')$ also holds; but $P(s,S')$ may hold for some s for which $P(s,S)$ does not.

It is simple to prove that I is a partial ordering on the subject-headings. Knowing this enables us to represent subject headings by means of a tree which facilitates search. We illustrate this in Figure 6.2. This tree summarizes many sentences. "California is included in the U.S." is an example of such a sentence. We can also infer that Ocean Blvd. in Santa Monica lies west of Dallas. This results from the transitivity of all the relations used in this tree.

To prove that I is a partial ordering, we must just show that for all triples of subject-headings—S, S', S''—$I(S,S')$ and $I(S', S'')$ implies $I(S,S'')$. The first relation asserts that the set of all s such that $P(s,S')$ holds includes the set of all s such that $P(s,S)$ holds. The second I relation asserts that the set of all s such that $P(s,S')$ holds is a subset of the set of all s such that $P(s,S'')$ holds. Hence it follows that I is transitive.

To show that I is a partial, not a total, ordering is to show that there is a pair of subject headings S, S' such that neither $I(S,S')$ nor $I(S',S)$. Since we have placed no restrictions on the relation P, there is no reason to preclude the existence of s, s', S, and S' such that $P(s,S)$ is true but (s,S') is false, and $P(s',S)$ is false but $P(s',S')$ is true. This proves the result.

Consider two examples. Newton's second law (s) pertains to the *acceleration of masses under external forces* (S), but not to *the propagation of inherited traits* (S'). Mendel's law (s') pertains to S' but not to S.

Such relationships among subject-headings as I are displayed in a thesaurus. It is often stated that the structure of a thesaurus can be represented by a lattice. This requires not only that there exists a relation such as I which is partially ordered, but that for any two subject-headings S, S' there is a greatest lower bound and a least upper bound.

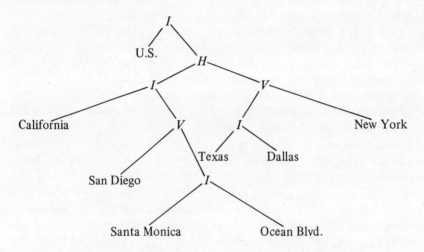

Figure 6.2. Representation of inferential relations.

If we are willing to include enough phrases in our authority list of subject-headings, these conditions could be met.

The basic mechanism by which fields of knowledge become more specialized is that by which every question which is answered generates further questions. Answers to such questions as "Is there a number whose square is −1" generate vastly more questions than do answers to other questions. Therefore, falling under the theory of complex variables are very many subtopics and sub-subtopics. The social process by which questions are created, formulated, posed, and answered and then beget offspring questions is at the very heart of a live information system. A question reflects knowledge. A good question reveals the querist's precise knowledge of what he does not know. A bad question reveals his ignorance. Posing but not answering a good question is a greater contribution than answering a bad question.

The number of good questions is probably proportional to the number of good querists-agents; also to the number of good documents.[†] The "goodness" of a query may also be related to the quality of documents and agents. We might expect high-quality documents to refer to and be referred to by a greater proportion of other good documents than is the case for lesser quality documents. An analogous remark could be made for questions. Let $P(q,q') = 1$ if the answer to q gives rise to q', and let it be 0 otherwise. Let $Q(q)$ be a positive real number to measure the goodness of a query. As in the case of document–document coupling, we define $Q(q)$ by the equation

$$Q(q) = \frac{1}{\lambda} \sum_{q'} P(q,q')Q(q')$$

We would expect the number of queries of quality Q to decrease with Q, probably according to a skew distribution such as Q^{-k}; insofar as a sufficient number of high-quality queries and answers which "belong together" define a topic, the number of topics specific to a generic topic is related to Q. So is the number of ancestor-generic topics per offspring-specific topic. The former quantity should continually grow with them, because we considered two topics in generic-specific relation no matter how many generations removed. The number of ancestor-generic topics per offspring-specific topic should also increase because topics are always being interrelated across classifications. Thus while the tensor calculus is an offspring of differential geometry, it can today also claim the theory of general relativity as an ancestor. Quantitative derivations and data pertaining to these variables remain for future investigations. What little is known is exemplified by the law of Willis in biological taxonomy.

In the previous discussion of the relation I, we used a pertinence predicate $P(s,S)$. There are two aspects in P, a logical one and a behavioral one. Consider a sentence, $s =$ "Not all that glitters is gold," and three subject-headings, $S =$ "gold," $S' =$ "superficiality," and $S'' =$ "proverbs." From a logical point of view, $P(s,S)$ holds and $P(s,S')$ or $P(s,S'')$ is very hard to ascertain by a purely logical analysis. On the other hand, $P(s,S')$ will be regarded as true by most people but not by others. Almost all people who consider $P(s,S')$ true will consider $P(s,S'')$ true. If we regard the function $P(s,S)$ as taking on not only the values 0 or 1 but any real number in $[0,1]$, then we can speak of a degree of pertinence on a ratio scale. At least an ordinal scale of more than two points may be easily justified. Such a function $P(s,S)$ will reflect individual differences to an even greater extent.

[†] De Solla Price has stated that the number of good documents varies as the square root of the number of documents. If $D(t)$, the number of documents, continues to grow, the *ratio* of good documents $\sqrt{D(t)}/D(t)$, will decrease to 0 as $(D(t))^{-1/2}$.

6.5. TOPIC–AGENT COUPLING: MANPOWER REGISTERS

This is the remaining interaction between the three main components of our conceptualization. Two functions specify it. The first is $E(t)$, the number of people who are *concerned* with a randomly selected topic at time t. The second is $E^{-1}(t)$, the number of topics with which a randomly chosen person is concerned at time t. In parallel with the previous results about averages, we have here

$$\bar{E}(t) S(t) = \bar{E}^{-1}(t) \mid U(t) \mid$$

How are users (agents) matched with the knowledge they utilize and add to? The fundamental concept underlying this question is *concern*. It is our central thesis that if people need an IR system, it is to help them cope with or solve a problem. All of us are faced with more problems than we recognize, and we recognize more than we can select to pay attention to at one time. Concern refers to the problems we heed. It means assignment of priorities to recognized problems.

If a parent has an autistic child and knows this to be a problem high on his priority list, then he is *concerned* with the topic of "autistic children." His question might be "Is there a successful treatment for my child," but an article entitled "Behavior Modification of an Autistic Child" might be of concern to him, too. The nature of this parent's concern differs from that of a scientist investigating the behavior of autistic children. Generally, the consumer of knowledge has different concerns from those of the producer. The latter has not only concern, but expertise as well. He supplies answers. The consumer has not only concern, but purchasing power as well. He demands answers.

One vital function of a directory is to bring together people who can supply answers with people who demand answers to specific questions. How can such a directory be built and maintained? If a question is well-defined—that is, is specified by a set of possible solutions, a set of properties a solution should have, and a data base of knowledge and methods necessary to find a solution—then it can be assigned to an indexable topic or field. If it is ill-structured, it can perhaps still be assigned to one or more explorable fields.

A directory to help match consumers with producers on well-defined questions can take the form of a manpower register, which posts people against the index terms characterizing the indexable fields. For example, both a producer and a consumer of information about the lattice parameters of Zn_3As_2 are concerned with "crystallography." A directory which lists all producers of knowledge in this field might then be scanned by the consumer, who could then call or write these people or search for publications by them in author indexes. Of course, crystallography may be too broad a term, and list far too many people who are not concerned with the very specific question of concern. The key to the effectiveness and efficiency of such a directory is the specificity of its index terms.

A directory to help match consumers with producers on ill-structured questions must be more personalized. It is likely to resemble a grapevine over which confidential recommendations are transferred. The problem may be a psychiatric syndrome which the patient, who is the consumer, cannot name. Possible producers of professional expertise to help him cope with the problem include psychiatrists, clinical psychologists, social workers, and perhaps others. It matters perhaps more which particular helper is assigned to the patient—in terms of the helper's personality—than what profession or specialty area he belongs to. A register to effect such matches must therefore obtain a wealth of reliable, confidential information about both the consumers and the producers.

An important use of such registers is to help an editor select referees to evaluate manuscripts submitted to a journal for publication (Kochen, 1969). The choice of referees is a major determinant of the quality of literature published in that journal. A reasonable procedure to control quality is the following. The editor indexes (or edits index terms supplied by the author) the manuscript on receipt, if the paper is an indexable field. If it is not, he obtains data to characterize the author. Using the resulting profile of the paper (or the author), he then tries to locate all potential referees from a large register of these whose profiles match. The referee's behavior—in the promptness, thoroughness, objectivity, etc., of his review—is recorded to assess the extent to which his concern and expertise with the question raised and answered in the manuscript equal those of the author; this behavioral data, plus numerous other data—for example, the referee's load and time schedule—all enter into the matching decision. The referees must also be a representative sample of the journal's readership in addition to their competence as judges.

An ongoing experiment of this nature, with the *Journal of the Association for Computing Machinery* (Information Retrieval), is yielding a continuous record of data to be used for assessing the effectiveness of such a quality-control device.

6.6. QUESTION-ANSWERING

In Sections 3.4 and 3.5 we viewed fields of knowledge as representable by a language. We now pursue the possibility of automatically answering certain questions in mechanizable fields that can be represented by a competent technical language and a well-structured data base. This includes questions which can be answered by direct lookup of the answer, or by looking up facts from which the answer can be deductively or inductively inferred. Such questions are most likely to occur and be of value when the user has well-defined problems.

A technical or formal language is specified as the seven-tuple $\{VT, VA, RF,$
$RT, WF, AX, RI\}$ defined in Section 3.8. To illustrate the principles of a system
for answering English-like questions directly, consider a hypothetical specialty
topic called "Vertical Relations Among Eight Light and Dark Dots on a Line."
This might evoke an *image* in your mind such as is shown in Figure 6.3. Suppose
that it is possible to label the dots so that no two get the same label and each dot
is labeled. Call the labels *1, 2, ..., n*, where *n* is the number of dots. The only
two-place relation we consider is that previously denoted by $V(a,b)$, which states
that configuration *a* is just above configuration *b*; a configuration may, in turn,
consist of two other configurations, one just above the other, or of single dots.
The only one-place relation we consider is $D(a)$, which asserts that each dot in
configuration *a* is dark. If we label the dots in the picture from bottom to top,
then we can also represent the data by

$$V\left\{V[V(8,7), V(6,5)], V[V(4,3), V(2,1)]\right\}$$

Figure 6.3. Light and dark dots on a line.

This can also be represented by a tree (as shown in Figure 6.4) in which

$$\overset{V}{\underset{a \quad b}{\diagup \diagdown}}$$

stands for $V(a,b)$. The advantage of the tree representation is that we can easily
determine that *8* is *somewhere* (as distinct from *just*) above *1*, by detecting a
path up from *8* entering the top vertex *V* from the left and down to *1*. The tree
embodies the transitivity of the *V*-relation in a form convenient for finding such
paths (Kochen, 1969).

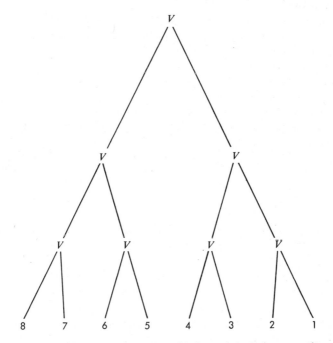

Figure 6.4. Tree representation of light and dark dots on a line.

We can also describe this data by sentences such as "*8* is above *7*," "*8* is dark," "*7* is above *6*," and "*7* is light." We would also like to be able to state the empirically *verifiable* generalization, "Each dot which is dark is above a dot which is light." We should like to be able to pose questions such as "Is it true that each dot which is light and below a dot which is dark is above a dot which is light?" To construct a grammar that generates sentences such as these, let:

VT =   { each, a, is, dark, light, above, below, dot, which, not, and, or, *1,2,3,4,5, 6,7,8,9,10* }

VA =   { QUA,QUE,IS,REL1,REL2,etc.}

RF   includes the items shown in Figure 6.5: QUA→each, VAR→dot, W→which, IS→is, REL1→light, AND→and, REL2→below, QUE→a, REL1→dark, REL2→above, ANT→VAR, CONS→REL1; WF→(QUA) (IMP), ANT→(ANT)(CL), CL→(W)(IS)(CONS), CONS→(CONS) (AND)(CONS), CONS→(REL2)(QUANT), QUANT→(QUE)(ANT), IMP→(ANT)(IS)(CONS), ANT→(VAR)(CL)

Suppose now that an IR system has a data base which consists of Figure 6.3 or its equivalent expressed as a string. Suppose further that a question such as the above enters. The first step is to scan the question sentence from left to right, searching a dictionary for applicable rules of formation. Thus the first word encountered in Figure 6.4 is "each," and a dictionary reveals that it is used in the rule *QUA→each*. If there is more than one rule, all must be tried, but various devices to shorten such an exhaustive search can be applied when parsing has progressed further. The first word is replaced by a symbol from *AT* which could have generated it; thus QUA appears as the first symbol of the second line of Figure 6.4. The dictionary which indicated what formation rule is applicable to *each* also indicates which of several possible building blocks of a flow diagram for a computer program should be used. In the case of *QUA→each* this is a black box (Figure 6.6) with two inputs and two outputs. Input C_1 is a lead for a control signal which starts the subroutine designated by this box. Input C_n is a signal to test whether search through a list of n items (that is what this sub-routine does) should continue or cease. Output C_Q activates transfer of the question to a specified other box (usually ANT). Output C_Y is a signal indicating that the subroutine succeeded in matching the data in the question with something in the list being searched.

After the first line in Figure 6.4 has been completed, the same process is repeated with the second line. For example, a search for formation rules involving QUA will uncover WF→(QUA)(IMP). In this way a phrase-marker (Figure 6.5) is generated, which is completed when the entire sentence is shown to be generated from just the symbol WF. During the process of constructing this phrase-marker, all the necessary subroutines are specified, appropriate variables

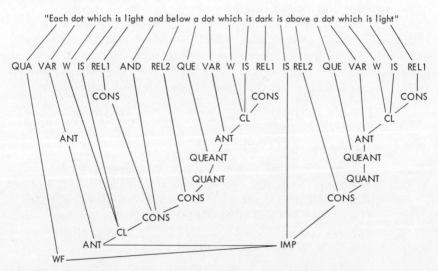

Figure 6.5. Phrase marker or parsing tree for a sentence.

and constant are inserted into places calling for such insertions before the specifications are completed, and designated interconnections among the subroutines are made.

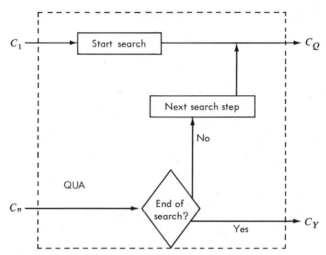

Figure 6.6. Translation rule for *each* or QUA in forming a question-answering program.

The result is the flow diagram of Figure 6.7. This specifies a computer program. If that program were implemented and run, it would search the data base of eight objects, substituting $1, \ldots, 8$ for x_1, x_2, and x_3 as specified, and produce a Yes or No answer to the original question of whether or not the sentence of Figure 6.4 is true.

Note that this program could be made to answer certain questions requiring deductive inference, such as "Is 8 somewhere above 1," by adding special rules of inference such as the following. For all x_1, x_2, x_3, "from $V^*(x_1, x_2)$ and $V^*(x_2, x_3)$, infer $V^*(x_1, x_3)$," and "from $V(x_1, x_2)$ infer $V^*(x_1, x_2)$"; for $V^*(x_1, x_2)$, read "x_1 is somewhere above x_2." If n is large, applying these rules efficiently to check an inference is a problem, which becomes more severe in more general cases of theorem-proving. There exist, however, computer programs which can, in principle if not efficiently, ascertain the truth or falsity of any decidable proposition in the first-order predicate calculus with equality (Robinson, 1967).

An inductive inference is assigning a probability measure to the Yes and No exits to the flow diagram in Figure 6.7 corresponding to the sentence of Figure 6.4 interpreted as a *hypothesis*; here n, the number of dots, is so large that a sample must be taken. The problem would be one of statistical inference if the hypothesis referred to random variables. An example of such a statistical hypothesis is: "The number of dots, which, if they are light and under a dark dot, are then above a light dot, has a Poisson distribution with a mean of $n - 1$." The statement in Figure 6.4 is not of this nature, and techniques of inductive inference other than statistical ones—for example, weighting of two types of confirmation (Kochen, 1960)—must be employed.

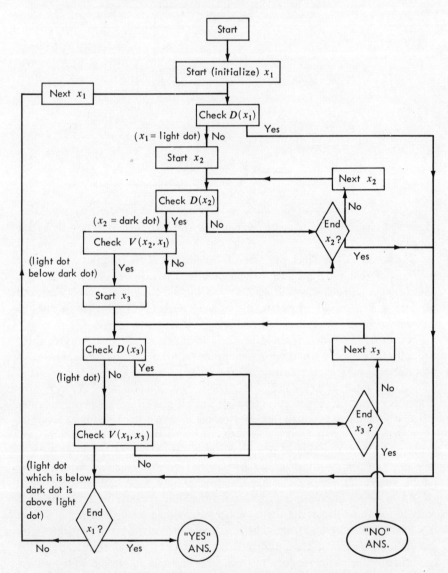

Figure 6.7. Flow diagram for forming a question-answering program.

Some question-answering systems are used primarily for deriving answers as logical consequences of what is in the data base. Hayes points out that, if the data base contains any inconsistency—or even worse, a false statement—then *any* answer can be deduced. Deductive question-answering systems are far too error-sensitive. It is indeed a most important problem to explain how we do and how we should use data bases that contain errors and inconsistencies. There has been some work on systems that not only retrieve answers, but that detect contradictions and gaps as well, but it has just begun.

Chapter Seven

Specifying an Information Retrieval System

In this chapter we bring together all the analyses and comments of the preceding chapters. We use them to formulate a set of design principles in Section 7.6. First, we sketch a model of an IR system and examine the key variables and parameters characterizing the performance of an IR system in its effectiveness, then in its efficiency. These are used to classify IR systems for the purpose of matching them with user classes and fields.

7.1. MODEL OF AN IR SYSTEM

An IR system consists of three major units:

1. A data base, which stores documents or recorded data, and from which they are retrieved.
2. A communication system, which allows users to update and access the data base.
3. A system of representation.

The *data base* is a set of documents. For purposes of this discussion let us regard a sentence representing a recorded datum as a special case of a document, with the author, references, name, and validating agency implicit. All retrievable items in the data base are documents, and each document is retrievable. A document is retrieved if it is displayed in response to a request. A document may be a string of other documents. Each *document* is a string of the following *parts*, in order: Tag, Title or name; Author; Relevance-indicators or substance (for example, descriptors); Significance-indicators or substance; a Claim, which is the main substance or authorization; Validity-indicators or substance; Novelty-indicators; and References (Figure 7.1). If any of these facts are not explicitly stated, they are taken to be the same as the corresponding document of which this document is a *member*.

132

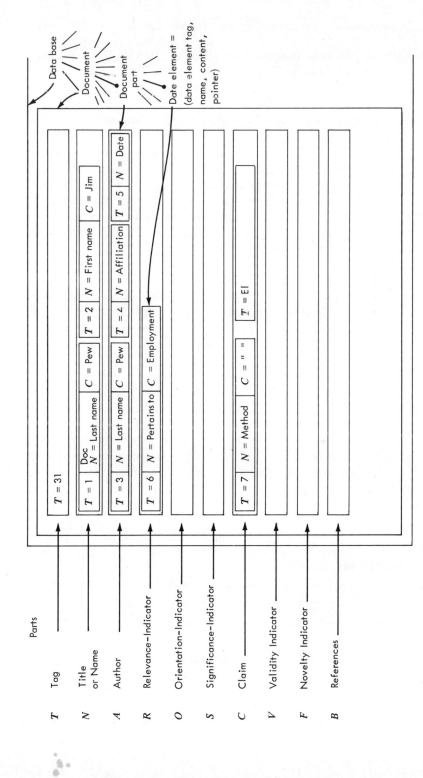

Figure 7.1. Example of a data base of just one document, say a resumé.

The labeled parts may, themselves, be documents. There may be two kinds of tags, internal and external. An external tag is a pointer to another document or part. All of the variables, $T, N, \ldots, B$ range over strings of alphanumeric characters. A *data element* is a concatenation of strings corresponding to a tag, the name, the actual content, and possibly a pointer. A *part* is a concatenation of strings corresponding to data elements, and a *document* is a string of parts. A *file* is a concatenation of documents in some order, as defined in Section 3.5.

The data base can be structured in various ways. This refers to structural relations among the data elements, as implemented by pointers. A data structure can be visualized as a directed graph, with each data element represented by a node; a directed edge links one node to another if the data element corresponding to the first has a pointer which names the data element of the second. A file, as defined in Section 3.5, is an example of a *linear list*.

The linear lists are further classified (Knuth, 1968) into (*a*) stacks, where all insertions and deletions (and most accesses) are made at one end of the list; (*b*) queues, where all insertions (and most accesses) are made at one end of the list and deletions are made at the other end; (*c*) deques (double-ended queues), which include stacks and queues; (*d*) circular lists, where the last item is linked with the first, with all links in one direction; (*e*) doubly linked lists, in which links can be directed both ways; and (*f*) arrays, such as matrices.

Trees are another, more complex, kind of data structure. A family tree is a simple example.

Among the most complex kinds of data structures[†] are multilinked ones, with many interconnections. AMNIPS (Adaptive, Man–machine Nonarithmetic Information Processing System) was one of the first IR systems with such a structure (Kochen, 1967). It embodied many of the features used in the several relational and set-theoretic data structures in use today.

The communication system is specified by a formal language,[*] among other things. The following commands or their equivalents have to be in any such language:

1. Create a file, document, part, or data element.
2. List an entire file.
3. Search a specified file for a specified document, part, or data element.
4. Form a temporary file of items retrieved by command 3.
5. Display a specified response to a request.
6. Perform specified operations on retrieved items.
7. Check that retrieved items satisfy specified relations.

[†]There is a significant literature on file organization (Hayes, 1965; Salton, 1968; Warheit, 1967), but we represented it primarily by the approach exemplified in Section 3.5.
[*]For a comparison of languages see Soergel (1967).

These are commands for a user to express his need and to instruct the IR system in forming a useful response. Question-answering systems, such as discussed in Section 6.7, accept questions in a much more English-like formal language. This is far less constrained than a constrained language with commands such as the above and rather rigid rules of syntax.

The AMNIP system specified such a language which permitted a limited amount of conversational interaction as well. The central idea in AMNIPS was its "adaptiveness." It incorporated the idea of a "growing thesaurus," one in which new terms and various connections between these and words already in the thesaurus would be entered as they were encountered in use of the system. The entire data structure, and to some extent the vocabulary, was designed to be modified so as to converge, with use and accumulating input, toward an optimal design tailored to its users, topics, and documents.

A most important aspect of an IR system is provision for protection of private data, of confidentiality (van Tassel, 1972). One way of providing this is by means of protection keys and other checks and balances during the process of using an IR system. If the IR system is computerized, the use process typically begins with a "Sign-on" command, whereby the user presents the computer account identification number. He is then asked to supply his password. The password is a document part that can have many data elements in it. Some are:

1. His degree of security risk.
2. His general security classification; if it is high, a variety of double-checking or cross-checking procedures are invoked later.
3. Which classes of operations or commands are forbidden to this user.
4. Which classes of data or sets of data specified by properties are disallowed for this user.
5. Special disallowances.

He may then be asked his name and other data to identify himself. This, together with the time and place where the use occurs, is automatically recorded so that it can be traced in case of a violation.

The request is then accepted and processed. The protection codes of documents which are retrieved are then checked prior to display.

Systems of representation for an IR system were already discussed in Chapter Three. This is closely related to choice of structuring the data base and to choosing the commands and predicates in the communication system. In its deeper sense, representation has to do with the organization of the knowledge contained in the data base and the user's questions. In the context of question-answering system's representation refers to the choice of variables, axioms, and special rules of inference. It has been shown that the efficiency of a system for answering questions about the missionary-and-cannibals puzzle is significantly affected by how the problem is formulated (Amarel, 1971).

7.2.   EFFECTIVENESS

The effectiveness of a literature-search system for an indexable field is usually characterized by h, the hit-rate or recall ratio, and a, the acceptance-rate or precision ratio. These are most applicable to a straightforward recall situation. Suppose that on January 10, 1970, a personnel department clerk files two batches of 110 and 90 resumés that he has just received, by the people's names. He is told the first batch are physicists and the second are chemists. He also has an index by professional fields, and he assigns to each resumé one or more classes, such as physicist, astrophysicist, or chemist. The resumé identification number of a person classified "physicist" and the date of filing are then posted under the index term "physicist." An hour later, the clerk wants to get all these 110 resumés of the first batch back from the file, and *recalls* that they were all physicists. But his recall is imperfect. When he indexed all 200 resumés, he labeled some resumés of the second batch "physicists" and failed to label some resumés of the first batch "physicists." But he does not recall this, because both types of "errors" were rather small. Nonetheless, his search may uncover not 110 but only 100 resumés under "physicists." On inspecting these, he now judges only 99 of these to be physicists. Evidently, he had labeled resumés "physicist" an hour ago, and would not do so now. The acceptance rate for this search is 99/100 or 0.99. But he expected to get 110 physicists, and got only 99, so that his search had a hit−rate of $99/110 = 0.90$. Evidently, he had failed to label 10 resumés "physicists" an hour ago. Perhaps he would not revise his judgment about these ten. But he *recalled* having been told that all 110 of the first batch were physicists.

An even better application of these measures is to show a person a list of n words for 2 minutes and ask him to memorize them. An hour later, he is asked to write down all the words he recalls, reminding him that there were n. Suppose he writes down m, with no restriction on m, of which k are in the original list. The hit or recall rate is $h = k/n$, and the acceptance or precision rate is k/m. If his reward were $u \cdot k$ dollars, with no cost, he might make m as large as possible. If all the words or the original list were common, he could, by listing as many common words as he can think of, hit upon most or all of the k by guessing if not by recall. Perhaps when he guesses a word in the list he did not recall, he recognizes it as being in the list. Thus as m increases, h increases slowly, though a decreases rapidly.

The following very simple, yet plausible and experimentally testable, model implies the much discussed tradeoff between a and h. Assume that $n > 7$. Repeat the above experiment on a sample of human subjects, and let each one produce a list of words in the order in which he recalls them. The n target words are drawn with equal probability from a list of V words, and all subjects have this list; V is very large. The probability is high that each of the subjects' first 7 words will match words on the target list. The expected value of k should be just m for $m \leq$ 7. For $m > 1$, assume that any subject lists a word on the target list only once in every $V/(n-7)$ guesses. Thus the expected value of k, $F(k) = 7 + [(n-7)/V]$ $(m-7)$, may be a plausible hypothesis. If n is large compared with 7, then $E(k) \doteq 7 + [(n-7)]/V \, m$ and the average value of h and a, $\bar{h} \doteq 7/n + [(n-7)/Vn] \, m$, $\bar{a} \doteq 7/m + (n-7)/V$. Express m in terms of h and then in terms of a and set the two equal:

$$\frac{\bar{h} - 7/n}{(n-7)/Vn} = \frac{7V}{\bar{a}V - n + 7}$$

Cross-multiply to obtain $(\bar{h} - 7/n)(\bar{a}V - n + 7) = 7(n-7)/n$. For example, if $V = 200$, $n = 21$, then $(\bar{h} - 1/3)(200\bar{a} - 14) = 14/3$ or $(\bar{h} - 0.33)(\bar{a} - 0.07) = 7/300$. Thus if $\bar{h} = 1$, $\bar{a} = 21/200$; if $\bar{h} = 2/3$, $\bar{a} = 28/200$; and if $\bar{h} = 1/2$, $\bar{a} = 42/200$; while for $\bar{a} = 1$, $\bar{h} = 100/279 \doteq 0.36$. This is shown in Figure 7.2.

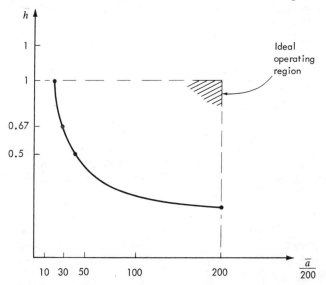

Figure 7.2. Illustrating the recall–precision tradeoff law.

Human recall is limited to from five to seven "chunks" (Miller, 1956). To recall items from a list much beyond this, external aids to recall are needed. If a list of n words is stored in cards, a book, or a computer, recalling it an hour later should have an effectiveness of $\bar{h} = 1$, $\bar{a} = 1$ *provided the list were precisely specified*. The tradeoff does not apply to storage devices with perfect recall for single, unambiguously named lists, and these measures of effectiveness do not directly apply to situations other than recall.

If we take the purpose of information retrieval to be providing responses which meet a stated need for documents, then effective responses must be relevant or sensitive to the stated need, significant or useful for the user in his need, valid or documented, timely, and in a form matched with his ability to use the needed documents.

Much has been written about *relevance*. One of the early proposals (Maron and Kuhns, 1960) defined it as the probability of a document satisfying a given request. Operationally (Cleverdon, 1965), a document was considered relevant to a question which was chosen in an experiment because its answers are known to be in that document. This introduces a bias into the relationship between the question and the source-document (Swanson, 1965). Estimating hit-rate by adding to the k retrieved items the user judges relevant all the nonretrieved documents the user knows to be relevant before the search, and taking the ratio of k to that, introduces a similar bias.

It is important to distinguish between relevance as a relation between propositions and the recognition of relevance or its judgment by a user, which resembles a utility or significance judgment (Cooper, 1971).

If the user is willing to abide by the following axioms of utility theory, then it is possible to assign, for a given user U with a given request Q, a utility to each document in the collection.

A1. For any two documents d and d', U should be able to state unambiguously whether he prefers d to d', d' to d, or that he is indifferent.

A2. If U prefers d to d', and d' to d'', then he prefers d to d'' for any such d, d', d''.

A3. If U prefers d to d' and d' to d'', then he can specify a probability P such that, for all d, d', d'', he is indifferent between the option of d' for sure versus the option of using a method which retrieves d with probability P and d'' with probability $1 - P$.

A4. If U is indifferent between d and d^* and d^* is substituted for d in a strategy (d with probability P or d'' with probability $(1 - P)$) as in A3, then U is indifferent between that strategy and (d^* with probability P or d'' with probability $(1 - P)$).

From these axioms, it follows that there exists a utility function $u(d;U,Q)$ which assigns a number to each document d for a given U and Q such that if U prefers d to d', then $u(d) > u(d')$ and the expected utility of a strategy is the expected utility of the documents in it.

The most serious limitation is A1. A given user U with a given question Q may slightly prefer d to d' one day, but be indifferent between them or even prefer d' to d on another day, depending on context. Learning may change his preferences; so may the order in which documents are encountered. Moreover, to extend a utility function beyond documents U has seen on the basis of an estimate for a sample, it must be possible to characterize all documents so that utilities can be assigned to them.

To design an IR system is to specify values for a large number of variables. To make it effective is to pick values that do not violate constraint relations which have to hold among these variables and which are in accordance with all the princples. The following is a brief list of effectiveness variables for use in one particular and simple design model for a given class of users and requests in an indexable field.

u   *Utility* of documents judged by users, averaged over all users, questions, and retrieved documents from a sample.

t   Total *turnaround time,* or *promptness* measured from when a user first expresses his need to when he makes a utility judgment, averaged over all requests.

b   *Completeness* of the data base, estimated by the ratio to the number of different documents cited by or citing documents in the data base, of the number of such documents which are in the data base.

r   *Recency* of the data base, measured by the time elapsed after a document is published and its earlist availability from the data base, averaged over all documents.

f   *Fitness*, estimated by $\sum_s [f_q(s) - f_d(s)]^2$, where $f_d(s)$ is frequency with which topic-descriptor s is used in the topic profile of documents in the data base, averaged over all $\cup_d R(d)$, and f_q is the frequency with which topic-descriptor s is used in the topic profile, averaged over all questions posed to the system.

ρ   *Reach*, or the extent to which the documents in the IR system reach users to whom they are of potential value. This resembles hit-rate, while f resembles acceptance-rate.

7.3   EFFICIENCY

One IR system is more efficient than another if it attains the same effectiveness at a lower total cost. If effectiveness were a differentiable function of total cost, we could define efficiency as the derivative, that is, as the marginal increase in effectiveness attained by adding the last dollar to the total cost. This may imply a value of total cost at which the efficiency is maximum, that is, an optimum investment level; unfortunately the resulting effectiveness may be unacceptably low or the cost unacceptably high by other criteria.

There may be levels of effectiveness that are unattainable at any cost. Some of these limits are practical ones, governed by organizational, technological, or economic factors. In time, they may increase. But there may be theoretical upper bounds to effectiveness as well, governed by the same basic laws that specify the dynamics of the institution into which the IR systems have to be grafted.

The total cost has three major components: the cost of building the system amortized over the system's life so that it appears as a rate $(C_1$ \$/hr); the cost of maintaining the system, including updating, maintenance, and servicing clients $(C_2$ \$/hr); and the direct cost to the client for his effort in using it other than the system costs which are passed on to him $(C_3$ \$/hr). We examine these in turn.

The prime determinant of C_1 is D_1, the initial number of documents and their surrogates in the system. For a library, we could take a unit cost of c_1 \$/document for the construction of shelving, land, housing, and acquiring the document, indexes or catalogs, equipment, and software (for example, specially developed computer programs and operating protocols). The detailed costs will, of course, differ depending on whether the documents or their surrogates are stored and processed in bulk form, microform, or digitally. Various mixes are possible, and there may be an optimal mix.

The major two variables affecting C_2 are L, the request *load* or demand, in number of requests/hour, and D', the rate at which the document collection grows.

For a completely computerized system, the operating cost is no greater if it is fully utilized than if it is not used at all; so that L and D' do not affect C_2 at all. But then the entire cost, other than hardware/software maintenance and power, is absorbed in C_1. The salaries of such operators, resident programmers, supervisors, and other human elements of the system as are needed to the extent the system is not *fully* automated are all part of C_2. If people have to index incoming documents, or if they merely have to prepare input that is suitable for an automatic indexing system, their wages are part of C_2.

In a well-designed system, the number of people with various information-processing capacities and equipment of specified capacities are chosen so that all the units are neither idle nor congested too much of the time. These numbers are determined by L and D'. For example, if one reference librarian can process 10 questions per hour and $L = 30$ requests per hour, all of which require a reference worker's services, then three ought to be used. (Actually, probably four should be used because of fluctuations in the request rate.) If an indexer can handle 12 documents per hour and $D' = 48$ documents per hour, then at least four indexers are needed. If the hourly rate of a reference worker is c_{21} and for an indexer it is c_{22}, then $C_2 > 3c_{21} + 4c_{22}$.

The costs of certain maintenance functions, such as indexing, can be partially allocated to C_1 and C_2. A human indexer may spend a certain amount of time, say t_1 hours per document, in content analysis, leaving to a computer all the more clerical aspects of descriptive and subject cataloging, which require t_2

hours/document. If the computer costs c_{1C} \$/hr (part of C_1), then the indexing cost is $c_{22}t_1 + c_{1C}t_2$ \$/document. There may be an optimal mix (t_1, t_2), which minimizes this total and satisfies some additional constraints regarding the minimum quality of indexing, maximum time per document, etc. This is readily seen to be a linear programming problem.

Just as the cost of certain functions can be split between C_1 and C_2, the direct cost of serving the user can be split between C_3 and C_2 and possibly also C_1. Whenever a user presents a retrospective literature-search request, he must expend a certain amount of preparatory effort. Let us measure this by the time, t_u hours, he spends in preparing his request. Some users can arrive at the same level of preparedness with a more concentrated effort expended over a smaller time than others. Let us assume—this is probably unwarranted, but subject to empirical verification and replacement by a more realistic assumption—that the wage rate of such a more energetic or capable user is proportional to the intensity and quality of his effort. That is, if his rate is c_u \$/hr, then $c_u t_u$ is a constant which depends only on the request. Thus an inexperienced user employed at \$4/hour spends 10 minutes formulating a request for the lattice parameters of Zinc–Arsenic, while a more experienced user, employed at \$8/hour, can formulate the same request in 5 minutes.

The effort spent by the user is difficult to operationalize, because it is not clear when counting the time should begin or end. Nor is it total elapsed time, but effort on formulating a request is distributed over a considerable time period, including false starts, etc. Suppose, however, the total input effort, like $c_u t_u$, averaged over all requests, can be operationalized. The availability of reference workers could save the users some of this preparatory effort. This transfers costs from C_3 to C_2. A sophisticated computer program for query negotiation (Taylor, 1968) could also cut down $c_u t_u$, hence C_3, at the expense of an increase in C_1.

A similar tradeoff exists at the output end. The total effort that users have to expend in utilizing the response of an IR system can be diminished if more effort is expended in suitably preparing and presenting this response. Finally, more effort expended on indexing documents when they enter the system may decrease the effort required from users, reference workers, and computers at the time a request is processed. Let, as above, the terms denote the following:

t_1 Time per document spent by an indexer at rate c_{22}.

t_2 Time per document spent by a computer at rate c_{1C} in updating.

t_u Time spent by a user at rate c_u in preparing a request and interpreting or supplementing the output.

t_3 Time spent by a reference worker at rate c_{21} in helping with a request.

t_c Time spent by the computer at rate c_{1C} in processing a request.

The cost per request is thus $[(t_1 c_{22} + t_2 c_{1C})D'] / L + t_u c_u + t_3 c_{21} + t_c c_{1C}$. It may be possible to find an optimal mix $(t_1, t_2, t_3, t_u, t_c)$ which minimizes this cost and satisfies constraints on total time and quality.

7.4   TYPES OF IR SYSTEMS

Figure 7.3 gives an overall view of some of the major services which fall under *information retrieval*, broadly interpreted. They are classified according to a mixture of criteria. The most commonly provided service, retrospective searching, is subdivided according to the urgency of the request. Note that we do not distinguish between literature-search and question-answering; when answers are urgently needed, the questioner does not care whether he gets it directly or by first getting a document surrogate and then finding the answer in the document. He does care that the answer is valid or documented, even in an urgent crisis.

The most common kind of service now supplied is IA. This corresponds to class US1.1 of Section 5.4. The most prevalent kind of IR system supplying this service is the author-and-title catalog of a library. Because library users tend to recall titles with greater precision than they recall authors' names (Tagliacozzo and Kochen, 1970), the title catalog has greater potential effectiveness than the author catalog. Ironically, fewer known-item searchers use the title catalog than use the author catalog. Occasionally, the subject catalog is also used in known-item searches. For example, to locate *The Fabricated Man*, which deals with the ethics of genetic control, a user might try such subject-headings as "eugenics" and "cloning." Because there may be many books under "eugenics," and quite a few under the author's name, Paul Ramsey, of which the user may not be too sure (and most likely not recall it completely), his best strategy is to search the card catalog for the title, under "Fabricated."

If the user needs the exact citation to *The Fabricated Man* for use in a bibliography he is preparing for publication while in the midst of this, it hardly pays him to make the trip to the nearest library catalog, unless he can batch this request with all the others that make an errand to the library worthwhile. It is not merely the transit time between his work-place and the library that may be a cost, but also the possibly unwelcome disruption of his work schedule and the continuity of his thought. He should have the option of calling his request to the library, having a reference worker (or a computer) search the catalog for him while he waits on the telephone line, and supply the answer. Even if the respondent at the other end calls back—as much as 24 hours later—it would seem effective.

Some university libraries—for example, the University of Michigan Library—provide such a service to the faculty. Some public libraries—for example, the Detroit Public Library—have portable telephones that can be plugged into ports

TYPE OF SERVICE	TYPICAL REQUESTS	DESIRED RESPONSE
I Retrospective Searching		
A. Known-Item Search	I would like The Fabricated Man; What is π to 10 decimals?	Produce book; give number
B. 24 - 250-hour search	Produce an annotated bibliography on the effect of radiation on the production of cancer in mice; of patents on lasers in microscopy; what measurements of the speed of light are reported	List of titles & authors; patent numbers; table of numbers
C. ½ - 24-hour search	Has the N.Y. Times ever reported a meeting between Messrs A & B	News clippings or summaries
D. $1/_{10}$ - ½-hour search	Has Mr. A previous arrest record	Direct answer; display of record
E. 10 Sec. to 6 minutes	Antidote to Cobalt Poisoning	How to get it in a hurry
F. Less than 10 seconds	Response from an on-line machine, e.g. telephone, computer, TV	Some acknowledgment signal
II Current Awareness		
A. Standing Request, Monthly - Annual	Abstracts of all new publications on X, at most 1 year after they came out; Names of all people hired or dismissed by gv't. of X.	List of Abstracts Names.
B. Standing Request, Daily - Weekly	Citations of all articles which cited one or more articles on a target list; Values of monitored social or economic indicators; Stocks; weather	Bibliography Tables of data.
C. Standing Request for unique event, in less than a minute after detection	Heartbeat of patients in intensive care; attacking enemy missiles	Warning signal
D. On-demand Request for unique event, in less than an hour after request	Missing person alarm; lost passport	Report
III Bibliographic & Editorial Control	"Is The Fabricated Man by Paul Ramsey in this collection, and where is it?"	Yes/No; call number
IV Tutorial - Orientation	I am an engineer concerned with coding messages for transmission I would like to learn what is now known about the 4-color conjecture as it might connect with coding theory that might help me design better codes	Directory to hierarchical network of tutorial passages, which provides orientation.
V Aid to Research	If the average rainfall in China is unknown, how can I infer it from something that is known?	Advice of a consultant, suggestion of what variables, data to search for.

Figure 7.3. A classification of IR systems.

in the catalog room for such a service. Computerized systems, such as that at Ohio State University, allow for on-line search of the card catalog. The costs of a computerized system or of enough full-time telephone reference workers to handle the load is considerable, and whether the benefits are sufficient to offset them is an open question.

An alternative to remote access to catalogs over communication channels is to disperse copies of the main catalog into branch libraries or into further decentralized units. A microform copy of the entire catalog in "book" form together with a microfilm reader could be purchased by each potential user, perhaps at an initial cost of $100 plus $5 per year for annual replacements of the updated catalog copy. Considerable effort (and initial cost) is, however, required to produce an original "book" form acceptable version of a sizable catalog suitable for making microform copies.

Another kind of IR system for known-item searching is the permuted title index. *The Fabricated Man* would be found twice if "the" is stripped off: under "Fabricated" and under "Man." Such an index to a million titles with five index words per title on the average would have five million entries. If each entry takes a line—the title plus an identification number—and each page is 50 lines, then this would take a book of 100,000 pages or 500 volumes. Quite probably, there will be several pages with the main entry "Man" and several pages with "Fabricated." In addition, the complete citation corresponding to the item with the appropriate identification number must also be looked up in a set of about 12 volumes. For such sizes, a printed permuted title index does not seem effective relative to its cost. A much more cost-effective alternative is a computer-stored list of titles. Permuting them helps little, since it is easy to use editing programs to search a list of titles for specified words wherever they occur in the title.

For retrospective subject searching in indexable fields, there are numerous IR systems. There appears to be a market for systems that search for statutes and cases, with law firms willing to pay $200,000/year for appropriate services. One of the oldest systems, which is in principle the permuted title idea applied to all sentences in a text, is the use of a concordance. If the full text of each document in a large data base can be computer-stored and searched for the presence of any specified word to print, within a few seconds, all sentences containing that word, this would be an effective system. It may not be efficient.

Consider a data base of texts with N word-tokens. The 200 or so most frequently occurring word-types (for example, "the," "a," "of," . . .) account for about half the N words. To account for the other half of the N word-tokens (occurrences), we can enumerate n different word-types, $n < N$, each of which is a possible query term. Let m be the average number of words per sentence or passage to be retrieved. Then there are N/m such passages.

A concordance-based IR system stores a table which has all the n words in alphabetic order, listing next to each the identification numbers for all passages which contain that word. If we consider it very improbable that one of the n words would be repeated very often in the same passage (plausible for m small). then we expect about N/n passages to be posted per word, on the average. A computer store that can be randomly and rapidly accessed should store $n(b_w + (N/n) b_p)$ bits, where b_w is the number of bits to store a word and b_p is the number to store a passage identification number. If the average word has 10 characters, and a code of 8 bits per character is used, then $b_w = 80$. If each passage identification number is to identify a passage uniquely, then b_p must be at least $\log_2 N/n$, with some extra check bits to detect and correct errors. To use the system, a listing of the full text next to each passage identification number must be stored for serial printout after a whole batch of searches has amassed.

Random-access storage is more costly (say c_{ra} \$/bit/hour) than serial access storage (c_{sa} \$/bit/hour). From the viewpoint of storage alone, the cost of storing the full text in a random-access store is $Nb_w c_{ra}$ \$/hour. For a concordance, it is $n(b_w + (N/n)b_p)c_{ra} + (Nb_w + (N/n)b_p)c_{sa}$ or whichever is less, if $nc_{ra} + Nc_{sa} < Nc_{ra}$ and $(N/n)b_p(c_{ra} + c_{sa})$ is a small part of the total cost.

The ratio n/N is the type-token ratio, and characterizes the language of the data base in its statistical aspects. In text with a very varied vocabulary, such as James Joyce's *Ulysses*, it is close to 1. It is low if a few words are used over and over. For a text with varied, rich vocabulary, $(N/n)b_p(c_{ra} + c_{sa})$ is a modest number compared with $nc_{ra} + Nc_{sa}$. The cost of storing a concordance is therefore less than the cost of storing the full text for random access if $n/N + c_{sa}/c_{ra} < 1$. As long as random-access storage is *much* more costly than serial storage, this may be satisfied.

A great variety of devices for vocabulary control have been proposed and tried. They have been thoroughly discussed (Lancaster, 1972). It has been shown that effectiveness depends greatly on the specificity and ambiguity of the index terms. It is the most important determinant of acceptance rate: if a query uses a very specific, unambiguous term, such as Zinc–Arsenic, and this matches an index term, it is very unlikely that a search would retrieve many irrelevant documents. "For maximum effectiveness, a controlled vocabulary must be carefully tailored to the requirements of a particular organization or user community" (Lancaster, 1972, p. 224).

Systems differ by the extent to which their list of index terms is supplemented by a thesaurus, a cross-reference structure, or something equivalent. Whether these differences bear significantly on effectiveness and efficiency is not yet clearly understood. It is clear, however, that a system for use by industrial chemists or the pharmaceutical industry with precise and specific index terms, such as the names of compounds, their synonyms, and the names of compound classes, differs from a subject catalog in a library. Whether or not the chemistry system differs fundamentally from a biographic file in which the index terms are primarily proper names (with a few aliases) is difficult to determine.

A thesaurus for a chemical or pharmaceutical data base is easier to construct than one for a biographic data base, because these are well-structured fields. But the expert user of a chemistry data base hardly needs a map to orient him, while the user of a biographic data base does.

Direct question-answering services in indexable fields use systems of the above types. The unit that is stored is frequently a documented proposition, sentence, or datum, in place of a full-text document. In formatted files, each data entry can be interpreted as a sentence. To be able to retrieve the value of π to ten decimals, it is necessary to first locate a table or record labeled "π," and the total record is equivalent to the sentence "The value of π is approximately 3.1415925636." Question-answering systems differ primarily in the representation of their data base, the way the stored data is structured for ready access and updating, and the associated inference techniques.

In Sections 7.2 and 7.3 twelve variables characterizing the performance of an IR system were listed. If the values of each of these variables were considered to be high, medium, or low, then 3^{12} or over a billion IR system-types would be possible. In Figure 7.4 we chart just seven IR system-types, according to such a breakdown of the 12 variables.

Note that six of the variables, above the dark line, represent assets: high values are preferred to low. The six variables below the line are costs: low values are preferred, except perhaps for load. Some other points are noteworthy, indicated by notes in the figure.

Suppose a person had to cope with the problem of finding a job. He wants to use an IR system for getting an answer to the specific question: "What was the median salary in 1972 of a computer programmer with a B.S. and 10 years of experience in industry?" This is a well-defined question in a mechanizable topic. If a question-answering system with a data base of salaries existed and could present him with a number, this would be preferable to a literature-search system which gave him leads to published statistics. A directory system, which forced him to delve into all kinds of qualifications—B.S. in what?, experience in what industry?, what computers?, what kind of programming?—would not be useful for the precise question of the user.

Had the same user asked, "What kinds of jobs are available for a person with a B.S. in electrical engineering and 10 years of programming and supervisory experience in the accounting department of an automobile manufacturing company?", a directory system might have been most effective. Had he asked about opportunities for professional growth as a computer scientist, about the intellectual environment, and the productivity of professional colleagues at a particular organization he is considering to join, then a literature-search system, giving him references to publications by people who work in that industry, might be most helpful.

	Journal System Data Base is all articles Access by Indexes	Report System No refereeing; Limited circulation	Books + catalogs	Current Awareness Systems e.g. Current Contents	Retrosp. Search System e.g. Medlars	Quest-Ans. Service e.g. New York Times	Orienting Directory e.g. Yellow Pages or I & R Center
u : How valuable is the average response to user?	Medium–High; quality varies greatly	High[a] for those with need to know	Med–High	Med–High	Med–High	Med–High	High
t : How quickly are needs attended to?	Medium (trip to library or own collection)	High	Low	Irrelev. (High where relev.)	Medium	High	High
b : How complete is Data Base?	Medium (Many refs. to book)	Low	Medium	High	High	Med–High	Medium
r : How up-to-date is Data Base?	Too low for science, e.g.	High	Low	High	Medium	High	Low
f : How many of its requests does it match?	Too low	High	Medium	High	Medium	Med–High	Medium
p : How many potential users does it reach?	Medium	Too low	Med–High[b]	Medium[c]	Medium	Medium	Low–Med
L : Does it get many requests/ hour?	Low	Low	Low–Med	(Nr. of users) Medium	Medium	High	Medium
How fast does data base grow?	High	High	High	High	High	High	Medium
Size of data base	High	High	High	High	High	High	Medium
Amt. of preparatory effort required of the user	High	High	Med–High	Med–High	Med–High	Low	Low
Judgment and effort expected of user	Med–High	High	Medium	Med–High	Med–High	Low	Low
Amt. of preparatory effort required of the system	High	Med–High	High	High	High	Med–High	Medium

Figure 7.4. Comparison of IR system types. Notes: [a]Since readers of reports do their own critical reviewing, we rated their judgment and effort higher than users of the journal system. Journals usually have a fixed circulation, while reports have smaller distribution or are supplied on demand. [b]Openly marketed books reach a wide readership. [c]All seven systems try to extend their reach by advertising—books most, reports least. Report distributors seek out those most likely to benefit. Book distributors rely on potential users to seek them out.

How helpful? One article uncovered by the literature search might just inspire the job-seeker to such an extent that, in his enthusiasm, he makes up his mind to accept a job offer from the employer of that article's author. This is unusual, but possible. The literature-search system will have contributed enormously to help him make a decision, to cope with his job-seeking problem. (We could have reversed the problem to one of a recruiter having to decide on a potential applicant on the basis of his publications.) The answer to the precise question is far less likely to have helped the job-seeker. Perhaps, while settling on a salary when a job offer is being negotiated, knowledge of salary distribution in that organization can help the applicant. The directory system is most likely to lead the user into experiences which "click" with him to help him cope.

7.5 SECULAR TRENDS

Trends in some of the key variables describing the institutional environment of IR systems have already been noted. The number of users, and with that, the number of documents and topics, continues to grow, though not as fast in advanced countries as it has in the past. Growth in these variables should originate from developing countries, such as China. Insofar as the gap in average per capita income between developed and developing countries may continue to increase, IR system users may increasingly belong to an elite, to the world's "informationally privileged." IR systems will be maintained only as long as they have their users' support because they meet their informational needs, or supply demand, whether recognized by the users themselves or by their government.

A countertrend—information for the community—may be appearing, at least in the U.S. It is evidenced by the burgeoning of thousands of *information and referral (I&R) centers* to serve the needs of the poor, the alienated, and the disadvantaged (Kochen and Donohue, 1974). Though this is very significant, it is a local U.S. phenomenon. Its support stems from the current American commitment to correcting inequities and injustices in the distribution of privilege and opportunity among its citizens. American taxpayers, through such government programs as the Model Cities' projects, are funding some information and referral centers to serve the population of a model cities community, who are often poorer blacks, with a high unemployment rate, disrupted families, and low educational level. Other I&R centers are staffed by altruistically motivated volunteers. To what extent the users' real needs are being met by such services is an open question. Support seems to be accumulating for the hypothesis that people with middle-class backgrounds are most likely to benefit from the services of an IR system.

The number of agencies established in any sizable U.S. community to meet an untold number of needs is far beyond what most people realize. The middle-class citizen is not only aware of these but knows how to orient himself, which to utilize when. Directories are of greatest benefit to him, though they ought to be of greatest benefit to the less advantaged citizens. Many of the latter do not, however, have the motivation, the attitudes, or the habits of seeking information or even considering to become consumers of information services.

In the rest of the world, the less privileged do not even have the option of becoming consumers of information if they wanted to. The key to major change is education. In the foreseeable future, education and information services for the less privileged will be directed by national governments. These aim at nationalistic goals more frequently than at humanitarian ones. The key factor in the success of an information service is the choice of people who design and deliver it. As always, these people are accountable to those who keep them in their positions (sometimes only to themselves). A fundamentally political process underlies this.

As the advances in technology make our world more complex, the problems we face tend more to be ill-structured rather than well-defined. High-speed and high-throughput transportation systems generate numerous problems that did not exist in simpler transportation systems, and many of these are complex systems problems, organizational and psychological. Though many more decisions can now be analyzed with the help of operations research and decision theory than was possible three decades ago, many more decisions that people were not faced with three decades ago cannot be so analyzed. Consider only the command and control systems in modern international defense establishments. If an automatic early warning system indicates that missiles are heading toward certain targets, with the possibility that it is a surprise attack, then there are only minutes left to decide if this is a false alarm or a genuine attack. An error of omission—failing to recognize the imminence of an attack—can have disastrous consequences. An error of commission—mistaking a false alarm for a real attack—can also have serious consequences. Payoff matrices can be set up and probabilities estimated, drawing on all the best information in an IR system. A decision has to be made within minutes. To be sure, some aspects of the decisions could be computed with more thoroughness, reliability, and speed than by a human, using programs whose designer very carefully thought through, in advance, every contingency that could be anticipated. Nonetheless, the decision-maker is under pressure from other people. He is conscious that even the best computer program may be imperfect and that he is ultimately responsible.

While there is increasing demand for directory-type systems to help people cope with ill-structured problems, it is not yet being met. A significant trend toward serious concern with alternative futures, with the application of science and technology to planning, appears to be starting. The Club of Rome and increasingly numerous enterprises like it are actively concerned with world problems. There are now at least three information-network indexes on world problems, which might indicate a start in the direction of directory systems. The *Yearbook on World Problems and Human Development*, for example, is to be a

" 'mapping' operation. . .knowledge of areas. . .for future efforts to result in maximal benefit." It is to appear in January 1974 as the result of a collaborative, computer-based effort by Mankind 2000 and the Union on International Associations.

Research in the computer sciences and more particularly in artificial intelligence is progressing toward maturity, and question-answering systems as aids to research are already a practical possibility. Decreasing costs of computer memories and processors, combined with increasing costs of human labor, will increase the demand for such systems.

Perhaps the most important trend affecting literature-search systems is the increasing availability of documents in computer-processable form. This could have a significant effect on the development of citation indexing, which is perhaps the most effective type of IR system.

7.6 DESIGN PRINCIPLES

The overriding principle underlying any IR system, whether evolved by nature or designed by us, is that it be governed by the laws of the host organization it is to serve. Only then will it be viable. In our discussion so far, the embedding host has been a system for the organization of knowledge that exists to help people recognize and cope with an increasing variety of problems. The laws of that host pertain to conditions under which the growth of knowledge remained normal and functional, so that it helps people cope at least as well as they did before.

Some of these laws, as discussed in Chapters Two through Six, will now be applied in specifying rules for choosing or building IR systems. In the preceding sections of this chapter we described variables and parameters specifying IR systems. This implied a vast number of possible IR systems. These are to be matched with an equally vast number of user classes and topic classes. This makes it unfeasible to list specific rules for each kind of IR system. What follows, therefore, is a list of general statements that apply to most of them. These statements summarize the experience of designers, operators, and users of viable (and nonviable) IR systems to help designers and users.

1. Specify the user class to be served. Distinguish between direct users and beneficiaries. For example, a person looking for records pertinent to his estate for purposes of making a will is the direct user, but the heirs are the beneficiaries. If there is more than one user or beneficiary class for the same IR system, assign and announce clear-cut priorities, on the basis of matching the characteristics of the system with those of the user class. For example, if the IR system gives a rapid response (rates high in t, row 2 of Figure 7.4) and one of the user groups is impatient (row 4 of

Table 5.2), give them priority on the fast system. Assigning these priorities often involves moral and ethical judgments, such as the degree of attention given to a document of greater value to beneficiaries than to direct clients. It also involves balancing difficult tradeoffs, where the individual values of the system's policy-makers provide the weights assigned to conflicting variables.

2. Specify the uses and problem-classes for which the system is intended, and allocate priorities over these. The five use-classes of Section 5.4 should be first grossly matched against the system types of Figure 7.3. Thus for checking whether a solution to a given problem-statement already exists (user-class US1), a system of Class I in Figure 7.3 is indicated. Then a second discrimination can be made. Topics classified into mechanizable, indexable, or explorable can be matched with IR systems that are primarily based on question-answering, catalogs or indexes, or directories, respectively. A finer discrimination yet can be made by deciding on what mix of problem-classes $A-N$ of Table 5.1 the system will respond to, and selecting from Figure 5.1 one (or a mix) of the seven IR systems, IS1–IS7, that fits best. For example, for a system which aims to service best the problems of class E (ill-structured), system IS4 is best. The salient characteristics of such a system are (a) it should stimulate its user to ask significant questions he would not have asked without the help of the system, to shift his representation of his problem; (b) it helps him become more aware of how his problem relates to other problems, of alternative solutions, and of the consequences of various possible decisions; and (c) it directs him to special aids in coping with unsolvable problems.

3. Specify the documents necessary to help users in the selected class cope with problems of the selected class. This includes documents that indicate the consequences resulting from various decisions likely to be made by users. It includes documents necessary to reduce the risk in predicting the consequences. If the problem-class for which the system is intended is an indexable field, then documents can be collected by matching their profiles (set of index terms) against the profiles of the topics to be covered. Citation indexes would be excellent devices to both specify and build a data base.

4. In specifying the forms for collecting data for the data base (which may contain both documents and recorded data) state clearly, for each data element, who is to use it, for what purpose, and how. Make sure that direct users concur with this specification if they did not participate in drafting it. If the same data element has multiple uses, identify possible conflicts and assign priorities. This applies more to recorded data than to documents in the technical sense in which we defined them. It applies to

bibliography, too, however. It is wise to ask for each data element on a new record form corresponding to a catalog card, for example, who is to use it, for what, and how. Decisions about which data elements to include are then based on a judgment of importance and frequencies of these uses.

5. Provide for cross-validating and checking all inputs to the data base. This means specifying who can update the data base and with what criteria. Only documented items should be admitted. Screening for well-formedness, relevance, validity, and authenticity can be partially accomplished by independent judgments from several reliable sources. Significance of an item cannot easily be screened for, because it depends on its relation to many other items, and its novelty depends on its relation to specific users. What is novel to one user-group may not be to another.

6. Make it cost-effective to test, restructure, and edit the data base for significance (utility), relevance, validity, well-formedness, and redundancy, periodically or when a flaw occasions it. Items which have not served in producing useful and significant responses for a long time should perhaps be weeded out. Nonauthentic items that passed screening during input may be detected later. Irrelevant and unnecessarily redundant items will, in time, appear as such and should sometimes be weeded out. This is especially important for a directory to, say, service agencies, where the values of such recorded data elements as telephone numbers and addresses change often. Weeding is one of the costliest, least studied operations on a data base. Because of its great importance, it should be designed into an IR system.

7. Be sure to provide for means of controlling with checks and balances who can use the system and how. The question of who has access to what files is a legal, ethical, political question more than it is a technical one. In (5), to keep the data base unpolluted by undocumented items, we suggested disallowing all but the most reliable sources from contributing to it. But this raises the question of who judges source reliability. The patient with data about the quality of a doctor's services may be considered an unreliable source, but he is often the only source. Similar, independent reports from several patients increases the reliability of each source.† A counterpart of this problem occurs in trading the cost of erroneously denying someone access to certain files when he should have

---

†This suggests an interesting mathematical model analogous to models for how a reliable device can be designed with less reliable components (Kochen, 1959; Moore and Shannon, 1956; von Neumann, 1956).

it against the cost of erroneously permitting someone access to a file that he should be denied. The system policy-maker must judge this tradeoff by his values and explicitly make the needed decisions.

8. Users of the system should participate in planning it. This is particularly the case for policy-decisions. In case of conflicting interests or values, attempts should be made to seek that common ground on which there is agreement. Differences should be stated explicitly and de-emphasized. Conflicts should be resolved by negotiations toward agreement on the common grounds rather than by adversary proceedings, confrontations, or advocacy. If insufficient common ground exists or negotiations fail, separate IR systems should be allocated to the largest user groups which meet this condition.

9. If users, uses, and needed documents can be a priori specified with little uncertainty and considerable precision and accuracy, and if they are not likely to change over the life of the system, then as many design decisions as possible should be made at the outset. A special-purpose dedicated IR system may be best. But such certainty rarely exists. The price of uncertainty is the cost of greater flexibility, of a more general-purpose system that can be adjusted as the requirements become better known. If patterns of future use fluctuate randomly or if the IR system has to cater to user groups with diverse use patterns, then the data structures, algorithms for updating and search, and formats and languages in which to accept inputs and present outputs must also be flexible so that the system can adapt as patterns of use converge or so that it can be readily adjusted. In particular, procedures for packaging items should allow considerable flexibility, and zooming up and down levels in a directory is most helpful in orienting users in explorable fields.

10. Most policy decisions and rules governing the use of an IR system should be stated explicitly and in such precise operational terms that it requires a minimum of interpretation to ascertain whether a user has violated a rule or not. Designed into the system should be procedures for enforcing those rules with close to 100% consistency. These include most of the decisions called for in (1)–(9). Such questions as the planned or expected life of the IR system are perhaps best settled by implicit rather than explicit decisions.

Reaching any of the above decisions requires numerous trades, many of which were already mentioned. If the trade between recall and precision warrants the status, as Ziman suggested, of the (first) law of information science, then no IR system can expect to get around it. Design decisions must take it into account. If maintaining a proper balance between users who use and who add to

MECHANIZABLE FIELDS ← INDEXABLE FIELDS → EXPLORABLE FIELDS

Problem or use Classes / User Class	US1 - Checking (see Sec. 5.4) US1.1 knows sol'n exists (F,N see Table 5.1)	US1.2 not sure sol'n exists (F,N)	US2-Search for Analysis US2.1 seen before (F,N)	US2.2 not seen before (F)	US3 - Seeks knowledge & methods (F,K,L,M)	US4-Needs help with analysis (F,I,J)	US5-Calls for shift; needs, understanding (F,G,H)	US6-Ill-defined needs, understanding (C,E)	US7-Unrecognized, non-problems (A,B,D)
Specialist who adds to-	IA (see Table 7.3)	IB	IB	IB,IIB	IB,IIB	V	II,A,V	IV	II,A,B
Specialist who adds to- but switched fields	IA	IB,IV	IB,IV	IIB,IB,IV	IIB,IV	IV,V	IIA,IV,V	IV	IV,IIA,B
Generalist who adds to- or Librarian	IA,III	IB,III	IB,IV	IIB,IB,IV	IIB,IV,III	IV,V, Consult.	IIA,IV,V, Consult.	IV, Consult.	IV,IIA,B
Staff problem-solver, professional who is expert user.	IA	IC,ID	ID	IC,IIB	IC,IIB	IV,V, Consult.	IV,V,IIA Consult.	IV, Consult.	II,IIA,B
Professional Novice user	IA	IC	ID,IV	IC,IIB,IV	IC,IIB,IV	IV,V, Consult.	IV,V,IIA Consult.	IV, Consult.	IV,IIA,B
Top Executive or Aide	IA	IE,IIC	IE,IV	IE,IIC,IV	IE,IIC,IV	IV,V, Consult.	IV,V,IIE Consult.	IV Consult.	IV,IIC
Middle-level manager or Aide	IA	IE,IIB	IE,IV	ID,IIB,IV	ID,IIB,IV	IV,V, Consult.	IV,V,IID Consult.	IV, Consult.	IV,IIC
Automated intelligence Early Warning Decision-Aids	IA	IF,IID	IF	IF,IID	IF,IID	V (automated)	V (Autom.)	-	IID

Figure 7.5. Illustrating a way of matching IR systems with user classes and use classes. Each column denotes one of the user classes A – N from Table 5.1. The prevalence of tutorial IR systems (Type IV) suggests an important direction for the development of future IR systems.

knowledge is another (the second) law of information science, then IR systems
that contribute to upsetting this balance have their own obsolescence built in. IR
systems grafted to nonfunctional or decaying organizations at best prolong their
life when the same resources might better have been invested in embedding the
IR system in viable, functional organizations and letting the others die gracefully
and naturally. If the pervasive appearance of skew, long-tailed distributions is a
third law of information science, taking them into account has very important
implications for the above design decisions. Designing for average or peak performance, as suggested in much of the above, has its dangers. But very little is as
yet known about the mathematical statistics, the engineering, or the analysis of
natural phenomena where such skew distributions appear.

An impressive body of data about human memory has, however, accumulated. The design of IR systems should certainly take into account what is
known about how its users remember. The IR systems users carry in their minds
should in some sense be matched with the IR systems created by designers.

Psychologists have classified human memory according to what is to be remembered: images, sentences, skill performances, emotional responses. They
view the memorization process to consist of three stages: (1) registration and
trace formation, (2) trace retention, (3) trace retrieval in response to cues. How
people understand sentences is most relevant for our purpose.

According to G. Bower (Sigma Xi Lecture at Stanford University, February
14, 1974), the following findings favor a model in which a sentence comprehender hypothesizes a speaker's intention and then brings his conceptual rules
and his world knowledge to bear. The findings contradict a model of a comprehension based on syntactic analysis of a sentence.

1. We (people, users of IR systems) tend to remember the gist rather than the
   words or structure of a sentence.
2. We use our world knowledge to fill in normative consequences. If told that
   "John fell out of a boat," we may remember that John got wet.
3. We tend to particularize. Hearing that "the container held apples," we may
   remember that the *basket* held apples.
4. On hearing interrelated sentences, we tend to integrate them into a model or
   coherent overall picture, and lose the details we heard.
5. We tend to react to conveyed rather than to literal meaning. Thus a speaker
   who hears "there are people sitting on the floor" may accept it as a compli-
   ment. The janitor may hear it as an order to get more chairs.
6. We find it more difficult to remember sentences we do not understand.

Chapter Eight

Problems and Issues

In this chapter we present a sample problem of interest in designing some specific aspects of an IR system. The purpose of this exercise is to show how further mathematical analysis of some of the concepts in the preceding chapters leads to interesting and useful results.

We choose the recall–precision tradeoff because of its centrality in information retrieval theory.

We also discuss some of the major issues related to the design and use of IR systems.

8.1. RECALL VERSUS PRECISION

Consider a model for an IR system with the following variables:

D	Number of documents in its data base.
P	Probability that a randomly chosen document is relevant to a given request, expressed as a conjunction of m index terms.
m	Number of index terms, $w_1, \ldots, w_m$.
M	Number of words in each of the D documents.
r_i	Rank of the ith of the m words in the request, according to a ranking of words by frequency of use, $i = 1, \ldots, m$.
$c(w_1, \ldots, w_m)$	Conditional probability that $w_1, \ldots, w_m$ are all in randomly chosen word-positions of a randomly chosen document, given that it is relevant.
$c'(w_1, \ldots, w_m)$	Condition of probability that a randomly chosen document contains $w_1, \ldots, w_m$ in randomly chosen word-positions, given that it is judged irrelevant.

We wish to derive expressions for recall and precision rates and to show how they are related. This is related to the analyses in Sections 4.5 and 7.2. We prefer to replace the terms recall and precision ratios by hit- and acceptance-rate, to keep in mind the relation to signal detection theory (Swets, 1963). The simplest way to define these is to use the following contingency table. The hit-rate h is the fraction of all relevant documents which are retrieved. The acceptance-rate a is the fraction of all the retrieved documents which are relevant.

$$h = \frac{\text{Expected number of hits}}{\text{Expected number of hits} + \text{Expected number of misses}}$$

$$a = \frac{\text{Expected number of hits}}{\text{Expected number of hits} + \text{Expected number of trashes}}$$

	Retrieved	Not retrieved
Relevant	Hit	Miss
Irrelevant	Trash	Pass

For an ideal IR system, both $h = 1$ and $a = 1$. Empirical evidence suggests that a and h cannot both be 1. The point of this section is to show some theoretical considerations why very high (close to 1) a results in very low h and vice versa. If large h is gained at the expense of a, then cost-effectiveness considerations can provide some guidance about how to trade one for the other. It is probably more important for h to be near 1 than for a to be near 1. This means that many users would prefer not missing any relevant documents to assurance that all the documents they receive are relevant. Users may tolerate an error of commission, which forces them to judge a document they receive from the IR system irrelevant and to ignore or discard it. They may be less tolerant of an error of omission, if they know that such an error had been committed.

We make the following assumptions in this model:

1. Word w_i is specified by its rank r_i according to decreasing use frequency, given by $f(r_i) = [1/\zeta(1 + \alpha)]r^{-(1+\alpha)}$, where ζ is the Riemann Zeta function.

To simplify notation, we let Z denote $\zeta(1 + \alpha)$ from now on. Though there is a great deal written about this function in the mathematical literature, only its name is used here. It arises as a normalizing coefficient for this Zipf–Bradford distribution, to make $\sum_{i=1}^{\infty} f(r_i)$ equal to 1. All the reader needs to know about it is that for most English text, α lies between 0.1 and 0.6, and $Z(1 + \alpha)$ is approximately $1/\alpha$ and $f(r) \doteq \alpha r^{-(1+\alpha)}$.

This assumption is widely supported by data. It asserts that the most frequently used word, "the" in English, accounts for about 10% of all the word-tokens in a text. If $f(r) = 0.1r^{-1.1}$, then, very approximately, $f(2) = 0.05$. That is, the word that is the second most frequently used accounts for the next 5% of all the words in a text. (This approximation is quite poor when the parameter is as small as 0.1.) The original form of "Zipf's law" was $f(r) = K/r$, as if the parameter were 0.

2. A document is retrieved only if it contains each of the words $w_1, \ldots, w_m$.

Thus if a user wishes to retrieve all documents reporting the lattice parameters of Zinc–Arsenic, then m could be 4, and he asks for all documents which contain *each* of the following four words: $w_1 = $ Zinc, $w_2 = $ Arsenic, $w_3 = $ lattice, and $w_4 = $ parameters.

3. The occurrences of $w_1, \ldots, w_m$ in one document are statistically independent.

4. $c'(w_1) = Ar_1^{-(1+\alpha)} \exp -r_1/R,^\dagger$ where r_1 is the rank of word w_1 and A and R are constants, and $\sum_{r=1}^{\infty} c'(r) = 1$, where $c'(r) = c'(w_1)$ and $r = r_1$.

We now derive* expressions for h and a in terms of p, m, M, α, R. Using only assumption (2), it follows that

$$h = C \quad \text{and} \quad a = \frac{Cp}{Cp + C'(1-p)} \tag{8.1}$$

where C and C' correspond to c and c' except that they refer to the event of $w_1, \ldots, w_m$ all being *somewhere* in the document.

The equation $h = C$ stated that the fraction of all relevant documents which are retrieved in response to a query is equal to the probability that a relevant document will contain somewhere in its text each of the words in that query.

To prove the second equation, note that the expected number of hits is D times the joint probability that a randomly chosen document is both relevant and retrieved (contains $w_1, \ldots, w_m$). By assumption (2) this is CP. The probability that it is both irrelevant and retrieved is $C'(1 - P)$ for the same reason. Hence $D(CP + C'(1 - P))$ is the expected number of retrieved documents, and the result follows.

Let $m = 1$. The probability that word w_1 in a given query occurs in a particular but randomly chosen word-slot in a randomly chosen document is

---

†We have followed the standard convention where e^x is expressed as exp x.
*The nonmathematical reader may wish to skip to p. 163.

$c(w_1)p + (1 - P)c'(w_1)$. This must also be equal to $f(r_1)$, where r_1 is the rank of w_1 by assumption (1). We shall write $c(r_1, \ldots, r_m)$ in place of $c(w_1, \ldots, w_m)$ and set this equal to $\Pi^m_{i=1} c(r_i)$ by assumption (3). We do the same for c'.

From $(1/Z)r^{-(1+\alpha)} = c(r_1)P + (1 - P)c'(r_1)$ and assumption (4), it follows that

$$c(r_i) = \frac{r_i^{-(1+\alpha)}}{P}\left[\frac{1}{Z} - (1 - P)A \exp -\frac{r_i}{R}\right] \qquad i = 1, \ldots, m \qquad (8.2)$$

We now introduce one more assumption.

5. All the M word positions in a document can be occupied by w_1 with the same probability, and statistically independently.

It follows that

$$h = C = 1 - (1 - c)^M \qquad (8.3)$$

or

$$h = 1 - \left[1 - \frac{r_i^{-(1+\alpha)}}{P}\left(\frac{1}{Z} - (1 - P)A \exp -\frac{r_i}{R}\right)\right]^M \qquad i = 1, \ldots, m \qquad (8.4)$$

$$a = \frac{hP}{hP + (1 - P)\left[1 - \left(1 - Ar_i^{-(1+\alpha)} \exp -r_i/R\right)^M\right]} \qquad (8.5)$$

The constants R and A can be related by observing[†] that if w_1 is the most frequently used word (for example, "the"), then

$$r_1 = 1 \quad \text{and} \quad f(1) = \frac{1}{Z} \quad \text{and} \quad A \exp -\frac{1}{R} = \frac{1}{Z} \qquad (8.6)$$

For words of moderately high rank, c is small, and

$$h \doteq 1 - \exp -M(r_i^{-(1+\alpha)}/P)\left[1/Z - (1 - P)A \exp -\frac{r_i}{R}\right] \qquad (8.7)$$

[†]The most frequent word in English is "the." Only articles by linguists are likely to pertain to "the" as their subject matter. Hence c', the probability that the article contains "the" given that it is irrelevant to "the" is, plausibly, the same as the probability of "the" being used at all (in one word-position).

If r_i is very large, $\exp -r_i/R \doteq 0$ and $h \doteq 1 - \exp Mr_i^{-(1+\alpha)}/ZP$, which is close to 1 as long as $MR_i^{-(1+\alpha)}/ZP \gg 1$. When $r \gg (M/ZP)^{1/(1+\alpha)}$, h tends to 0. Typically, M may be about 10^4 words (word-tokens, positions), $1/Z = \alpha \doteq 1/3$, and $P \doteq 10^{-4}$, which makes $(M/ZP)^{1/(1+\alpha)} = (3 \times 10^8)^{3/4} \doteq 1 \cdot 7 \times 10^6$; there are hardly any words whose rank exceeds a million. The hit-rate becomes low only if there is probably a relevant document for a query with a very rarely used query term, which is plausible.

We can approximate a, when r_i is large, by noting that $C \doteq 1 - \exp(-MAr_i^{-(1+\alpha)} (\exp -r_i/R))$, which is close to 1 as long as $Mar_i^{-(1+\alpha)} \exp -r_i/R \gg 1$. This makes $a \doteq [hP/hP + (1-P)]$ or 1 for questions for which a relevant document is likely. When a word is so frequent—when its rank is so low—that $(\exp r_i/R) r_i^{(1+\alpha)} \ll MA$, then C' can drop to zero, and $a \doteq 1$. The acceptance rate drops if, for a question with a rarely used query term, the probability of a relevant document is low. Then $a \doteq hP/(hP + 1)$, for P small. That is just where the hit-rate h is high, indicating the tradeoff between a and h.

When the hit-rate is very low, the acceptance-rate is high, because we are searching for documents containing very rarely used topic words; the appearance of such rarely used words in a document is likely to make it relevant. Hence retrieving documents containing such a word is likely to produce few irrelevant documents. On the other hand, the probability of a *very* rarely used topic word even in a relevant document is low, because the author may not have known or thought of using the same word that the querist uses years later, or because there are more likely to be near-synonyms or circumlocutions for such rarely used words. Hence there will be many relevant documents that will be missed if only those containing the specified word in the query are retrieved.

Let us now proceed beyond the case $m = 1$.

$$h = 1 - \left[1 - \prod_{i=1}^{m} c(r_i)\right]^M = C$$

This is, approximately,

$$h \doteq 1 - \exp -M \prod_{i=1}^{m} r_i^{-(1+\alpha)}/PZ \left[1 - (1-P) ZA \exp -\frac{r_i}{R}\right] \tag{8.8}$$

$$= 1 - \exp -M(PZ)^{-m} \prod_{i=1}^{m} r_i^{-(1+\alpha)} \exp -(1-P)AZ \sum_{i=1}^{m} \exp -\frac{r_i}{R}$$

From (8.6) we have $AZ = \exp 1/R$. Call $\prod_{i=1} r_i = k(q)$, a characteristic of question q. To simplify the unwieldy expression (8.8), assume that

$\exp -(1-P)AZ \sum \exp r_i/R$ is close to 1, which is plausible if R is large or if the query terms are rare or if P is near 1. Then

$$h \doteq 1 - \exp -M (PZ)^{-m} k^{-(1+\alpha)} \qquad (8.9)$$

Suppose that all terms have rank exceeding r_0. Then $k > r_0^m$ and the exponent in (8.9) cannot exceed $M[r_0^{-(1+\alpha)} PZ]^{-m}$, and

$$h \leq 1 - \exp -M [r_0^{-(1+\alpha)} PZ]^m \qquad (8.10)$$

As m increases, the exponent goes to 0 because $r_0^{-(1+\alpha)}PZ < 1$, so that this upper bound on h decreases (toward 0). The hit-rate is less for queries with many terms in conjunction. This is so because it is less likely to find a document containing each of several specified words than one containing just a single word.

The acceptance rate is given by expression (8.1), into which we substitute $C' = 1 - [(1 - \Pi_{i=1}^m c'(r_i))]^M$, which is approximately

$$C' \doteq 1 - \exp\left(-MA^m k^{-(1+\alpha)}\left(\exp - \sum_{i=1}^m \frac{r_i}{R}\right)\right) \qquad (8.11)$$

Let $k'(q)$ be another characteristic of question q: $k' = \sum_{i=1}^m r_i$, where $r_1, \ldots, r_m$ are the ranks of all the words used in q. Let r_* be the rank of the rarest word in q. Then $k < r_*^m$ and $mr_0 < k' < mr_*$. To get an upper bound on C', note that the exponent cannot exceed $MA^m r_0^{-(1+\alpha)m} \exp - mr_0/R$. To get a lower bound on C', note that the exponent exceeds $MA^m r_*^{-(1+\alpha)m}\exp -mr_*/R$. We can thus bound a by

$$\frac{hP}{hP + (1-P)MA^m r_0^{-m(1+\alpha)} \exp - mr_0/R}$$

$$< a < \frac{hP}{hP + (1-P)MA^m r_*^{-m(1+\alpha)} \exp - mr_*/R} \qquad (8.12)$$

As m increases, $C' \to 0$ and $a \to 1$.

This accentuates the inverse relation between a and h.

Among the m words representing a question could be several words that are near-synonyms. If a user presents a query of three terms, and each term has n

near-synonyms, as determined by the thesaurus, then the data base of documents is searched for all those which contain each of these $m = 3n$ words. By analyses like the above, it can be estimated that if 30% of the relevant documents are missed by retrieving those containing a single word, the miss-rate $(1 -$ hit-rate) can be decreased to about $(0.3)^3$ or 2.7% if two near-synonyms are adjoined to that single word. In general, the use of near-synonyms in a conjunction increases hit-rate and decreases acceptance-rate. This still decreases as m increases, but for any m we can select a sufficiently large n that will make h as large as possible. Of course, the bigger m, the greater the smallest n required, and so many near-synonyms may not exist.

The assumption that the terms of a query in conjunction are statistically independent is unrealistic. Two terms such as "temperature" and "moon" are more likely to co-occur in a query than "temperature" and "theft." The assumption that near-synonyms occur in the same paper *independently* is even more unrealistic. The simplest way to drop the independence assumption is to stratify the subject-heading terms (and the documents). Assume that the probability of a relevant document containing two near-synonyms of rank r and r' is, instead of $C(r)C(r')$, a fixed number c_s. Suppose further that the probability of a relevant document containing at least one of the near-synonyms all chosen from the same set of $n + 1$ near-synonyms is also c_s. Thus we imagine our vocabulary of T words partitioned into $T/(n + 1)$ "clusters" of near-synonyms. For each such cluster there would be a different c_s, depending possibly on the rank r_{min} of the most frequently occurring synonym in it. In computing the hit-rate, we would now state that the probability that a word position of a randomly chosen relevant document contains at least one of the $n + 1$ near-synonyms is $c_s(r_{min})$ instead of as before. If all these clusters were equiprobable, then h would increase with n, decrease with T. That is, the greater the indexing vocabulary, the lower the hit-rate; the greater the maximum number of near-synonyms/term, the higher the hit-rate.

To compute acceptance-rate, let c_s' be similarly defined as the probability of an irrelevant document containing at least one of the $n + 1$ synonyms. Then

$$a = \frac{hP}{hP + (1 - P)\left[1 - (1 - c_s')\right] M}$$

with the linear approximation,

$$a = \frac{Mc_s P}{Mc_s P + (1 - P)Mc_s'} = \frac{1}{1 + \left[(1 - P)/P\right]c_s'/c_s}$$

To the extent to which the probability of a relevant document containing at least one of the $n + 1$ synonyms exceeds the corresponding probability for an irrelevant document, the closer the acceptance rate is to 1.

The $(n + 1)/T$ near-synonym clusters must, however, not be considered independent either. Suppose that these clusters, each designated by a most representative word, group themselves in such a way that terms such as "temperature" and "moon" are "closer" than "temperature" and "theft." We must examine such groupings and their theoretical structure more closely before we can begin to drop the assumption of independence among conjunction terms in a query.

8.2. ON IR SYSTEM DESIGN

Designing an IR system is largely an engineering problem. Like many other engineering problems, such as the design of aircraft, circuits, and chemical refineries, the design of an IR system involves problems of analysis and problems of synthesis. Synthesis or design proper, could be approached as an art rather than analytically. The major trend in engineering has been to subject to analysis many of the design features that were once achieved via art. This is not to say that design could or should be achieved entirely analytically, without art.

An objective of analyzing IR systems is to arrange a set of feasible IR systems in a partial ordering,[†] so that for any two which can be compared, we can say which is preferred. For example, if one IR system is both more effective and more efficient than another, it is preferable; if it is more effective but much less efficient, the two may not be comparable. Or else, for a given level of effectiveness, the efficiency of the most efficient feasible system may be determined. A human judge then examines how this maximum efficiency varies with effectiveness, and decides—by a political process—on an operating point. Such a partial ordering of the feasible system can help the designer.

In design, it is most important not to violate such basic principles as are understood. These are generally in the form of constraints. *It is our fundamental thesis that if an IR system is viable, it conforms with basic principles governing the processing of information in the host institution. If it violates these principles, it does not remain viable.* This is analogous to the design of a heart–lung machine, which must take into account constraints and limits on basic physiological variables.

[†]For some interesting analytical and empirical findings of this kind for SDI (selective dissemination of information) systems, see a recent Ph.D. dissertation by Carl M. Drott, of Drexel University, Philadelphia, in the Department of Industrial Engineering at the University of Michigan, 1973.

One of the key problems in the design of an IR system is specifying the job-slots that people should fill, then assigning appropriate people into these slots. This is, of course, a universal organizational problem. If the qualifications for each job slot can be accurately specified, and the qualifications of applicants can be reliably assessed, then the suitability of each applicant for each job can be arrayed as a matrix. This can be used to compute (the assignment problem) an assignment of applicants to jobs which maximize the total suitability score.

For certain IR services, however, qualifications for jobs can neither be clearly specified nor readily assessed. Consider, for example, a system to help users find psychiatric help. The counselor with the job of referring the client to someone most likely to match the client's need must, with some sensitivity, explore the client's need. In communication between counselor and client, *what* they say may not be as important as *how* they say it to bring out the need. Specifying the qualifications such a counselor should have might be phrased in such terms as "good interviewing skills," "psychoanalytically perceptive," and "sensitive in interpersonal relations," but this is hardly of the precision required to set up an assignment matrix.

The first problem of analysis is determination of feasibility. The precise definition of feasibility depends on the model used for specifying a class of IR systems. To take a simple example, we can model an IR system for an indexable field as consisting of:

N_1 Indexers, who take t_1 hours/document and earn c_{22} \$/hour.

N_2 Reference workers, who take t_3 hours/document and earn c_{21} \$/hour.

N_3 Other IR system personnel, who earn c_{23} \$/hour.

A computer facility with a random access capacity of K bits which costs c_{1C} \$/hour, and takes t_u hours/document for updating and t_c per request to help provide a response.

Other fixed capital, such as land, buildings, and equipment for storing, transporting, and displaying documents, amortized as c_{11} \$/hour.

The users should be treated as part of the system, and the quality of the data base should be specified as well. But this makes it too complex for utility as an example. The environment in which the IR system has to operate is specified by L requests per hour to be serviced and D' documents per hour to be indexed for updating the data base.

Several constraining relations may be known. For example, $t_1 = f_1(c_{22})$, $t_3 = f_3(c_{21})$, $c_{1C} = f_C(K, t_u t_c)$. This oversimplified model has 15 variables. Suppose that only L and D' are known. If the remaining 13 variables are to satisfy the above three constraints, only 10 variables can be chosen by the designer. But these, too, are related. For example, a plausible constraint is that $N_1 \geq D'/t_1$. If the number of indexers is less than what is required to clear the incoming documents to be indexed, then arrearages build up, and effective-ness (at least the recency aspect) decreases. Similarly, $N_2 > L/t_3$.

A feasible solution is any mix of the as-yet-unspecified variables which does not violate any of the constraints or necessary relations.

Another class of design problems involves optimization. The simplest ex-ample of that is finding a feasible solution which minimizes cost. In the above case, the total hourly cost (excluding the user) is $C = N_1 c_{22} + N_2 c_{21} + N_3 c_{23} + c_{1C} + c_{11}$. Suppose we let $N_1 = D'/t_1$ and $N_2 = L/t_3$. Then

$$C = c_{22} D'/f_1(c_{22}) + c_{21} L/f_3(c_{21}) + N_3 c_{23} + f_c(K, t_u, t_c) + c_{11}$$

Suppose further that N_3, c_{23}, c_{11}, c_{21}, D', L are all specified. A solution then consists of values for (K, t_u, t_c) or the choice of a computer system. Obviously, $(0, 0, 0)$ is feasible and least costly, if there are no constraints that express the necessity of a computer. The constraints could be a relation between t_1, t_u and a minimum level of f (fitness), or a lower bound on t_c to ensure a minimum level of t (promptness). If $f_c(K, t_u, t_c)$ is a linear combination of these variables and all the constraints are linear, then the optimization problem is one of linear programming.

8.3. OPTIONS

The impressive advances achieved in the information technologies in recent years have provided people concerned with all stages of the information storage and retrieval process, above all else, with options. According to Harvey Brooks, a technology is a specifiable and reproducible as well as communicable way of doing something. It resembles know-how, except that know-how may not be specifiable, reproducible, or easily communicated. Information technologies, such as computers with large-scale integration, CATV, or microform readers at low cost enlarge the range of choices available to designers of IR systems, source-recording methods, storage systems.

In this section we discuss some of the desiderata for choosing among these options. For this purpose it is useful to analyze the overall process of storing and retrieving information into seven separable stages or subprocesses. Each subpro-cess can be implemented in the various ways that the technologies make option-al.

The entire storage and retrieval process begins when a person decides to record his explicit representation of some event, action, discovery, emotion, idea, or when the event leaves its own record in a natural way. The burial of a dinosaur several millenia ago by volcanic ash or the fosselization of ancient molluscs illustrate nature's way of recording both the facts that dinosaurs or ancient molluscs existed and the particular events of their deaths. Both the pyramids and hieroglyphs carved in stone record some ancient Egyptians' esteem for their departed ancestors.

The first stage begins by a decision of some author to record something. He will have had to select, from all the details he might have recorded, a specific aspect of the event or emotion, etc. that he did record. Most important, he had to decide on an explicit representation and design of the record. The main options provided by technology at this first stage are different modes of representation for record storage. In choosing a representation, it is desirable that it should:

1. Allow for the expression of as many diverse data, events, ideas, etc., as the author can *imagine* himself wanting to express on that topic. This could lead to an extreme in which there is a different representation for each topic and each author.

2. Be consistent or identical with the representations chosen by as many authors on as many topics as possible, to help preserve the homogeneity of culture, to help smooth over discontinuities and gaps. This desideratum may conflict with desideratum (1), in which case compromises or trades must be worked out. One form of compromise is to have multiple representations. One kind of representation for, say, nuclear physics, would be the highly technical language that is necessary for and understood by the most advanced specialists at the research frontier but by no one else; this representation would hardly fit any other topic. Another kind of representation is a less specialized language of science that could be understood by humanists as well; this would fit very many topics, but none as well as a special language.

3. Allow authors to express most of what is known in their topic with considerable ease. Here they must trade between all they can imagine themselves expressing and the little that the leading experts have already expressed.

4. Be readily learned by those most likely to use it. It should resemble lightly constrained natural languages so that people with different linguistic backgrounds and skills can readily interpret what is most relevant and significant for them.

5. Allow for deductions and deep inferences.

6. Allow for broad inferences, such as the kind of parallel data retrieval and correlation that *we* seem to do when we recognize a face.

7. Be flexible and easily changed so that it can adapt to the growth of knowledge and the changing needs implied by it.

Stage two consists of actually recording the record. It is a physical process of transforming the blueprint for the record, which may exist only in the author's mind, into a physical record such as the familiar microgroove recording or sound tape recording. If an artisan rather than the author performs this second subprocess, then the author must of course supply the recorder with a "manuscript" or explicit directions about what to record. This is just another record, though it is temporary and private, while the latter is more permanent and available for many to use and reuse. The options afforded by technology for recording are well-known, ranging from the sculptor's craft to bleaching of color centers in a cubic centimeter of alkali halide. Some desiderata for a recording process are:

1. It should be easily used by those skilled in the art.
2. It should depend only on readily available, easily replaceable and repairable tools, energy sources, materials.
3. It should minimize the amount of repetitive human labor, and require as little human attention as possible.
4. It should facilitate many rapid passes in which the author or recorder can compare his conception of the record he designed with the way it is coming out, about how it will appear to some others.
5. It should allow him to erase, and give him freedom and flexibility to change his design.
6. It should permit operation under diverse environmental conditions.
7. It should allow for simultaneous recording with several input channels, possibly of different technologies (e.g. eye and ear), and provide for some insurance against errors of various kinds, possibly by distributed and redundant storage.

The third stage is that of maintaining the record on a medium. Here the options are among the various media. Some desiderata are:

1. Not too much energy should be required to record.
2. Not too much energy should be required for reading.
3. Reading should not destroy or render unusable the record.
4. Not too much energy should be required for erasure and restoration.
5. The highest possible spatial recording densities.
6. The largest possible number of simultaneous read and write channels.
7. Storage should be physically stable during the predicted lifetime, and the lifetime should be controlled, i.e., as predictable as possible, and in some cases as long as possible, with minimum requirements on preventive maintenance of the storage medium.

8. Errors due to accidental erasure, decay, environmental damage, etc. should be minimum.

9. Times for recording, reading, erasure, recovery should be minimum.

In the fourth stage, a stored record is being considered for retrieval. This is what it was intended for. Even a time capsule or a spacecraft sent out of our solar system with a message about our existence is intended for retrieval by someone, sometime. Hiding a record forever, so that it is irretrievable, seems inconsistent. Records may become irretrievable in practice. Whether it is possible, in principle, to create, encode, and store a record so that it is irretrievable, even by its author, is an interesting conjecture that might be mathematically provable (or proved to be undecidable). It is not necessarily the case that what is buried can be extracted. Certain burying processes may be irreversible. If a record were strictly irretrievable, however, in what sense could it be said to be stored?

To make a record more easily retrievable, its custodian must enter it into an organized collection, make its existence known to those likely to be concerned, and finally present the object or its information contents to users who request it or who would benefit. The options available to a custodian are the various existing collections, into any one of which he might enter his new record, or the ways of organizing collections if he has to start a new collection. He also has the most important options about where and how to store it so that it will be in desired relations with all the other objects in the chosen collection. Some desiderata about where and how to store are:

1. It should reach the users who need it as quickly as possible. If transporting users to the site where the record is located or the record to them is an important factor, then copies of the record should be kept at locations close to where such users are concentrated. The optimal number and dispersion of copies can be calculated by minimizing an expression of the total cost, in which one term represents the cost of keeping n copies, and the second term is the cost of the users' time in getting to the nearest site where a copy is stored or waiting for a copy if it has to be sent to them.

2. The inconvenience of locating and using the record should be offset by the utility of the average record to its users.

3. The likelihood that someone who would benefit from using the record overlooks it or fails to see it at the right time should be minimized.

4. Though no special efforts need be made to keep records from people who have no use for them, they should not affect them adversely either; no one should be subjected to an overload of more records than he can assimilate, or be bewildered by huge and chaotic collections they cannot appreciate.

5. The user should easily be able to make both deep and broad inferences from the record and the collection in which it is stored.

6. The custodian should be able to keep track of each record at all times, efficiently and rapidly, without errors, arrearages.

The fifth subprocess is that in which both the custodian and the user try to remain informed about what new (and related old) records exist and how to best retrieve them. This involves a map to the organized collections. It should have the following properties:

1. The custodian should be able to update it conveniently and rapidly, as well as to locate and retrieve not only uniquely identified records, but records specified by their content as well.

2. The map should be easily usable and readily learnable by as great a number of potential users as possible.

3. The map should teach and orient the user to the collections' contents in addition to directing him and assisting him in location.

4. Like automobile road maps in U.S. service stations or stack maps in some libraries, such maps should be widely available and kept up-to-date with very little delay.

The penultimate stage is the actual presentation of the record or its contents. This has two parts. The first is the process of transferring the record or its contents from where it is normally stored to where the user takes it in. The relevant technologies are those of communications and transport, and they offer a wide variety of options in bandwidth, speeds, etc. The second part of stage six is the actual display, which involves technologies of display and buffering with its numerous options. The desiderata have been much discussed in the human factors literature, and deal with such factors as color, flicker, brightness, contrast, resolution, upper- or lowercase print, etc., for visual displays, and corresponding factors for auditory or tactile presentations. The key consideration is that there be effective coupling between the perceptual characteristics of the user, and the corresponding variables of the channels and the terminals.

The last stage is in many ways analogous to stage one. Here the user has to internalize the contents of the record. He has to interpret his input by means of his internal system of representation. Technology may provide him with options among various systems of representation that he might adopt and use. It does this by means of computer-aided instruction of a more sophisticated kind and by special IR systems aimed at triggering shifts of representation. The desiderata for choosing among the options are complementary to those in stage one. Where in stage one, a representation was desirable if it allowed an *author* to *express* many diverse ideas, etc., here it is desirable if it allows a *user* to *internalize* many diverse ideas, etc. The key consideration is that there be effective conceptual rather than perceptual coupling between the cognitive characteristics of the user and the corresponding properties of an acquired way of looking at a set of records.

Most of these desiderata conflict with one another and in nearly all cases with cost minimization. Among all the trades this requires, one stands out. A great deal of effort can be expended when records are first generated and first brought into storage. A far-sighted recorder who can anticipate the users and uses of his records can attain the benefit of large returns on an initial investment in planning and preparation. Even if the custodians do not expend a great deal of preparatory effort in the early stages of the storage and retrieval process, so that users face a less organized collection, the users can, by correspondingly greater search efforts, derive the same benefits as if the collection had been better organized. The archeologist-historian who researches and retrieves such records as nature happens to leave has no choice between paying for the preparatory services of a custodian or expending his own search effort. In man-made storage and retrieval processes, however, the choice of how the effort should be distributed is a matter of policy. This policy can be enlightened by a careful cost analysis of the tradeoff between letting the custodian invest most of the preparatory effort initially or letting the customers pay, in terms of greater search effort, as they use the system.

8.4. ISSUES

Privacy. IR systems are now being used increasingly to store and process information about people rather than natural data. Computerized tax returns, insurance files, medical records, police and security files, and bank files are but a few of the as-yet-scattered systems which, if unified, would constitute an enormous file of dossiers on each of us, usable for intelligence (Miller, 1971). Individuals are and should be concerned about their rights to control how and by whom information about them will be used. This issue is primarily legal, with important political, social, ethical, and technological aspects (Feistel, 1973; Westin and Baker, 1972).

If it is not already the overriding issue in designing IR systems, it soon will be. It involves a most delicate tradeoff between errors of omission and commission (analogous to errors of types I and II in statistics). One purpose of IR systems with data and documents about people is to control the amount of deviation in a population from social norms. An error of omission is made if deviants likely to decrease social welfare significantly are not apprehended and their negative contributions prevented. For example, if drivers with a record of repeated accidents, carriers of a communicable disease with a record of having infected others repeatedly, or criminals with a record of repeated offenses are not detected and prevented from repeating their damage to society, errors of omission have been made.

To apprehend potential deviants, IR systems have to extend their tentacles into the social fabric to such an extent that errors of commission begin to pose a threat. An error of commission is made when an innocent person is erroneously arrested and a record of this arrest[†] is a permanent part of his dossier. Similarly, a falsely positive identification of a person as a disease carrier and of an unidentified flying object as an enemy missile are errors of commission. In some cases, such as injuring an innocent man, an error of commission is regarded by many people as more serious than an error of omission.

At a time when all people connected with an IR system are called on to be more accountable, it is essential that this issue be clarified and that as many affected and concerned people as possible be educated so that they can resolve it wisely.

Quality. As information processing rates and capacities of information technologies are approaching their natural limits, which exceed most requirements known now, it is tempting to record, in computerized form, most of the data and documents being generated from now on.[‡] Yet there is some truth to the GIGO cliché: Garbage in, garbage (or worse, gospel) out.

Again we face a trade between errors of commission and omission. Rigorous quality control of documents such as scientific papers submitted for publication risk the error of failure to accept a useful paper. Less rigorous control risks the error of publishing worthless papers. The latter, errors of commission, can perhaps be rectified subsequently by weeding, by critical reviewing, and by disuse,

---

[†] Ninety percent of all U.S. nonwhite urban males will be arrested at some time during their lives, according to the 1967 report of the President's Commission on Law Enforcement. The figure is 58% for white urban males. Close to half of those arrested are not convicted and presumed innocent. Yet "they often suffer consequences as grave as if they had been guilty" (Neier, 1973).

[‡] This seems more sensible than undue stress on converting accumulated recorded data and documents into computer-readable code. Many books, journals, and newspapers are now produced by linotype, monotype, or other machines that are driven by perforated paper tapes or similar information-storage media. Such media already contain information in coded, potentially computer-processible form. There are, of course, economic obstacles in using such tapes directly in IR systems. These stem from the high error rate in uncorrected tapes, the incompatibility of codes used, and the scarcity of effective and efficient computer programs to process such large volumes of text to generate a useful output.

The idea of creating an on-line question-answering system with the *New York Times Index* as a data base was first seriously proposed by the author in collaboration with F.J. Damerau. Computer-based aids in maintaining this index were also studied. This is feasible primarily because so many of the entries in the *New York Times Index* are proper nouns, and programs for detecting and using proper nouns in a text have been investigated.

There are also some reasonably efficient programs for the automatic detection and correction of spelling errors in text. This is related to automatic hyphenation and justification. Operational programs for these two functions have been used by a number of newspapers for some time.

or they may turn out not to be errors. It is possible to produce a useful synthesis of several documents which would, if judged individually, be regarded as worthless. A good synthesis could raise the worth of each document it cites. This is analogous to synthesizing a reliable (higher-quality) machine with less reliable components. Here again, useful works of synthesis that are possible can fail to be produced (an error of omission), and worthless works of synthesis can clutter the literature (errors of commission).

Certainty that only authentically valid and significant data updates the data base is bought at the cost of missing a great deal of potentially useful data.

Control.   One way to resolve actual or potential conflicts that arise when varied users have to share an IR system is to divide the users into smaller groups or individuals and give each its own IR system.† Some people perfer to have complete control over the IR system they use: deciding what goes in, controlling vocabulary, who may use it, etc. Both rational and emotional factors affect this position. A personal IR system is more responsive to its owner-user's need and may contribute more to increase his productivity than a more centralized, multipurpose system over which that user has less control. His manager may decide that this user's increase in productivity resulting from buying him a personal IR system over what it would be if he used a central system is worth more to the organization than the extra cost (Kochen and Deutsch, 1969, 1973).

Omission–commission error-trading appears once more. The individual with a personal IR system pays for his greater control by giving up the benefits of a larger data base, greater variety of languages in which to communicate, and superior processing power that a more centrally controlled IR system could provide.

In an IR system that is shared by many users, there is the issue of whether the person who authorizes use and controls the accounts should also be able to enter the user's files. Does control stretch to the point where the boss can violate the privacy of the job-related files of his subordinates? How broadly and widely should control be distributed among not only users of an IR system but the indirectly affected third parties as well?

Technology.   Whether or not to automate is an issue facing nearly everyone responsible for an IR system. Too many managers (and salesmen) approach the introduction of information technology into an on-going system primarily on a cost-displacement basis. Rarely does the introduction of technology pay for itself in a few years. It is true that the costs of some technologies have been dropping dramatically even while their capacities have improved, at the same time that the costs of the human labor they would displace have been rising. But technology begets more technology as well as its own, expensive, new labor.

---

†A census of files and catalogs at the Library of Congress revealed more than 1200, many of them duplicating, and most of them personal IR systems for use of the library staff.

Besides large initial capital investments, operating costs are often higher than those of the manual system they replace, and the improvement is not always economically justified if all the new technology does is to perform the old functions, albeit faster, more accurately, and more comprehensively.

At issue is the extent to which we should try to realize the potential of the new technology.† Not to utilize the technology for all it has to offer in performing useful new functions of which the manual IR system was in principle incapable is once again an error of omission. Bold technological innovations that fail to bring return on the investment are errors of commission. For example, it is very difficult to surpass by automation the gossip gravevine for exchanging expressions and recommendations about potential doctors, lawyers, teachers, employers, and even computer systems.

A reasonable approach is to search for an optimum or at least the smallest desirable level of investment in technology for an IR system. Unavailability of needed personnel, now or in the projected future, constraints on resources and know-how, and other factors such as timing must, of course, be taken into account.

Active versus Passive IR.   To intervene or not to intervene, that is a key question today. If we accept the major message of this book, that the primary purpose of IR systems is to help people recognize and cope with problems, then we tend to favor active systems that reach out, to passive ones that respond only when a user initiates a request. But does an IR system or the person whom it helps most have sufficient wisdom, and the right, to prescribe for others, perhaps even future generations, what they should do (Medawar, 1960)? On the other hand, does a person (an IR system) not have an obligation, if he (it) is wiser than others, to withhold his (its) recommendations, advice, and prescriptions (Kochen and Cason, 1973)?

Upper- and middle-class people are more likely to be users of IR systems than people at lower socioeconomic and educational levels. The former are already well oriented and possess the critical amount of understanding to ask questions and enrich their understanding. The information-rich get richer, widening the gap between themselves and the information-poor.

This contributes to the very inequities that lie at the roots of many problems with which both groups must cope. If IR systems are to help, they must somehow reach those who are not now likely to use them.

Unity.   Throughout several of the above issues ran the theme of fragmentation: one centralized, multipurpose IR system versus many personal ones; an integrated IR system of personal dossiers or several possibly redundant, conflicting,

---

†By a technology we mean, with Brooks, a specifiable, reproducible, and communicable way of doing something. Technology is, like science, a form of knowledge. It is knowledge about how to make something or about how to perform a service.

uncoordinated files containing bits and pieces of a dossier. Fragmentation versus integration is indeed a major theme that runs through this book.

People, as processors interacting with the knowledge system, are aggregated into professional and other groups. Some are specialized. Others are inter- or multidisciplinary.

In the knowledge system, topics are aggregated into several hierarchies. Documents, too, are aggregated. The primary purpose of all this structure and organization is to help people use and add to the knowledge system to recognize and cope with a greater variety of problems, at a rate that matches how fast these problems arise.

Is the organization of knowledge adequate for this? Is it overfragmented, or is it overorganized, or is it just right? How far can it depart from being just right and come back?

These large questions should be settled by theoretical and empirical research. This may take long. Till then, people should take a position about the likely answer as a philosophical basis for the kind of IR system they feel is most needed. *We take the position that the knowledge system is overfragmented, but not beyond repair by nature's self-regulating mechanisms. Properly designed IR systems that help restore the right degree of organization are most needed. They and their designers may be nature's instruments to effect self-regulation and self-repair.* Directories with novel features seem to us the needed systems of this kind.

8.5. RESEARCH

How nature has maintained its knowledge system functioning as well as it has is a continuing source of wonder and challenge to understanding. There is some danger that, in an age when crises and concern with the possibly irreversible damage that current (and past) actions may cause are paramount determinants of intellectual trends, the sense of wonder that sparks man's spirit of inquiry will take second place. If history and precedent contain lessons for us today, then the fundamental principles of information retrieval are more likely to arise from inquiry inspired by the sense of wonder than by an organized program toward clearly identified goals that persuasive people are convinced are necessary.

A good deal but not all of research must, of course, be directed toward goals of contemporary social relevance. Understanding what features of an IR system will increase the likelihood of its being used by the information-poor, and learning how to design such IR systems, should be a top-priority problem. The first step is to conceptualize information-poverty more clearly. We suggest that it relates to question-asking. An IR system that stimulates question-asking is part of an educational system. We need basic theoretical investigations into the process of question-asking and how people learn it. We need parallel experimental and field studies of children and adults in continuing education. A key research problem is to discover the theoretical limits on the ability of various individuals to ask good questions, to ascertain whether there are unsurmountable boundaries on information-poverty of individuals.

The considerable amount of current research on how to organize and search very large data bases is still largely motivated by the interests of information technologists and information industries rather than by the needs of users. Concern with the nontechnological aspects of the privacy issue, for example, should begin to parallel the advances towards potential unification of all dossier files.

The outlines of three possible laws or basic principles of information retrieval were sketched here. They are actually classes of laws, and their status as laws is merely suggested, to be established by further research. The first are tradeoff laws. The best known is the recall–precision trade, or the inverse relation between hit- and acceptance-rate, as we called it in Section 8.1. It was Ziman who called this the fundamental law of information retrieval. We may question whether hit-rate and acceptance-rate are of central and fundamental significance. But even if they are not, tradeoffs of all kinds pervade the analysis and design of IR systems.

The second class of laws concern the critical values of such variables as the ratio of users who *use* to those who *add to* knowledge, and nature's self-regulating principles for maintaining the knowledge system so it helps people recognize and cope with problems sufficiently fast. This is a fruitful and exciting area of mathematical modeling. It should be connected more closely to research on the research process and to the empirical work on invisible colleges. Controlled psychological experiments on how people recognize, pick, and formulate problems (Kochen, Badre, and Badre, 1973) appear to have considerable promise. A better understanding of how a scientist picks his problems can shed considerable light on the growth of knowledge.

The third class of laws are descendants of the laws of Zipf, Pareto, Berry, and Bradford, referring to phenomena in which a random variable has a very long-tailed distribution, such as the log-normal, the negative binomial, or the one used in Section 8.2. These phenomena are central to much of the behavioral and social sciences, and especially to the information sciences. An important theoretical problem for future research is to develop the mathematical statistics for such distribution to a level comparable to what was done for the normal distribution.

Bibliography

ABRAHAM, C.T. (1965). "Graph-theoretic Techniques for the Organization of Linked Data," in KOCHEN, M. (editor), *Some Problems in Information Science*. Metuchen, N.J.: Scarecrow Press, p. 225.

ALLEN, T.J., and MARQUIS, D.G. (1963). *Problem-Solving by Research Groups: Factors Influencing Technical Quality in the Preparation of Proposals for Government Contract*. Working paper No. 20–63, M.I.T. School of Industrial Management, Cambridge, Mass. See also working papers No. 68–64 (1964) and 130–65 (1965).

AMAREL, S. (1971). "Representations and Modeling of Problems of Program Formation," in MELTZER, B., and MICHIE, D., (editors), *Machine Intelligence*. Edinburgh: Edinburgh University Press.

AUERBACH, I.L. (1971). *Need For an Information Systems Theory*. Pamphlet, Address before the International Federation of Information Processing Societies, Amsterdam, Philadelphia: Auerbach.

AUGUSTSON, J.G., and MINKER, J. (1970). "An Analysis of Some Graph Theoretical Cluster Techniques." *J. ACM* **17** (4), 571–588.

AYER. A.J. (1965). *The Problem of Knowledge*. New York: St. Martin's Press.

BADRE, A.N. (1973). "On Hypotheses and Representational Shifting in Ill-Defined Problem-Situations." Ph.D. Thesis, University of Michigan, Ann Arbor.

BAKER, D.B. (1966). "Chemical Literature Expands." *Chem. Eng. News* **44** (23), 84–87.

BARBER, B. (1962). *Science and The Social Order*, 2nd ed. New York: Collier.

BARBER, B., and HIRSCH, W. (1962). *The Sociology of Science*. Glencoe, Ill.: Free Press.

BARCAM, A. (1964). "The Battle of the Bulk." *N.Y. Times*, Section 12, March 28, p. 8.

BAR-HILLEL, Y. (1959). "The Mechanization of Literature Searching." *Proceedings, Symposium in the Mechanization of Thought Processes.* London: H.M. Stationery Office.

BAR-HILLEL, Y. (1960). *Some Theoretical Aspects of the Mechanization of Literature Searching.* Jerusalem: Hebrew University.

BARR, K.P. (1967). "Estimates of the Number of Currently Available Scientific and Technical Journals." *J. Doc* **23**, 2.

BAXENDALE, P. (1966). "Content Analysis, Specification, and Control," in CUADRA, C. (editor), *ARIST, I.* New York: Wiley, p. 73.

BECKER, J., and HAYES, R.M. (1963). *Information Storage and Retrieval.* New York: Wiley.

BELZER, J., and GOFFMAN, W. (1964). "Theoretical Considerations in Information Retrieval." *Comm. ACM* **7** (7), 439–441.

BERGE, C. (1964). *The Theory of Graphs and Its Applications.* New York: Wiley.

BERGE, C. (1973). *Graphs and Hypergraphs,* Amsterdam: North-Holland.

BERNAL, J.D. (1939). *The Social Functions of Science.* London: Routledge.

BOOTH, A.D. (1967). "A 'Law' of Occurrence for Words of Low Frequency.' '*Info. Contr.* **10**, 4. Reprinted in SARACEVIC, T. (editor), *Introduction to Information Science.* New York: Bowker, p. 219.

BORING, E.G. (1950). "Great Men and Scientific Progress." *Proc. Amer. Philos. Soc.* **94** (4), 359.

BORKO, H. (1962). *Evaluating the Efficiency of Information Retrieval.* SDC Report SP 909/000/00, Systems Development Corporation, Santa Monica, Ca., August.

BORKO, H., and BERNICK, M.D. (1963). "Automatic Document Classification." *J. ACM* **10** (2), 151–162.

BOULDING, K. (1956). *The Image: Knowledge in Life and Society.* Ann Arbor: University of Michigan Press.

BOULDING, K. (1966). "The Economics of Knowledge and the Knowledge of Economics." *Amer. Econ. Rev.* **56** (2), 1–13.

BOURNE, C.P. (1963). *Methods of Information Handling.* New York: Wiley.

BRADFORD, S.C. (1953). *Documentation,* 2nd ed. London: Crossby Lockwood and Son. First edition, 1948.

BRADY, E.L., and BRANSCOMB, L.M. (1972). "Information for a Changing Society." *Science* **179** (March 3), 961–966.

BRILLOUIN, L. (1962). *Science and Information Theory,* 2nd ed. New York: Academic Press. First edition, 1952.

BRITTAIN, M. (1970). *Information and Its Uses.* Bath: Bath University Press.

BROADBENT, D. E. (1971). *Decision and Stress.* London: Academic Press.

BROMLEY, D.A. (1972). "Physics in Perspective." *Physics Today,* (July), 31.

BROOKS, H. (1973). "Knowledge and Action: The Dilemma of Science Policy in the '70's." *Daedalus* (Spring), 125–143.

BROOKS, H. (1968). *The Government of Science.* Cambridge, Mass.: M.I.T. Press.

BROWN, G.W., MILLER, J.G., and KEENAN, T.A. (1967). *EDUNET, Report of the Summer Study on Information Networks* (EDUCOM). New York: Wiley.

BROWNSON, H.L. (1960). "Research on Handling Scientific Information." *Science* **132** (3444).

BRUNER, J.S., OLVER, R.R., GREENFIELD, P.M. (1966). *Studies in Cognitive Growth,* New York: Wiley.

BUCHHOLZ, W. (1963). "File Organization and Addressing." *IBM Systems J.* **2** (June), 86–111.

BUNGE, M. (1967). *Scientific Research,* New York: Springer Verlag.

BURKS, A.W., GOLDSTINE, H.H., VON NEUMANN, J. (1946). *Preliminary Discussion of the Logical Design of an Electronic Computing Instrument.* Princeton, N.J.: Institute for Advanced Study.

BUSH, V. (1945). *Science, The Endless Frontier.* A Report from the U.S. Office of Scientific R&D to the President. Reprinted by NSF, Washington, D.C., 1960.

BYRNE, W.L. (1970). *Molecular Approaches to Learning and Memory.* New York: Academic Press.

CADWALLADER, M. (1968). "The Cybernetic Analysis of Change in Complex Social Systems," in *Modern Systems Research for the Behavioral Scientist,* W. Buckley (ed.), Chicago: Aldine.

CARNAP, R. (1934). *Logische Syntax der Sprache;* enlarged English translation. New York: Harcourt Brace Jovanovich, 1937. See also "Logical Foundations of the Unity of Science," reprinted in KOCHEN, M. (editor), *The Growth of Knowledge.* New York: Wiley, 1967, p. 161.

CARROLL, J.B., and FREEDLE, R.O., editors (1972). *Language Comprehension and the Acquisition of Knowledge.* New York: Wiley.

CARR-SANDERS, A.M., and WILSON, P.A. (1933). *The Professions.* Oxford: Clarendon Press.

CARTER, L., editor (1967). *Recommendations for National Document-Handling Systems in Science and Technology.* New York: Wiley. See also Committee on Scientific and Technical Communications (COSATI), *Scientific and Technical Communication: a Pressing National Problem and Recommendations for its Solution.* National Academy of Science, Washington, D.C. 1969.

CHANDLER, G. (1963). *How to Find Out*. New York: Macmillan.

CHEYDLEUR, B. (1964). *Technical Preconditions for Retrieval Center Operations,* Washington, D.C.: Spartan.

CHURCHMAN, C.W. (1970). "The Problems of Representation in Problem-Solving and Inquiry," in MESAROVIC, M. (editor), *Proceedings of Fourth Systems Symposium on Formal Models and Nonnumerical Problem-Solving by Computers.* Cleveland, Ohio: Case Western Reserve University Press.

CHURCHMAN, C.W. (1971). *The Design of Inquiring Systems.* New York: Basic Books.

CLEVERDON, C.W. (1965). "The Testing and Evaluation of the Operating Efficiency of the Intellectual Stages of Information Retrieval Systems," in ATHERTON, P. (editor), *Proceedings International Conference on Classification Research.* Munksgaard, Copenhagen. See also SWANSON.

CLEVERDON, C.W. (1967). "The Cranfield Tests on Index Language Devices." *ASLIB Proc.* **19** (6). Reprinted in SARACEVIC, T. (editor), *Introduction to Information Science.* New York: Bowker, p. 608.

COLEMAN, J.S., KATZ, E., and MENZEL, H. (1966). *Medical Innovation: A Diffusion Study.* Indianapolis: Bobbs–Merrill.

COOMBS, C.H. (1967). *A Theory of Data.* New York: Wiley.

COOPER, W.S. (1971). "Definition of Relevance for Information Retrieval." *Information Storage and Retrieval* **7**. 19–37.

CRANE, D. (1969). "Fashion in Science: Does It Exist?" *Social Problems* **16** (4).

CRANE, D. (1972). *Invisible Colleges: Diffusion of Knowledge in Scientific Communities.* Chicago: University of Chicago Press.

CRAWFORD, S., editor (1971a). *Informal Communication Among Scientists: Proceedings of a Conference on Current Research.* American Medical Association, February 22.

CRAWFORD, S. (1971b). "Informal Communication Among Scientists in Sleep Research." *J. ASIS* (Sept.–Oct.), 301–310.

CRICK, F. (1967). *Of Molecules and Men,* Seattle: Univ. of Washington Press.

CUADRA, C., editor (1966–1972). *Annual Review of Information Science and Technology (ARIST),* I–IV American Documentation Institute, New York: Wiley; VI, VII, Encyclopedia Britannica.

CUADRA, C., and KATTER, R. (1967). *Experimental Studies of Relevance Judgments,* Final Report. SDC TM–3520/001–002, Systems Development Corporation, Santa Monica, Ca., June.

DAHLBERG, I. (1972). *Literatur zu den Informationswissenschaften, Das Informations-Bankensystem,* **3**. Cologne: Carl Heymanns.

DALEY, D.J., and KENDALL, D.G. (1965). "Stochastic Rumours." *J. Inst. Maths. Applics.* **1**. 42–55.

DAVIS, H.T. (1941). *The Analysis of Economic Time Series.* Chicago: Principia Press.

DEUTSCH, K.W. (1958). "Scientific and Humanistic Knowledge in the Growth of Civilization," in BROWN, H. (editor), *Science and the Creative Spirit.* Toronto: University of Toronto Press.

DOYLE, L.B. (1965). "Is Automatic Classification a Reasonable Application of Statistical Analysis of Text?" *J. ACM* **12** (4), 473–489.

EDMUNDSON, H.P., and WYLLYS, R.E. (1961). "Automatic Abstracting and Indexing: Survey and Recommendations." *Comm. ACM* **4** (5), 226–234.

EGAN, M.E. (1956). "Education for Librarianship of the Future," in SHERA, J., KENT, A., and PERRY, J. (editors), *Documentation in Action.* New York: Reinhold.

ELIAS, P. (1974). "Efficient Storage and Retrieval by Content and Address of Simple Files." *J. ACM.*

ELSASSER, W. (1958). *The Physical Foundation of Biology.* New York: Pergamon Press.

ETZIONI, A. (1972). "Understanding of Science." *Science* **177** (4047), 391.

FAIRTHORNE, R.A. (1955). "Essentials for Document Retrieval." *Special Libraries* **46**, 340–53.

FAIRTHORNE, R.A. (1956). "The Patterns of Retrieval." *Am. Docum.* **7**, 65–70.

FAIRTHORNE, R.A. (1958). "Delegation of Classification." *Am. Docum.* **9**, 159–164.

FAIRTHORNE, R.A. (1961). *Towards Information Retrieval.* London: Butterworths.

FAIRTHORNE, R.A. (1965a). "Use and Mention in the Information Sciences," in HEILPRIN, L., MARKUSON, B., and GOODMAN, F. (editors), *Education for Information Science.* Washington: Spartan, pp. 9–12.

FAIRTHORNE, R.A. (1965b). "Some Basic Comments on Retrieval Testing." *J. Doc.* **21** (4).

FAIRTHORNE, R.A. (1969). "Empirical Hyperbolic Distributions (Bradford–Zipf–Mandelbrot) for Bibliometric Description and Prediction." *J. Doc.* **25**, 4. Reprinted in SARACEVIC, T. (editor), *Introduction to Information Science.* New York: Bowker, p. 521.

FANO, R.M. (1961). *Transmission of Information.* Cambridge, Mass.; M.I.T. Press and New York: Wiley.

FEISTEL, H. (1973). "Cryptography and Computer Privacy." *Sci. Am.* **228** (5), 15–23.

FELLER, W. (1950, 1966). *An Introduction to Probability Theory*, 1 and 2. New York: Wiley.

FIKES, R.E., and NILSSON, N.J. (1971). "STRIPS: A New Approach to the Application of Theorem-Proving to Problem-Solving." *Artif. Intell.* 2 (3/4), 189–208.

FISCHER, M. (1966). "The KWIC Index Concept: A Retrospective View." *Am. Docum.* 17 (2).

FLOWER, R.A. (1973). "Computer Updating of a Data Structure," Quarterly Progress Report No. 110, MIT Research Laboratory of Electronics, July 15, 147–154.

FOSKETT, D.J. (1970). *Classification for a General Index Language*. London: Library Association.

FUBINI, E.G., MCKAY, K., HILLIER, J., and HOLLOMON, J.H. (1969). "Electronically Expanding the Citizen's World." *IEEE Spectrum* July, 30–39.

GARDIN, J.C., DE GROLIER, E., and LEVERY, F. (1964). "L'Organisation de la Documentation Scientifique." Paris: Gauthiers–Villars.

GARFIELD, E. (1955). "Citation Indexes for Science." *Science* 122 (3159), 108–111.

GARFIELD, E. (1963). "Citation Indexes in Sociological and Historical Research." *Am. Docum.* 14 (4), 289–291.

GARFIELD, E. (1964). "Citation Indexing: A Natural Science Literature Retrieval System for the Social Sciences." *Amer. Behav. Scientist* 7 (10), 58–61.

GARFIELD, E. (1972). "Citation Analysis as a Tool in Journal Evaluation." *Science* 178 (4060), 471.

GARNER, R. (1967). "Graph Theory as an Information Retrieval Tool–An Example from Citation Indexing," *Levels of Interaction Between Man and Information: Proceedings of ADI*, New York, pp. 80–83.

GASTON, J. (1970). "The Reward System in British Science." *Amer. Soc. Rev.* 35 (4), 718–732.

GIULIANO, V.E., and JONES, P.E. (1966). *Study and Test of a Methodology for Laboratory Evaluation of Message Retrieval Systems*, Report ESD–TR–66–405. Cambridge, Mass.; Arthur D. Little,

GOFFMAN, W. (1966). "Mathematical Approach to the Spread of Scientific Ideas–The History of Mast Cell Research." *Nature* 212 (Oct.), 5061. Reprinted in SARACEVIC, T. (editor), *Introduction to Information Science*. New York: Bowker, p. 65.

GOFFMAN, W. (1969). "An Indirect Method of Information Retrieval." *Information Storage and Retrieval*, 4. New York: Pergamon Press, pp. 361–373.

GOFFMAN, W. (1970). "A General Theory of Communication," in SARACEVIC, T. (editor), *Introduction to Information Science*. New York: Bowker, pp. 724–747.

GOODMAN, F., and HEILPRIN, L. (1965), "Analogy Between Information Retrieval and Education," in HEILPRIN, L., MARKUSON, B., and GOODMAN, F. (editors), *Education for Information Science*. Washington, D.C.: Spartan, p. 13.

GRAY, D.E., editor (1957). *American Institute of Physics Handbook*. New York: McGraw-Hill.

GRIFFITH, B.C., and MILLER, J.A. (1970). "Networks of Informal Communication Among Scientifically Productive Scientists," in NELSON, C., and POLLOCK, D. (editors), *Communication Among Scientists and Engineers*. Lexington, Mass.: Heath, pp. 125–140.

GRIFFITH, B.C., and MULLINS, N.C. (1972). "Coherent Social Groups in Scientific Change." *Science* 177 (4053), 959–963.

HAGSTROM, W.O. (1965). *The Scientific Community*. New York: Basic Books.

HANSON, N.R. (1958). *Patterns of Discovery*. Cambridge, England: Cambridge University Press.

HARARY, F., CARTWRIGHT, D.Z., and NORMAN, R. (1965). *Structural Models: An Introduction to the Theory of Directed Graphs*. New York: Wiley.

HARRAH, D. (1963). *Communication: A Logical Model*. Cambridge, Mass.: M.I.T. Press.

HAVELOCK, R.G. (1971). *Planning for Innovation Through Dissemination and Utilization of Knowledge*. Report, Institute for Social Research, University of Michigan, Ann Arbor.

HAYES, R.M. (1965). "Theory for File Organization," in KARPLUS, W. (editor), *On-Line Computing*. New York: McGraw-Hill.

HAYS, D.G. (1967). *Introduction to Computational Linguistics*. New York: American Elsevier.

HENDERSON, M.M., MOATS, J.S., and STEVENS, M.E. (1966). *Cooperation, Convertibility, and Compatibility Among Information Systems: A Literature Review*. National Bureau of Standards–Miscellaneous Publication 76, Superintendent of Documents, U.S. Government Printing Office, Washington, D.C., June.

HERNER, S., (1970). *A Brief Guide to Sources of Scientific and Technical Information*. Information Resources Press, Washington, D.C.

HERNER, S., and HERNER, M. (1967). "Information Needs and Uses," in CUADRA, C. (editor), *ARIST, II*. New York: Wiley, pp. 30–31.

HERNER, S., and VELLUCCI, M. (1973). *Selected Federal Computer-Based Information Systems*. Information Resources Press, Washington, D.C.

HILLMAN, D. (1964). "Two Models for Retrieval System Design," *Am. Docum.* **15** (3). Reprinted in SARACEVIC, T. (editor), *Introduction to Information Science*. New York: Bowker, p. 157. See also *Studies of Theories and Models of Information Storage and Retrieval*, a series of continuing reports. Lehigh University, Bethlehem, Pa.

HIMSWORTH, H. (1966). *The Science of Science*. New York: Penguin.

HIMSWORTH, H. (1970). *The Development and Organization of Scientific Knowledge*. London: Heinemann.

HOLT, A.W. (1963). "Some Theorizing on Memory Structure and Information Retrieval." *Proceedings ACM National Conference*, Denver.

HORVATH, W.J. (1959). "Applicability of the Lognormal Distribution to Servicing Times in Congestion Problems." *Opns. Res.* **7** (1), 127–128.

HUTCHINS, R.M., BUCHANAN, S., MICHAEL, D.N., SHERWIN, C., REAL, J., and WHITE, L., Jr. (1963). *Science, Scientists, and Politics*. Occasional Papers Series, Center for the Study of Democratic Institutions, Fund for the Republic, Santa Barbara, Ca.

KAC, M., and ULAM, S. (1969). *Mathematics and Logic*. New York: Mentor.

KASHER, A. (1967). "Data Retrieval by Computer—A Critical Survey," in KOCHEN, M. (editor), *The Growth of Knowledge*. New York: Wiley.

KEMENY, J. (1966). "The Knowledge Explosion: A Mathematician's Point of View," in *The Knowledge Explosion*. New York: Farrar, Strauss & Giroux, p. 89.

KENT, A. (1963). *Textbook on Mechanized Information Retrieval*. New York: Interscience.

KESSLER, M.M. (1965). "Comparison of the Results of Bibliographic Coupling and Analytic Subject Indexing." *Am. Docum.* **16** (3), 223–233.

KILGOUR, F. (1967). "Implications for the Future of Reference/Information Service," in LINDERMAN, W. (editor), *The Present Status and Future Prospects of Reference/Information Service*. Chicago: American Library Association Press, pp. 172–184.

KING, D.W., and BRYANT, E.C. (1970). "A Diagnostic Model for Evaluating Retrospective Search Systems." *Inform. Stor. Retr.* **6** (3), 261–272.

KING, D.W., and BRYANT, E.C. (1972). *The Evaluation of Information Services and Products*. Washington, D.C.: Information Resources Press.

KING, G.W., EDMUNDSON, H.P., FLOOD, M.M., KOCHEN, M., SWANSON, D., and WYLLY, A. (1963). *Automation and The Library of Congress*. Washington, D.C.: Library of Congress.

KNIGHT, D.M., and NOURSE, E.S. (1969). *Libraries at Large*. New York: Bowker.

KNUTH, D.E. (1968). *The Art of Computer Programming, 1 Fundamental Algorithms*, Chapter 2 (Information Structures). London: Addison-Wesley.

KOCHEN, M. (1959). "Extension of Moore—Shannon Model for Relay Circuits." *IBM J. Res. Develop.* **3** (2), 169.

KOCHEN, M. (1960). "Experimental Study of 'Hypothesis Formation' by Computer," in CHERRY, C. (editor), *Information Theory*. London: Butterworths, pp. 377–403.

KOCHEN, M. editor (1965). *Some Problems in Information Science*. Metuchen, N.J.: Scarecrow Press.

KOCHEN, M., editor (1967). *The Growth of Knowledge: Readings on Organization and Retrieval of Information*. New York: Wiley. See particularly "Adaptive Mechanisms in Digital 'Concept'-Processing," p. 185.

KOCHEN, M. (1969a). "Automatic Question-Answering of English-Like Questions About Simple Diagrams." *J. ACM* **16** (1), 26–48.

KOCHEN, M. (1969b). "Stability in the Growth of Knowledge." *J. ASIS* **20** (3), 186–197.

KOCHEN, M. (1970), "Quality Control in the Publishing Process and Theoretical Foundations for Information Retrieval," in TOU, J. (editor), *Software Engineering*, **2**. New York: Academic Press, pp. 19–54.

KOCHEN, M. (1971, 1973). "Cognitive Learning Processes: An Explication," in FINDLER, N., and MELTZER, B. (editors), *Artificial Intelligence and Heuristic Programming*. Edinburgh: Edinburgh University Press, pp. 261–317; also later revised version, German translation.

KOCHEN, M. (1972a). "Directory Design for Networks of Information and Referral Centers," *Lib. Q.* **42** (1), 59–83. Also in SWANSON, D., and BOOKSTEIN, A. (editors), *Operations Research: Implications for Libraries*. Chicago: University of Chicago Press.

KOCHEN, M. (1972b). "WISE: A World Information Synthesis and Encyclopedia." *J. Doc.* **28** (4), 332–343.

KOCHEN, M. (1973a). "Information Systems for Urban Problem-Solvers," in *Artificial Intelligence,* TOU, J. (editor), *Proceedings of COINS-IV*. 1974.

KOCHEN, M. (1973b). "Representations and Algorithms for Cognitive Learning." *Artificial Intelligence*.

KOCHEN, M. (1973c). "Views on the Foundations of Information Science," in DEBONS, A.T. (editor), *Proceedings of 1972 NATO Conference on Information Science*. Pittsburgh: University of Pittsburgh.

KOCHEN, M. (1974). *Integrative Mechanisms in Literature Growth*. Westport, Conn.: Greenwood.

KOCHEN, M., and BADRE, A.N. (1974). "Question-Asking and Shifts of Representation in Problem-Solving." *Am. J. Psychol.*

KOCHEN, M., BADRE, A.N., and BADRE, B. (1973). "The Process of Formulating Mathematical Problems: Assessment and Improvement." Delivered at the *Fourth Annual 'Invitational' Meeting on Structural Learning*, April 6–7 (J. SCANDURA, Chairman). Accepted for publication in *J. Struc. Lrng.*

KOCHEN, M., and CASON, D. (1973). "A Cost–Benefit Analysis of an Information System to Help People Plan Their Families." *Proceedings Sixth Hawaii International Conference on System Sciences, Urban and Regional Systems*, Western Periodicals Company, Los Angeles, p. 32.

KOCHEN, M., and DEUTSCH, K.W. (1969). "Toward a Rational Theory of Decentralization." *Amer. Polit. Sci. Rev.* **63** (3), 734–749.

KOCHEN, M., and DEUTSCH, K.W. (1972). "Pluralization: A Mathematical Model." *Opns. Res.* **20** (2), 276–292.

KOCHEN, M., and DEUTSCH, K.W. (1973). "Decentralization by Function and Location." *Management Science: Applications,* **19**, No. 8, April, 841–856.

KOCHEN, M., and DONOHUE, J., editors (1974). *Information for the Community*. Chicago: American Library Association.

KOCHEN, M., MACKAY, D.M., MARON, M.E., SCRIVEN, M., and UHR, L. (1967). "Computers and Comprehension" (RAND Report '64), in KOCHEN, M. (editor), *The Growth of Knowledge*. New York: Wiley, p. 230.

KOCHEN, M., and TAGLIACOZZO, R. (1968), "A Study of Cross-Referencing: The Notion of Structural Level." *J. Doc.* **24** (3), 173–191.

KRUZAS, A.T. (1968). *Directory of Special Libraries and Information Centers*, 2nd ed. Detroit: Gale Research.

KUHN, T. (1962). *The Structure of Scientific Revolutions*. Chicago: University of Chicago Press.

LAKATOS, I., and MUSGRAVE, A.E., editors (1970). *Criticism and the Growth of Knowledge*. Cambridge, Mass.: Cambridge University Press.

LAMBERTON, D.M., editor (1971). *Economics of Information and Knowledge*. New York: Penguin. Also a forthcoming issue of *Ann. Amer. Acad. Polit. Soc. Sci,* "The Information Revolution," March 1974.

LANCASTER, F.W. (1968). "Evaluation of the MEDLARS Demand Search Service." Bethesda, Md.: National Library of Medicine.

LANCASTER, F.W. (1969). "MEDLARS: Report on the Evaluation of Its Operating Efficiency." *J. ASIS* **20** (2). Reprinted in SARACEVIC, T. (editor), *Introduction to Information Science.* New York: Bowker, p. 641.

LANCASTER, F.W. (1972). *Vocabulary Control for Information Retrieval.* Washington, D.C.: Information Resources Press.

LEARNES, D.H. (1953). Letter in Communications Section of *Econometrica* **21**, 630.

LEDERBERG, J., SUTHERLAND, G.S., BUCHANAN, B.B., and FEIGENBAUM, E.A. (1968). "Mechanization of Inductive Inference in Organic Chemistry," in KLEINMUNTZ, B. (editor), *Formal Representation for Human Judgment.* New York: Wiley.

LEIMKUHLER, F.F. (1967). "The Bradford Distribution." *J. Doc.* **23** (3). Reprinted in SARACEVIC, T. (editor), *Introduction to Information Science.* New York: Bowker, p. 509.

LICKLIDER, J.C. (1965), *Libraries of the Future.* Cambridge, Mass.: M.I.T. Press.

LIPETZ, B.A. (1966). "Information Storage and Retrieval." *Sci. Am.* **215** (3).

LUCE, D.R. (1950). "Connectivity and Generalized Cliques in Sociometric Group Structure." *Psychometrika* **15** (2), 169.

LUHN, H.P. (1953). "A New Method of Recording and Searching Information." *Am. Docum.* **4** (Jan.). 14–16.

LUHN, H.P. (1957). "A Statistical Approach to Mechanized Encoding and Searching of Literary Information." *IBM J. Res. Develop.* **1** (4) 309–317.

MACHLUP, F. (1962). *The Production and Distribution of Knowledge in the U.S.* Princeton: Princeton University Press.

MACKAY, D.M. (1961). "The Informational Analysis of Questions and Commands," in CHERRY, C. (editor), *Information Theory.* London: Butterworths.

MANDELBROT, B. (1959). "Information Sans Interpretation Dans la Description des Langues Réelles." *Synthèse* **11** (2) 160.

MANDELBROT, B. (1960). "The Pareto–Levy Law and the Distribution of Income." *Intl. Econ. Rev.* **1** (2), 79.

MANDELBROT, B. (1963). "Word Frequencies and the Log-Normal Function." IBM Research Note NC–265, IBM Research Center, Yorktown Heights, N.Y., May 15.

MARON, M.E., and KUHNS, J.L. (1960, 1961). "On Relevance, Probabilistic Indexing and Information Retrieval." *J. ACM* **7** (3). Also in *J. ACM* **8** (3).

MARSCHAK, J., and MIYASAWA, K. (1968). "Economic Comparability of Information Systems," *International Economic Review* **9**; 137–174.

MARSCHAK, J. (1971). "Economics of Information Systems," *Amer. Stat. Assn.* **66**, 192–219.

MARSCHAK, J. (1972). "Optimal Techniques for Information and Decision." in *Techniques of Optimization,* (J. Marschak, ed.), New York: Academic Press.

MARSCHAK, J. (1973). "Information and the Scientist," Western Management Science Inst. Working Paper Nr. 206, Univ. of Calif. in Los Angeles.

MCKENNEY, J.L. (1973). *A Taxonomy of Problem Solving,* Working Paper HBS73-3, Graduate School of Business Admin., Harvard Univ., Cambridge, Mass.

MEADOW, C.T. (1967). *The Analysis of Information Systems.* New York: Wiley.

MEDAWAR, P.B. (1960). *The Future of Man,* the 1959 Reith Lectures. Also in HARRISON, J. (editor), *Scientists as Writers.* Cambridge, Mass.: M.I.T. Press, 1965, p. 131. Also in *Induction and Intuition in Scientific Thought.* Philadelphia: American Philosophical Society, 1969.

MENDELSON, E. (1964). *Introduction to Mathematical Logic.* Princeton: Van Nostrand, p. 49.

MENZEL, H. (1966). "Scientific Communication: Five Themes from Social Science Research." *Am. Psychol.* **21** (10), 999–1004.

MERTON, R.K. (1938). *Science, Technology and Society in Seventeenth Century England* New York: Howard Fertig, 1970.

MIKHAILOV, A.I., PETROV, I.I., and VOSKOBOYNIK, D.I. (1966). "Informatics—A New Name for Scientific Information Theory." *Nauk Tekhn. Inform.* **12**, *35–39.*

MILGRAM, S. (1967). "The Small-World Problem." *Psychol. Today* (May), **1**, No. 1, 60–67.

MILLER, A. (1971). *The Assault on Privacy: Computers, Data Banks, and Dossiers.* Ann Arbor: University of Michigan Press.

MILLER, G.A. (1956). "The Magical Number of Seven, Plus or Minus Two: Some Limits on our Capacity for Processing Information." *Psychol. Rev.* **63** (2), 81–97.

MILLER, J.G. (1960). "Information Input Overload and Psychopathology." *Am. J. Psychol.* **116** (8), 695–704.

MINSKY, M., and PAPERT, S. (1969). *Perceptrons.* Cambridge, Mass.: M.I.T. Press, pp. 215–225.

MONTGOMERY, E.B., editor (1968). *The Foundations of Access to Knowledge: A Symposium.* Syracuse: Syracuse University Press.

MOOERS, C.N. (1951). "Zatocoding Applied to Mechanical Organization of Knowledge." *Am. Docum.* 2, (Jan.), 20–32. British Patent No. 681 902 (U.S. Application–September 17. 1947).

MOOERS, C.N. (1954). "Choice and Coding in Information Retrieval Systems," (1954 Symposium on Information Theory). *Trans. of IRE, PGIT-4,* The Institute of Radio Engineers, September 15, pp. 112–118.

MOOERS, C.N. (1959). "The Next Twenty Years in Information Retrieval." *Proceedings Western Joint Computer Conference,* March.

MOORE, E.F., and SHANNON, C.E. (1956). "Reliable Circuits Using Less Reliable Relays." *J. Frankl. Inst.* **262** (3 and 4). 191–208 and pp. 281–297.

MORISON, R.S. (1962). "Comments on Genetic Evolution," in HOAGLAND, H., and BURHOE, R.W. (editors), *Evolution and Man's Progress.* New York: Columbia University Press, p. 41.

MORSE, P.M. (1968). *Library Effectiveness: A Systems Approach.* Cambridge, Mass.: M.I.T. Press.

MULLINS, N.C. (1968). "The Distribution of Social and Cultural Properties in Informal Communication Networks among Biological Scientists." *Amer. Soc. Rev.* **33** (5). 786–797.

MYHILL, J. (1952). "Some Philosophical Implications of Mathematical Logic." *Rev. Metaphys.* **16** (2), 165–198.

NATIONAL ACADEMY OF SCIENCES (1972). *Libraries and Information Technology.* Washington, D.C.: National Academy of Sciences, See also *Applied Science and Technological Progress.* U.S. Government Printing Office, Washington, D.C., 1967.

NEEDHAM, R.M., and SPARCK-JONES, K. (1964). "Keywords and Clumps." *J. Doc.* **20** (1).

NEGOITA, C.V. (1970). *Sisteme de Inmagazinare Si Regasire a Informatiilor.* Bucharest, Rumania: Edit. Acad. Rep. Soc. (English summary at end).

NEIER, A. (1973). "Marked for Life: Have You Ever Been Arrested?" *N.Y. Times Magazine,* Section 6, Sunday, April 15, p. 10.

NEISSER, U. (1966). *Cognitive Psychology.* New York: Appleton-Century-Crofts.

NEWCOMB, T.M. (1966). *The Acquaintance Process.* New York: Holt, Rinehart & Winston.

NEWELL, A., and SIMON, H.A. (1972). *Human Problem Solving.* Englewood Cliffs, N.J.: Prentice-Hall.

O'CONNOR, J. (1965). "Automatic Subject Recognition in Scientific Papers: An Empirical Study." *J. ACM* **12** (4).

OECD (1971). *Information for a Changing Society*. Organization for Economic Cooperation and Development, Davis. See also Brady and Branscomb. See also *Science, Growth and Society*. Paris: OECD, 1971.

OETTINGER, A., Chairman (9172). *Libraries and Information Technology*. Washington, D.C.: National Academy of Sciences.

OPLER, A. (1964). "A Brief Survey of Topological Representations." *Proc. ADI* 499–502.

ORE, O. (1962). *Theory of Graphs*, 2nd ed. Colloquium Publications, **38**, Providence, R.I.: American Mathematical Society.

OTTEN, K., and DEBONS, A. (1970). "Toward a Metascience of Information: Informatology." *J. ASIS* (Jan./Feb.), 89–94.

OVERHAGE, C.F. (1966). "Plans for Project Intrex." *Science* **152** (3725).

PARKER, E.B., and DUNN, D.A. (1972). "Information Technology: Its Social Potential." *Science* **176** (4042), 1392.

PASSMAN, S. (1969). *Scientific and Technological Communication*. New York: Pergamon Press.

PETERSON, W.W. (1957). "Addressing for Random Access Storage." *IBM J. Res. Develop.* **1**, 130–146.

PIAGET, J. (1971). *Biology and Knowledge*. Chicago: University of Chicago Press.

POLANYI, M. (1958). *Personal Knowledge*. Chicago: University of Chicago Press.

POLISH ACADEMY OF SCIENCE (1970). *Problems of the Science of Science*, Wroclaw: Ossolineum.

POLLACK, I. (1968). "Information Theory," in SILLS, D.L. (editor), *International Encyclopedia of the Social Sciences*, **7** New York: Macmillan, pp. 331–337.

POLLOCK, S.M. (1968). "Measures for the Comparison of Information Retrieval Systems." *Am. Docum.* **19** (4). Reprinted in SARACEVIC, T. (editor), *Introduction to Information Science*. New York: Bowker, p. 592.

POOL, I. DE SOLA, and KOCHEN, M. (1958). *The Small World Problem* (or *Contact Nets*). Unpublished manuscript. See also *Handbook of Communication* (I. DE SOLA POOL and Wilbur SCHRAMM, eds.), Chicago: Rand McNally, 1973.

POPPER, K.R. (1959). *The Logic of Scientific Discovery*. New York: Basic Books.

POPPER, K.R. (1962). *Conjectures and Refutations: The Growth of Scientific Knowledge*. New York: Basic Books.

PRICE, D. DE SOLLA (1961). *Science Since Babylon*. New Haven, Conn.: Yale University Press.

PRICE, D. DE SOLLA (1965). "Networks of Scientific Papers." *Science* **149** (3683), 510–515. Reprinted in KOCHEN, M. (editor), *The Growth of Knowledge.* New York: Wiley.

PRICE, D. DE SOLLA (1970). "Citation Measures of Hard Science, Soft Science, Technology, and Nonscience," in NELSON, C.E., and POLLOCK, D.K. (editors), *Communication Among Scientists and Engineers.* Lexington, Mass.: Heath Lexington Books, pp. 3–22.

PRICE, D. DE SOLLA, and BEAVER, D. DE B. (1966). "Collaboration in an Invisible College." *Am. Psychol.* **21**, 1011–1018.

PRICE, D.K. (1962). *Government and Science.* New York: Oxford University Press.

PRICE, D.K. (1968). *The Scientific Estate.* New York: Oxford University Press.

RAMSEY, P. (1970). *The Fabricated Man.* New Haven, Conn.: Yale University Press.

RAWSKI, C. (1973). *Toward a Theory of Librarianship.* Metuchen, N.J.: Scarecrow Press.

REES, A.M. (1967). "Evaluation of Information Systems and Services," in CUADRA, C. (editor), *ARIST, II.* New York: Wiley, p. 81.

REISNER, P. (1965a). "Semantic Diversity and a Growing Man–Machine Thesaurus," in KOCHEN, M. (editor), *Some Problems in Information Science.* Metuchen, N.J.: Scarecrow Press, p. 117.

REISNER, P. (1965b). "Pre-test and Potential of a Machine-Stored Citation Index," in KOCHEN, M., (editor), *Some Problems in Information Science.* Metuchen, N.J.: Scarecrow Press, p. 161.

REUCK, A. DE, and KNIGHT, J. (1967). *Communication in Science.* Boston: Little, Brown.

ROBINSON, J.A. (1967). "A Review of Automatic Theorem-Proving." *Proceedings of Symposium in Applied Mathematics,* **19**. Providence, R.I.: American Mathematical Society, pp. 1–18.

ROGERS, D.J., and TANIMOTO, T.T. (1960). "A Computer Program for Classifying Plants." *Science* **132** (1115).

ROGET (1962). *International Thesaurus,* 3rd ed. New York: Crowell.

ROSTAND, J. (1960). *Error and Deception in Science,* translated by A.J. POMERANS. New York: Basic Books. Reprinted in HARRISON, J. (editor), *Scientists as Writers.* Cambridge, Mass.: M.I.T. Press, pp. 125, 130.

ROTHENBERG, D.H. (1969). "An Efficiency Model and a Performance Function for an Information Retrieval System." *Inform. Stor. Retr.* **5**(3). Reprinted in SARACEVIC, T. (editor), *Introduction to Information Science.* New York: Bowker, p. 707.

RUBINOFF, M. (1965). "Toward a National Information System." *Second Annual National Colloquium on Information Retrieval,* Washington, D.C.

SAATY, T. L., and BUSACKER, R.G. (1965). *Finite Graphs and Networks: An Introduction with Applications.* New York: McGraw-Hill.

SALTON, G. (1968). *Automatic Information Organization and Retrieval.* New York: McGraw-Hill.

SALTON, G. (1973). "On the Development of Information Science," *J. ASIS* **24** (3), 218.

SAMUELSON, K. (1968). *Mechanized Information Storage, Retrieval and Dissemination.* Amsterdam: North Holland.

SARACEVIC, T., editor (1970a). *Introduction to Information Science.* New York: Bowker.

SARACEVIC, T. (1970b). "Selected Results from an Inquiry into Testing of Information Retrieval Systems," in SARACEVIC, T. (editor), *Introduction to Information Science.* New York: Bowker, p. 665.

SCHEFFLER, I. (1963). *The Anatomy of Inquiry.* New York: Knopf.

SCHULTZ, C.K., editor (1967). *H.P. Luhn: Pioneer of Information Science.* New York: Spartan. Contains selected works; the earliest is 1952, "The IBM Electronic Information Searching System," p. 35; early patents in this area were 1948, "Record Controlled Data Storing Device;" 1952, "Sorting Machine;" 1953, "Optical Record Reading Device."

SHANNON, C.E., and WEAVER, W. (1949). *A Mathematical Theory of Communication.* Urbana: University of Illinois.

SHARPE, J.R. (1965). *Some Fundamentals of Information Retrieval.* London: Andre Deutsch.

SHAW, R.R. (1963). "Information Retrieval." *Science* **140** (3567), 606–609.

SHERA, J.H., KENT, A., and PERRY, J.W. (1956). *Documentation in Action.* New York: Reinhold.

SIEGFRIED, A. (1965). *Germs and Ideas.* London: Oliver & Boyd.

SIMMONS, R. (1967). "Answering English Questions by Computer: A Survey," in KOCHEN, M. (editor), *The Growth of Knowledge.* New York: Wiley, p. 264.

SIMON, H.A. (1957). *Models of Man.* New York: Wiley,

SIMON, H.A. (1960). *The New Science of Management Decision,* New York: Harper and Row.

SIMON, H.A., and SIKLOSSY, L., editors (1972). *Representation and Meaning.* Englewood Cliffs, N.J.: Prentice-Hall.

SLAMECKA, V., ZUNDE, P., and KRAUS, D.H. (1969). "On the Structure of Six National Science Information Systems." *International Forum of Informatics,* VINITI, Moscow, pp. 318–334.

SOERGEL, D. (1967a,b). "Mathematical Analysis of Documentation Systems: An Attempt to a Theory of Classification and Search Request Formulation." *Inform. Stor. Retr.* **3** (3), 129–173. See also "Some Remarks on Information Languages, Their Analysis and Comparison." *Inform. Stor. Retr.* **3** (4), 219–291.

SPARCK-JONES, K. (1970). "Some Thoughts on Classification for Retrieval." *J. Doc.* **26** (2), 89–102.

SPARCK-JONES, K., and JACKSON, D.M. (1967). "Recent Approaches to Classification and Clump-finding at Cambridge Language Research Unit." *Computer J.* **10** (1).

STEGMÜLLER, W. (1969). *Probleme und Resultate der Wissenschaftstheorie und Analytischen Philosophie.* New York: Springer.

STEVENS, M.E., GUILIANO, V.E., and HEILPRIN, L.B. (1965). "Statistical Association Methods for Mechanized Documentation." National Bureau of Standards Publication 269, Washington, D.C.

STORER, N. (1966). *The Social System of Science.* New York: Holt, Rinehart and Winston.

SWANK, R. (1970). "Interlibrary Cooperation, Interlibrary Communications and Information Networks: Explanations and Definitions," in BECKER, J. (editor), *Proceedings of Conference on Interlibrary Communication and Information Networks.* Chicago: American Library Association Press.

SWANSON, D.R. (1961). "Information Retrieval—State of the Art." *Proceedings Western Joint Computer Conference,* March.

SWANSON, D.R. (1965). "The Evidence Underlying the Cranfield Results." *Lib. Q.* **35** (1).

SWETS, J.A. (1963). "Information Retrieval Systems." *Science* **141** (3577). Reprinted in KOCHEN, M. (editor), *The Growth of Knowledge.* New York: Wiley.

TAGLIACOZZO, R., and KOCHEN, M. (1970). "Information-Seeking Behavior of Catalog Users." *Inform. Stor. Retr.* **6,** 363–381.

TAGLIACOZZO, R., KOCHEN, M., and EVERETT, W. (1971). "The Use of Information by Decision-Makers in Public Service Organizations." *Proceedings Annual Conference of American Society for Information Science,* Denver, pp. 53–57.

TARSKI, A. (1951). *A Decision Method for Elementary Algebra and Geometry,* 2nd Ed., Berkeley: Univ. of Calif. Press.

TARSKI, A. (1961). *Introduction to Logic and to the Methodology of Deductive Sciences,* New York: Oxford Univ. Press.

TART, C.T. (1972). "States of Consciousness and State-Specific Sciences." *Science* **176** (4040), 1203.

TAUBE, M. (1953). *Studies in Coordinate Indexing.* Bethesda, Md.: Documentation.

TAUBE, M., and Associates (1955). "Storage and Retrieval of Information by Means of Association of Ideas." *Am. Docum.* **6** (1), 1–17.

TAUBE, M., and WOOSTER, H. (1958). *Information Storage and Retrieval.* New York: Columbia University Press.

TAULBEE, O.E. (1968). "Content Analysis, Specification, and Control," in CUADRA, C. (editor), *ARIST,* III. American Documentation Institute, New York: Wiley.

TAYLOR, R.S. (1968). "Question-Negotiation and Information-Seeking in Libraries." *Coll. Res. Lib.* **28**, 178–194.

TEICH, A.H., editor (1972). *Technology and Man's Future.* New York: St. Martin's Press.

TOULMIN, S. (1971). "New Directions in Philosophy of Science." *Encounter* **35** (7), 53–64.

TUKEY, J.W. (1962). "Keeping Research in Contact with the Literature: Citation Indices and Beyond." *J. Chem. Doc.* **2** (1).

TULVING, E., and DONALDSON, W. (1972). *The Organization of Memory.* New York: Academic Press.

UNESCO (1971). *UNISIST: Synopsis of the Feasibility Study on a World Science Information System.* Paris: UNESCO.

VAN TASSEL, D. (1972). *Computer Security Management,* Englewood Cliffs, N.J.: Prentice Hall.

VICKERY, B.C. (1965). *On Retrieval System Theory,* 2nd ed. Washington, D.C.: Butterworths, First edition, 1961.

VIRGO, J. (1971). "A Statistical Measure for Evaluating the Importance of Scientific Papers." Ph.D. Thesis, University of Chicago.

VON NEUMANN, J. (1956). "Probabilistic Logics and the Synthesis of Reliable Organisms from Unreliable Components." *Automata Studies,* Annals of Math Studies No. 34, Princeton, N.J.: Princeton University Press, p. 43.

WARHEIT, I.A. (1967). "File Organization for Information Retrieval." Paper presented at *FID/IFIP Conference on Mechanized Information Storage Retrieval and Dissemination,* Rome, June.

WASSERMAN, P. (1965). *The Librarian and the Machine,* Detroit: Gale.

WAY, K. (1968). "Free Enterprise in Data Compilation." *Science* **159** (3812), 280–282.

WEINBERG, A. (1972a,b). "Science and Trans-Science." *Science* **177** (4045), 211. Also in *Minerva* **10** (Apr.), 209.

WEIZENBAUM, J. (1972). "On the Impact of the Computer on Society." *Science* **176** (May 12), 609–614.

WELLISCH, H. (1972). "From Information Science to Informatics: A Terminological Investigation." *J. Libnship* (Oct.).

WELLISCH, H. and WILSON, T.D. (1972). *Subject Retrieval in the Seventies,* Westport, Conn.: Greenwood.

WELLS, H.G. (1938). "World Encyclopaedia," in *World Brain*. Garden City, N.Y.: Doubleday & Doran. Reprinted in KOCHEN, M. (editor), *The Growth of Knowledge*. New York: Wiley.

WESTBROOK, J.H. (1960). "Identifying Significant Research." *Science* **132** (3435).

WESTIN, A.F., and BAKER, M.A. (1972). *Databanks in a Free Society*. New York: Quadrangle Books.

WHITE, H.C. (1970). "Search Parameters for The Small World Problem." *Soc. Forces* **49** (2), 259–264.

WILLIAMS, W.F. (1965). *Principles of Automated Information Retrieval*. Elmhurst, Ill.: Business Press.

WINOGRAD, T. (1972). *Understanding Natural Language*. New York: Academic Press.

YOVITS, M.C. (1969). "Information Science: Toward the Development of a True Scientific Discipline." *J. ASIS* **20** (Oct.), 369–376.

ZADEH, L.A. (1965). "Fuzzy Sets." *Inf. Contr.* **8** 338–353.

ZIMAN, J.M. (1969). "Information, Communication, Knowledge." *Nature* **224** (Oct. 25). Reprinted in SARACEVIC, T. (editor), *Introduction to Information Science*. New York: Bowker, pp. 76–84.

ZIPF, G.K. (1949). *Human Behavior and the Principle of Least Effort*. Cambridge, Mass.: Addison-Wesley.

Index